WET SOCKS
AND
DRY BONES

About the author
Nic Outterside was an award-winning newspaper journalist
and editor for 28 years and currently is the proprietor of
Time is an Ocean, the book publishing arm of **write***ahead*.
Wet Socks and Dry Bones is his twenty-seventh paperback book.

WET SOCKS
AND
DRY BONES

Nic Outterside

Time is an Ocean Publications

Time is an Ocean Publications
An Imprint of **write**_ahead_
Lonsdale Road
Wolverhampton, WV3 0DY

DEDICATION
Henry Wood for his help with this book
and all the former players, families and
friends who contributed their memories

Henry Wood

Contents

Foreword

"This is the most special place in all the world. Once a place touches you like this, the wind never blows so cold again. You feel for it, like it was your child"
Dr Archibald *Moonlight* Graham
Field of Dreams

It was while finishing my last football book **Death in Grimsby** that the blinding flash of light took place – a Road to Damascus experience if you like – which led me here.

The moment, to be precise, was Monday, 1st April 2019… the day I heard the news that my boyhood Brighton & Hove Albion hero Kit Napier had died just 12 hours earlier at his home in Durban, South Africa, aged 75.

There was a loud howl inside my head, as if part of my life was gone!

I was an impressionable 11-year-old kid in 1967 when I first saw Kit play, and for me, he was everything you wanted from a football hero… elegant and lithe, with tousled dark hair, fleet footed, devastatingly fast, a provider and a scorer of goals, a genius at riding tackles and ghosting past opposition defences in one move.

He could also deliver amazing in-swinging corners and scored directly from two of them against Barrow and Bury in March and December 1969.

Even if games were tough, you could bet your last sixpence that Kit would score. At times, he might look a little lazy but then he'd throw in a body swerve or a burst of pace and be away from whoever had been given the unenviable job of marking him.

Like all childhood heroes, I thought he would live forever.

So, when he died, I suddenly realised, that, like all of us, he was mortal; and when I got to know his family over the ensuing months, I discovered he was full of human flaws as well as being a football genius.

Then slowly, I came to realise that several of the stars from my first few seasons at the Goldstone Ground had also passed on – some well before their time.

1

Gone was fans' favourite Charlie Livesey; midfield creator Nobby Lawton; the goal-poaching Bobby Smith; mercurial winger Wally Gould; Jimmy Collins, Mel Hopkins and most recently, the human battering ram of a centre forward, Alex Dawson.

They were now all ghosts of the Goldstone's Field of Dreams.

Some months later, at the formal launch of my book **Death in Grimsby** at the Caxton Arms in Brighton, I stopped and chatted with the club's official historian Tim Carder.

I had not seen Tim for many years, and we talked non-stop about everything Albion related as well as his recently published book **Brighton & Hove Albion and the First World War**. Long forgotten names such as *Pom Pom* Whiting, Jasper Batey and Charlie Dexter seemed to fall into the space of our conversation as their tragic brief lives had fallen on the battlefields of Belgium and France more than 100 years earlier. All were legends of our football club.

It was then that the penny finally dropped, and the blinding light of the previous April started to make sense.

In something akin to WP Kinsella's **Shoeless Joe**, which inspired the movie **Field of Dreams**; this was our moment in time to bring home our own ghosts.

"Moonlight butters the whole Iowa night. Clover and corn smells are thick as syrup. I experience a tingling like the tiniest of electric wires touching the back of my neck, sending warm sensations through me. Then as the lights flare, a scar against the blue-black sky, I see Shoeless Joe Jackson standing out in left field. His feet spread wide, hands on hips, he waits. I hear the sharp crack of the bat, and Shoeless Joe drifts effortlessly a few steps to his left, raises his right hand to signal for the ball, camps under it for a second or two, catches it, at the same time transferring it to his throwing hand, and fires it into the infield."

(WP Kinsella)

In my mind I substituted football for baseball.

"It is a warm evening and the air was thick with cigarette smoke mingling with a steam of body odour, testosterone and Bovril. Voices chattered everywhere, broken only by guffaws of adult laughter, obscenities, and the occasional yell. The chants rose around us. Bodies massed and bodies swayed as the game got

underway. It was claustrophobic but exhilarating at the same time. A mist from the sweating bodies was beginning to swirl in the air under the white floodlights which shone brightly on the emerald-green turf, as the chanting became louder.

With less than 15 minutes to go, Kit Napier received the ball near the centre circle and broke forward at pace. A swift body swerve, he had split the Portsmouth defence and was racing into their half and towards the South Stand goal with the ball jiggling between his feet.

His marker was beaten for both pace and skill, when he suddenly reached out and grabbed Kit's number 7 shirt. The North Stand screamed "Foul" in one voice as the shirt was ripped from his back. With the Albion fans seething, Kit's torn shirt flapped behind him as he continued his run towards goal before the referee blew for a foul."

Fast forward to the winter of 2020-2021.

Snow is falling outside… and turning round from my office chair to the three-tiered bookcase to my right, I survey the many books about football which I had garnered over the years. Everything from Nick Varley's **Parklife** to Dick Knight's autobiography **Mad Man** seem to shout *"Hi, I'm here"*. Tim Carder and Roger Harris's encyclopaedic tomes **Albion A-Z** and **The Story of Brighton & Hove Albion FC** both stand tall like timeless bookends. But nowhere can I find anything about those legendary players from the Goldstone Ground who had passed on to our own **Field of Dreams**.

And there were hundreds of them!

So, with my own personal memories of the Goldstone Ground running around my brain, I begin the task of researching the lives and deaths of those players… those ghosts of the Goldstone.

It was probably the most enjoyable research I have ever done, as slowly this book began to come together… the ghosts started to make their journey home.

While the South Stand, erected in 1910, underwent two rebuilds - the second after a fire in 1980 - the West Stand was also extended and rebuilt twice, the North Stand was given a new roof, and as the East terracing crumbled, the bright green pitch in that oddly shaped stadium we called the Goldstone Ground, remained.

3

Two world wars were fought, a great depression occurred, 23 Prime Ministers were elected, England won the World Cup and man landed on the moon all during the 95 years of life of this hallowed place.

The Clark's bakery and Sackville Hotel stood like sentinels while traffic continued to rumble along the Old Shoreham Road and generations of families descended on this peculiar football ground in BN3 to watch their heroes play.

And over time, those heroes became legends and an everlasting part of countless ordinary lives.

The smell of Bovril
And cigarettes
The Old Bill
And Sally suffragettes
The night time's swirling mist
Under bright lights gently kissed
The blue and white
The emerald so bright
Yesterday's daze in the smoky haze
We score
Then the roar
The forward surge
And bodies merge
As one
Under the drenching sun
This game is already won
The songs and chants
The tribal dance
The love and passion
The replica fashion
No matter what the weather
The memories remain forever

Wet Socks and Dry Bones is not an objective encyclopaedia of all things Brighton & Hove Albion. Instead, by its very nature, it is

4

my own subjective collection of 50 stories of some of the most outstanding ghosts of the Goldstone era.

So, while you will find the expected legends of longevity such as **Charlie Webb, Len Darling** and **Tug Wilson,** and the goal scoring machines of **Tommy Cook, Bert Stephens** and **Jock Davie,** there are also the great characters of the Goldstone… **Frankie Howard, Bobby Farrell** and **Bill Cassidy.**

The drinking tales of **Alex Dawson, Brian Bromley** and **Tony Grealish** are legendary, but here you will also find how a naked **Charlie Livesey** made his way to bed after a night out on the town, how **Michael Robinson** hid his man boobs, the loveliness of **Steve Piper** and **Denis Foreman,** and the secret of **Hugh Vallance's** sudden departure after scoring 32 goals in just one season.

And there are also a few surprises: **Barrie Rees, Bobby Smith** and **Justin Fashanu** only made 75 appearances for Brighton & Hove Albion between them. But like the others, they deserve a place in this book for the legacy each left behind.

And there are so many more… may all these ghosts never be forgotten.

I hope you enjoy reading and remembering as much as I have enjoyed researching and writing.

NB

The original working title for this book was *Goldstone Ghosts*. But a few months before publication I remembered that Attila the Stockbroker (John Baine) published a book of his collected poems under that very same name some 20 years ago.

The title *Wet Socks and Dry Bones* was inspired by my good Albion friend and curator of the *Brighton Room*: Alan Willard. Thank you.

A Brighton & Hove Albion Centenary Lunch with some treasured
Goldstone Ghosts at Withdean Stadium in 2001.
Sitting round the table, clockwise, are Dave Sexton, John Shepherd, Des
Tennant's son Warren, Eric Gill, Glen Wilson and Johnny McNichol.

1

Arthur Hulme
(Joseph Arthur Hulme)
1877-1916
BHAFC 1902-1909
Full Back/Right Half
Appearances: 174
Goals: 7

Joseph Arthur Hulme can rightly be considered as Brighton & Hove Albion's first Goldstone legend.

And what a larger-than-life character he was.

Arthur was born in Leek, Staffordshire, and began his career in junior football in the local area, playing as an inside forward.

He signed for Lincoln City in June 1897, at the age of 20, and made his first-team debut on 4th September, the opening day of the 1897-1898 Football League season, in a Second Division match away at Newton Heath. Lincoln lost 5-0.

Hard working and physically strong with a happy personality, Arthur played regularly for the Imps, scoring 13 goals from 31 appearances in all competitions, but he was released by the club at the end of the season.

Arthur and Lincoln team-mate, goalkeeper William Wilkinson, were two of numerous new signings for Kent side, Gravesend United for the 1898-1899 Southern League season. But neither man was retained for the following campaign.

The club's committee publicly said it was keen to dispense with the services of *"men with drinking reputations, who proved such failures last season"*. However, there is no indication that Arthur was one of these wayward drinkers.

Arthur then played for Midland League club Wellingborough, before returning to the Southern League with Bristol Rovers in 1901-1902.

He signed for Brighton ahead of the club's second season in the Southern League and its first full year playing at the Goldstone Ground.

The club took up permanent residency at the Goldstone Ground for the 1902-1903 season and celebrated the move by winning the Southern League Division Two title.

Amateur side Hove FC had been the sole tenants at the Goldstone, but with their attendances barely raising enough money to pay the rent, they needed another club to share the burden.

They turned to the Albion, who made the switch from the Sussex County Cricket Ground in what proved to be a busy summer of 1902.

As well as moving homes, the club joined a new league. Division Two of the Southern League had only six clubs for the 1902-1903 season, so Brighton became members of the South Eastern League too, to flesh out their fixture list.

Albion manager John Jackson fielded his first team in both competitions, although there were occasions when he would use the South Eastern Competition to play younger players.

It also gave Brighton their first exposure to more established clubs. The likes of Tottenham Hotspur, Queens Park Rangers, West Ham United and Watford all fielded sides in the South Eastern League in addition to their own Southern League Division One commitments. Brighton ended their South Eastern League campaign in fifth place.

During the summer, Jackson brought in just two new faces as he looked to better the 1901-1902 season's third place finish and they both proved to be astute additions. Arthur Hulme, who had converted into a hard tackling defender, joined from Bristol Rovers and former England international Ben Garfield arrived from West Bromwich Albion. Garfield's signing was quite the coup given that the Albion had only been in existence for one season. He proved his worth, particularly in the FA Cup with five goals in five games.

Brighton racked up some big wins in the competition, hammering Brighton Amateurs 14-2 and Shoreham 12-0. The Shoreham game took place on Saturday 18th October 1902, the same day that the Albion also took on St Albans Amateurs in the South Eastern League. It remains the only occasion in Brighton & Hove Albion's history that two competitive games have been played on the same day, with Brighton winning 1-0 against the Amateurs.

Meanwhile, Arthur was to become one of the great characters in the Albion's early history and the club's first longest serving professional.

He scored from a penalty in a 2-2 draw away at Bedford Queen's on 27th September 1902 – one of only seven goals he scored for the club in his seven years at the Goldstone Ground, in an era where defenders were expected to defend rather than score goals.

Albion's official historian Tim Carder describes Arthur Hulme as *"highly influential"* in the club's successful campaign for promotion to the First Division, and he missed only one match in Brighton's first campaign at the higher level.

But during the 1904-1905 season, he played more frequently for the reserves than for the first team.

However, at the end of that season, Arthur was one of only three players retained by the Albion. He was subsequently appointed captain and this sturdy defender contributed to the club reaching the last 32 of the 1905-1906 FA Cup, in which they lost to Football League First Division club Middlesbrough – but only after two replays.

According to the **Daily Mirror's** match report, Arthur played *"splendidly"*.

But by 1907 he was once again in the reserves, standing in when first choice Arthur Archer was unavailable.

According to Tim Carder, Arthur was *"a great favourite"* with the supporters and combined a *"jovial personality"* with loads of *"honest endeavour"*.

The Thiepval War Memorial where Arthur Hulme is remembered

Then in recognition of his five years' service to the club, he became the first Albion player to be awarded a benefit match. The chosen game was a Western League fixture against Southampton. Unfortunately, the weather was extremely wet that day and the attendance was reported as *"barely two thousand"*.

Arthur played only one first team match in 1908-1909, and retired at the end of the season, having scored seven goals from 174 appearances for the Albion in first-team competition.

He then returned to his native Leek where he re-signed for Macclesfield. He later became trainer of nearby Leek United for the 1909-1910 season and only made two appearances for Macclesfield during that season, having been almost ever-present during the 1908-1909 campaign.

Arthur enlisted in the Royal Sussex Regiment at the start of World War One. He was serving as a corporal in the 7th Battalion at the time of his death in action on 3rd October 1916 at Gueudecourt, just south of Bancourt, during the bloody Battle of the Somme.

Joseph Arthur Hulme is commemorated on the Thiepval Memorial and on the Nicholson War Memorial in Leek.

2

Bob *Pom Pom* Whiting
(Robert Whiting)
1883-1917
BHAFC 1908-1915
Goalkeeper
Appearances: 320

A true legend of English football, Bob Whiting made 320 appearances in all competitions for Brighton & Hove Albion, a record total for an Albion goalkeeper which was not surpassed until the early 1970s.

In the highly successful 1909-1910 season, Bob conceded just 28 goals in 42 matches.

He is regarded by most football historians as *"one of the finest goalkeepers to ever play for the Albion."*

He was a giant of a man who earned his nickname of *Pom Pom* from his amazing kicking ability. It is reported that he had the power to kick a ball from one end of the pitch to the other, on one occasion clearing the opposition crossbar from a kick taken from his own goal area. His kicking power was compared to the force and range of the Royal Navy's two pounder rapid firing Pom Pom gun.

Robert Whiting was born on 6th January 1883 in Canning Town, London under the name of Robert Greenhough. His father - also named Robert - had been brought up by his stepfather Robert Whiting. He was so fond of him that he changed the family name to Whiting.

Today, Bob Whiting's sporting reputation is such that he is claimed by no fewer than four football clubs (West Ham United, Chelsea, Tunbridge Wells and Brighton & Hove Albion).

Bob followed the family tradition and entered the local shipyard as a labourer. Selected as goalkeeper for the works football team, Thames Ironworks, (West Ham United from 1900) he went on to play for South West Ham FC and Tunbridge Wells Rangers.

As a goalkeeper he was moving up, fast. He was scouted and asked to play in goal for Chelsea in 1906.

Chelsea fans revelled at his piston-like ability to kick deep into the opposition's half.

But team selection was a ruthless business and after only one season *Pom Pom* was dropped from the Chelsea side.

Aged 24, Bob married his fiancée Nellie in 1907. Then in 1908, with Nellie and his two sons living in Tunbridge Wells, he was transferred to Brighton & Hove Albion.

Within a year, Bob was enjoying huge success with his new club.

The Albion enjoyed a truly amazing 1909-10 season as manager Jack Robson led the club to both the Southern League Division One title and the Southern Professional Charity Cup, the first and only double season in the club's history.

The success was even more remarkable given that Brighton had finished the 1908-1909 campaign just one point above the relegation zone.

With the Southern League expanding to 22 teams for the 1909-1910 season and the increasing travel costs which came with being a part of the Western League, the Albion declined to defend their Western Division title, focusing their efforts entirely on the main Southern League competition.

Without the demand of two leagues, Robson could work with a smaller squad. Only four players arrived in the summer – Bill Hastings, Bullet Jones, Joe McGhie and Fred Blackman. All proved to be quality additions.

Blackman played every game, McGhie and Hastings only missed one apiece and Jones led the scoring charts with 22 goals in all competitions.

And behind them all was their rock of a goalkeeper Bob *Pom Pom* Whiting.

The Albion ended the season five points clear of Swindon and were deserved champions.

They proved to be extremely difficult to beat, losing just six Division One games all season. 11 draws from 21 games on the road went a long way towards securing the title, while Bob Whiting conceded just 28 times - by far and away the best defensive record of any side in the league.

Lifting the title gave Brighton the opportunity to take on Football League champions Aston Villa in the Charity Shield for the title of Unofficial Champions of England. That game would take place in the opening weeks of the 1910-1911 season, giving Albion fans plenty to look forward to over the summer of 1910.

Bob's football career flourished for seven seasons until the outbreak of World War One.

In recognition of his services to the Albion he was granted a benefit match in October 1914. However, with poor war-time attendances, the match was postponed, and Bob never lived to benefit from the game.

Bob made 253 appearances in the Southern League for Brighton & Hove Albion (320 in total in all competitions).

The 1914-1915 football season had started a month after war broke out. Nationally there was a massive outcry: should professional footballers be running around on the football pitch or they should be running around on the fields of Flanders, chasing the Germans?

The counter argument was that football provided an entertainment for the masses who were working in the munitions' factories - keeping morale up, giving them a bit of a release from their work.

There were moves to have football abolished, but in the end a special battalion of footballers was raised – the 17th Battalion of the Middlesex Regiment. And a lot of the Albion players joined that battalion. Bob Whiting was one of them. They trained at White City, which had been the home of the 1908 Olympics, and at the weekend a lot of them were released to play their football until the end of the season, when English professional football stopped completely.

The new soldiers went off to fight in France in November 1915.

After seeing action, Bob was given leave in May 1916. But when he came home, he found that he had scabies – a disease transmitted by lice in the trenches – and was admitted to hospital in Brighton.

While back at home he made his wife pregnant with their third child. So, when the time came for him to return to the front he was torn between loyalties to his pregnant wife and his duty to his country.

He then went Absent Without Leave for 133 days between June and October 1916. He was eventually arrested and given a court-martial in France and imprisoned for nine months with hard labour.

The **Brighton Herald** reported his case on 21st October 1916:
"On Saturday Robert Whiting, a private in the Footballers' Battalion of the Middlesex Regiment, was remanded to await an escort.

"He was charged with being an absentee since June last, but pleaded not guilty on the ground that he had been suffering from a complaint for which he entered hospital in May.

"Defendant told Detective-Sergeant Adlam that he had been treated in hospital, and that he was not in a fit condition to travel. Whiting was before the war the goalkeeper of the Brighton and Hove Football Club, and a very well-known figure in the football world."

But in 1917, the Army needed all the men it could get for a final push against the Germans, so Bob's sentence was suspended so he was posted back to the Front.

He was fighting on the line near Arras, in France, in April 1917, tending some wounded soldiers in Oppy Wood when a shell landed close by and he was never seen again.

Bob never saw the son that was born on the day that he was sentenced.

But it got worse than that: because of what had happened to him, going absent, there were rumours back at home that he had been shot as a deserter. His wife Nellie had to release letters from his Commanding Officer showing that her husband was, in fact, killed in the line of duty.

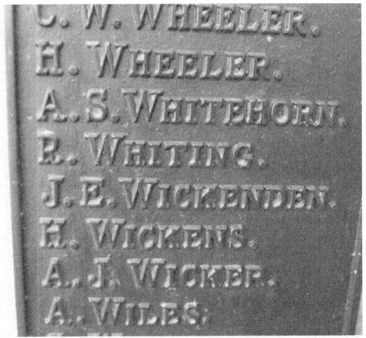

Bob Whiting remembered on the Tunbridge Wells War Memorial

The Army then formally stated that Bob was indeed killed in action by shell fire while attending to wounded colleagues at Vimy Ridge, a fortified German position during the Battle of Arras on 28th April 1917.

Robert *Pom Pom* Whiting is commemorated on the Arras Memorial and at home on the Tunbridge Wells War Memorial.

3

Charlie Webb
(Charles Graham Webb)
1886-1973
BHAFC
Inside Left
1909-1915 (Player)
Appearances: 265
Goals: 79
1919-1947 (Manager)

If ever the words *Albion Legend* was judged by longevity alone, then Charlie Webb would win hands down.

And if you ever cut him open, like a stick of Brighton rock, the words Brighton & Hove Albion would run right through him.

He played for the Albion for a modest six years; but after the end of World War One he managed the club for a further 28 years… giving a total of 34 years of his life to the club he loved.

But he was much more than that. He should also be judged by his manner and his remarkable achievements.

Charlie was born into a Scottish military family at the Curragh Camp in County Kildare, Ireland, where his father, Sergeant William Webb of the Black Watch, was stationed.

The family moved around following Sgt Webb's postings, so the young Charlie Webb spent some of his childhood in Edinburgh Castle before settling in the Worthing area.

As a 16-year-old, Charlie played first-team football for Worthing FC, and in his second season, he contributed to the club winning a treble of the Sussex Senior Cup, the West Sussex Senior League, and a local charity cup.

In 1904, he followed in the family's military tradition by enlisting in the 2nd Battalion of the Essex Regiment. His trade in the Army was a clerk, and while serving in Ireland, he furthered his football career playing for his regimental team in the Leinster Senior League, and later, in the Irish Football League for Bohemians.

He scored freely for his regiment – in November 1907 he scored all seven in a 7-4 defeat of Dublin University - and early the following year was the only player from outside the Irish League to be selected for the Leinster representative team to play Ulster.

He had a trial with Glasgow Rangers in 1908, and later that year was chosen to represent the Irish League in a match against the English League. In November, he was capped by the Ireland amateur national team in a match against the England amateurs in Dublin.

In January 1909, while on Christmas leave from his regiment, Charlie played and scored for Brighton & Hove Albion in a Southern League match against West Ham United. But on his return, the Army discovered he had appeared alongside professionals and he was banned from military football for 12 months.

The Football Association fined the Albion £5 (£620 in 2021 value) *"for having approached and played Webb in violation of the Rules of the Association."*

Rumours that the military authorities would prevent him playing for Bohemians in the semi-final of the Irish Cup proved unfounded, but when Charlie finished on the winning side, the **Irish Times** reported that Glentoran, the losing club, intended to protest his inclusion, on the grounds that playing in the Southern League made him ineligible to appear in the Irish Cup competition.

Forced to choose between his military and his football careers, Charlie bought himself out of the Army and signed for the Albion as an amateur.

A few days later he became the first Brighton player to be capped at full international level when he made his debut for Ireland against Scotland at Ibrox on 15th March 1909. Ireland lost 5-0.

At the end of the 1909-1910 season, the *Times* reported that: *"Brighton & Hove Albion have not had much difficulty in finishing at the head of the Southern League".*

Charlie played in every game - usually at inside left - as the Albion won their first and only major title.

This achievement earned them a place in the 1910 FA Charity Shield in which they faced reigning Football League champions Aston Villa at Stamford Bridge. At the time Villa were the biggest club in the land. Charlie described it as *"David versus Goliath".*

The only goal of the game was scored in the second half, following a corner kick taken by the Albion's Bert Longstaff. Villa's goalkeeper parried the ball into a knot of players, from where Bill Hastings touched it to Charlie Webb, *"who cleverly evaded a couple of Villa defenders and found the net with a rising cross-shot."*

The *Daily Mirror* reported some extra detail: *"Hastings eventually managed to get hold the ball, laying it off to Webb who danced around a couple of flaying defenders before firing high into the goal for 1-0."*

Villa then threw players forward and Albion manager Jack Robson responded by dropping Charlie in as an additional defender. It worked, and the Albion saw out the remainder of the match and upon the final whistle, the crowd surged onto the pitch to celebrate.

Huge crowds later packed the area around Brighton railway station to welcome the victorious team home at 11.30 pm, and the *Sussex Daily News* reported that the team could *"now be dubbed as Champions of England".*

A testimonial fund raised more than £120 which was distributed among the professional players. As an amateur, Charlie could receive no prize money, so the club presented him with a gold tie pin instead.

He turned professional soon afterwards and was at last able to reap the financial rewards as a player.

Charlie finished as the club's leading scorer in 1912-1913, with 13 goals in all competitions; and went on to set a club record for goals scored in the Southern League at 64.

Though his Ireland career was at an end, Charlie continued to be selected in representative teams. In September 1912, he scored for the Southern League as the Football League XI beat them 2-1 at

Old Trafford, and the following season, he was selected for a Southern Alliance XI to play that league's champions, Croydon Common. Sadly, a serious leg injury sustained in another match against Millwall in November 1914 effectively put an end to his playing career.

He did play five games towards the end of the season, but with Britain now at war and the Albion set to close for more than four years, Charlie's days as an inside forward were over.

On the outbreak of World War One, Charlie re-enlisted as a second lieutenant in the King's Royal Rifle Corps and served on the Western Front from July 1917.

Promoted to acting captain (the rank was confirmed after the war), he was leading a patrol near Nesle in March 1918 when they were challenged in French. Unfortunately for Charlie and his men, the French speakers were German troops. Preferring to avoid injury or death, Charlie surrendered.

He saw out the duration of the war as a prisoner of war in Mainz, Germany.

While awaiting repatriation, he received a letter from the chairman of Brighton & Hove Albion offering him the post of team manager, an appointment he took up on his demobilisation in 1919.

As the new manager, Charlie's first task was not only rebuilding the team but also involving himself with rebuilding the ground.

Proper competition resumed in 1919-1920, and the following season, Charlie led the team into the Football League as a Third Division was formed, largely comprising the Southern League First Division teams of the year before.

Awarded a testimonial in recognition of his service to the club, Charlie chose the League game against Watford in April 1921 as his benefit match. It attracted more than 10,000 spectators and raised nearly £500 – worth about £24,000 in 2021 values.

In the 1923-1924 FA Cup, Charlie led Albion to the fifth round, defeating First Division Everton on the way, in what he later described as: *"The best Cup exhibition of any Albion team under my management"*.

Charlie quickly earned a reputation as a sound judge of a player. Immediately after the war, the signing of former England international forward George Holley for a club record £200 fee was viewed as quite a coup.

Sadly, Holley suffered a career-ending injury, so hardly played, but Charlie replaced him with Jack Doran who finished as the club's top scorer despite joining halfway through the season.

He also brought Tommy Cook through from the juniors into the first team. Cook was top scorer in three seasons, but when he left the club to concentrate on his cricket career, Charlie brought in QPR reserve Hugh Vallance in 1929, who turned out to be a *"goalscoring phenomenon"* alongside Dan Kirkwood.

Again, when twice top scorer Arthur Attwood succumbed to appendicitis in 1933, Charlie signed former Norwich City centre forward Oliver *Buster* Brown from West Ham United. Brown produced 41 goals in his first two seasons.

Between the wars, Charlie Webb's teams finished in the top five of the Third Division South on 10 occasions but challenged seriously for promotion only in the latter half of the 1930s.

He led the team to third place in 1936-1937, despite an uneasy relationship with the club's board, the supporters, and the press.

The board came under criticism for alleged interference in team affairs, having undue influence over the manager in pressing the claims for selection of one player over another.

Letters to the local press suggested that Webb should *"be allowed greater freedom"*, while in the **Evening Argus**, the pseudonymous *Crusader* launched *"vitriolic attacks on the directors and management of Brighton & Hove Albion for their alleged lack of ambition and inept team selections"*.

It generated a massive readership response and led to near physical confrontations with Charlie Webb.

The club's relationship with the local newspaper worsened during the 1937-1938 season, to the extent that the *Crusader* was: *"either banned by the directors or was voluntarily taken off by the editor"*.

Charlie told the **Daily Express**: *"Here you have a town full of people with money, yet hardly one of them will give us a hand. Without attractive new players and a winning team you can't get gates and without gates you can't have money."*

Nevertheless, the national press recognised his achievements. A *Daily Mirror* feature in 1939 compared him to George Allison of Arsenal and Frank Buckley of Wolverhampton Wanderers,

A *Guardian* retrospective on the club, written in 1973, described how *"Brighton had a skilful team usually playing to the top six"* under Webb, *"whose transfer acquisitions were as often as not costed on the price of his train ticket and buffet sandwiches"*.

At the outbreak of World War Two and no longer of an age for active service, Charlie joined the Home Guard.

The Albion continued to compete in the various wartime leagues, and Charlie skilfully exploited the regulations allowing players to make guest appearances for the club nearest to their base.

He was particularly fortunate that the King's Liverpool Regiment's posting to Newhaven in 1941 gave him the pick of Liverpool's pre-war team. In their absence, he was reduced to selecting youngsters or soliciting members of the crowd to make up the numbers, as at Norwich City at Christmas 1940, when his travelling party of one senior player and three amateurs was supplemented by Jimmy Ithell of Bolton Wanderers, Norwich City juniors and local servicemen… the Albion lost 18-0.

At the end of the 1946-1947 season, at the age of 60, Charlie handed over responsibility for team affairs to Tommy Cook, remaining with the club on the administrative side, as secretary and general manager.

A few days after a 4-0 home defeat to Walsall left Albion at the bottom of the table, provoking a demonstration after the match, the directors appointed Don Welsh as secretary-manager.

Charlie stayed on until the end of the 1947-1948 season to assist his successor, then left the club and retired from football.

Such was Charlie's standing in the game that he was awarded a second testimonial. In September 1949, Portsmouth, reigning Football League title holders beat Arsenal, their predecessors as champions, by two goals to one in *"an exhibition of memorable football"* at the Goldstone Ground.

Charlie continued living in his house in Frith Road (just off Sackville Road) in Hove until shortly before his death in a local nursing home in 1973, at the age of 86 - a year after his beloved wife Minnie, to whom he'd been married for more than 60 years.

Their son, Ken, was married with a child and employed by the **Evening Argus**, when he was killed while training as a pilot during World War Two. Their daughter, Joyce Watts – born on the same day as the 1910 Charity Shield – survived her parents.

She spoke on screen at the club's centenary evening in 2001, at which her father was one of 24 former players and managers nominated as *legends* and in 2003, she helped unveil a memorial plaque at the former family home at 15 Frith Road. It was an appropriate location for the plaque, because for many years his home had acted as the club office.

The plaque was funded by the Albion's Collectors and Historians Society in recognition of Charlie's extraordinary service to the club.

Joyce said: *"On match days all the gate money used to come to Frith Road and we used to store it in our larder in a safe because the banks weren't open.*

"For cup ties we even sold tickets from the house!"

In 2017, Albion fan Danny Chapman raised a petition to Brighton & Hove Council to allow a memorial plaque to be placed at the base of a tree which was planted in memory *"of a true legend of the city in 1973"*. It currently stands unmarked in Hove Park opposite the former site of the Goldstone Ground.

A year later, in 2018, Charlie's granddaughter Ann Spike gave a revealing interview to the **Brighton Journal** about his life and legacy.

She said: *"His father didn't want him to play football at all, so he hid it, which is why he was amateur to start off with."*

She then referred to the Albion's Charity Shield triumph over Aston Villa, which became one of the club's greatest ever achievements.

"However, because he was an amateur at the time, he couldn't be rewarded with prize money for his efforts, instead he was given a tie-pin with a shamrock and there's a pearl in it.

"When he died, my mother made it into a little charm to go on a necklace – which I now have and often wear."

Well respected by everyone in the game Ann said: *"He was never called boss which they are called now, he was called 'Mr Webb', they all addressed him as Mr Webb."*

She also recalled a story which was told by her mother Joyce, about how the referee for one of Albion's matches ended up travelling with Charlie Webb and the Brighton & Hove Albion team to the game.

"Over Christmas they tended to have games away and at home in close proximity, and on this occasion, I think there was some bad weather," Ann recalled.

"It was very rare that the FA would allow the referee who was going to referee their match, to travel on the coach with the team.

"But because grandfather was so well respected and they knew that there'd be no trouble like bribery or anything like that, the referee travelled with them."

Of her own memories of her grandfather, Ann stated: *"Of course I was born in 1945, which was when he was just finishing – so I was really a baby.*

"But when I was growing up, I used to go around and see my grandparents all the time in Frith Road.

"What was lovely was as I got older, when we did sports days at school and did high jump and things - he used to train me to do high jump and things like that."

Her parents and grandparents also had season tickets.

"All those years ago, 20 minutes before the game ended, they used to open the gates and you could just go in. I knew where they (granddad and grandma) sat so I used to go in and join them and sit with them," she recalled.

"A lot of the players and former players knew him and respected him, there were several who actually lived in Frith Road when he was retired.

"Ex Brighton player Dave Sexton was always very respectful and would pop over and speak with him".

After his retirement, Charlie worked as an usher at the cricket ground in Hove and would show people to their seats.

Post war Charlie Webb (second left) with the Albion's directors

Ann recalled when football legend Jimmy Hill came to a match: *"This particular day it was quite a big match and Jimmy came to the stand. Grandad knew full well who he was, but he said to Jimmy Hill: "Oh could I see your ticket please", as though he didn't know him!*

"Because Grandad disliked people being pompous, so he made Jimmy root around for his ticket," she added.

On the Albion legend who had a remarkable football career, but also more importantly was her loving grandfather, Ann added: *"He was a lovely man, very quiet and unassuming and he wasn't very boastful at all.*

"It is amazing how many people who support the club know of him. I can't believe that he would even imagine that there's still so much interest in him and his history."

4

Jasper *Ginger* Batey
(Jasper Matthews Batey)
1890-1915
BHAFC 1913-1915
Left Half
Appearances: 40
Goals: 4

Nicknamed *Ginger* after the popular ginger beer of the time, Tyneside born Jasper Matthews Batey signed for Brighton & Hove Albion in the summer of 1913.

Red-haired Jasper had scored 26 goals as a centre forward for Portsmouth the previous season – including a hat trick for the reserves against the Brighton Lambs on Boxing Day 1912.

The local postman had initially impressed while playing part-time for his home-town club South Shields FC in the North Eastern League.

But after signing at the Goldstone Ground the Albion's manager Jack Robson decided to convert him into a left half.

One recollection of Jasper Batey as a player was: *"The lad was tall, quick and tough tackling. He was afraid of no-one and won the ball more often than he lost it."*

Another was: *"He always seemed to have a smile on his face and joke for his team-mates, although I am sure many could not understand a word he said, such was his north country accent."*

The Albion's star goalkeeper, Bob *Pom Pom* Whiting, said: *"He was a strong boy, always had a laugh when things were tough and a good one to have on our side."*

Ginger only played 10 times during his first season at the Albion but then made the left half position his own in 1914-1915, playing in 20 of the club's 23 games before league football came to a halt in May.

Everything had changed for Ginger and every other player, when a month before the Southern League Division One season kicked off, Great Britain declared war on Germany to enter World War One.

The call to arms was made and from Wednesday 5th August 1914 and hundreds of thousands of men rushed to sign up to fight for King and county.

These included the Albion's Gunner Higham who was an Army Reservist and was called up as soon as war was declared. By the time Brighton were making the long trip to Plymouth Argyle on Saturday 2nd September for the opening fixture, he was serving in France. Early in November 1914, the Goldstone's groundsman Fred Bates was killed in action serving for the Royal Scots Fusiliers.

Most of the Albion squad signed up for the 17th Battalion of the Duke of Cambridge's Own Middlesex Regiment, made up of professional footballers and nicknamed *The Footballers' Battalion*. The members trained at White City in London during the week, before being released at the weekends to represent their clubs.

Although football continued throughout World War One, the Albion decided to shut down at the end of the 1914-1915 season until the conflict was at an end.

The Goldstone Ground lay vacant and fell into a state of disrepair with the pitch being used to graze animals. In the Albion's place, a new club called simply Brighton & Hove were formed playing at Wish Park in Hove and many of the Albion's ex-players turned out for their side when on leave.

Then with the chaos of war ensuing, Albion manager Jack Robson was approached to become manager of the mighty Manchester United. It was an offer which was too good to turn down. So, Robson, the man who had turned Brighton & Hove Albion into the Champions of England in 1910, departed for Old Trafford.

With the war in the forefront of everyone's minds, Brighton decided against appointing a replacement for Robson so trainer Alf Nelmes was put in caretaker charge for the second half of the 1914-1915 season.

For Jasper Batey, World War One arrived just as his career as a professional player was taking off.

When he enlisted in the Footballers' Battalion in February 1915, his Albion career ended after 40 appearances and four goals. The battalion had been formed in response to the controversy over the continuation of league football after the outbreak of war. It had been thought that allowing the 1914-1915 season to proceed would help support public morale.

But the fact that young men were still playing football while others were fighting on the front line became a hot issue, with figures like Sherlock Holmes creator Arthur Conan Doyle calling for players to sign up to the forces.

At the outbreak of the war there had been an initial push by clubs for professional football to continue, to keep the public's spirits up.

This stance was not widely agreed with and public opinion largely turned against professional footballers.

One soldier, serving in France, wrote to a British newspaper to complain that *"hundreds of thousands of able-bodied young roughs were watching hirelings playing football"* while others were serving their country.

The suggestion was even made that King George V should cease being a patron of The Football Association.

A recruitment poster for the Footballers' Battalion used a quote from the German newspaper Frankfurter Zeitung that *"The young Britons prefer to exercise their long limbs on the football ground rather than to expose them to any sort of risk in the service of their country"*.

William Joynson-Hicks formed the Footballers' Battalion on 12th December 1914 at Fulham town hall.

England international Frank Buckley became the first player to join, out of 30 players who signed up at its formation, which was announced to the public on 1st January 1915.

During training, the players were allowed leave on a Saturday to return to their clubs to take part in games. However, the clubs found themselves having to subsidise the train fares as the Army did not pay for them.

By the following March, 122 professional footballers (including Jasper Batey) had signed up for the battalion. These footballing recruits included the whole of Clapton Orient (later to be known as Leyton Orient). Meanwhile, the entire Heart of Midlothian team in Edinburgh had signed up for the 16th Royal Scots (known as McCrae's Battalion).

In addition to footballers, officials and referees also joined the 17th Service Battalion, along with football fans themselves.

Jasper was then transferred to the Army XI Corps Cyclist Corps after his enlistment.

But he was tragically killed in action on 23rd October 1915 at the Pas-de-Calais aged just 25, while serving as a cyclist messenger.

The fields and valleys of France's Nord-Pas-de-Calais saw some of the most brutal and bloody battles of World War One.

Runners or Messengers, as they were officially named, were usually low-ranking non-commissioned officers, such as corporals, who were chosen for their fitness, stamina, and ability to read maps. Physically fit athletes, such as footballers were considered ideal for the job.

They also had to be tough and resourceful enough to find their destination in any sort of weather, and sufficiently lithe and agile to navigate obstacles.

As they ventured beyond their unit's position, they faced the risk of being shot or blown up before they got there, or on the way back.

Of all the jobs in the infantry, *"the runner's job was the hardest and most dangerous,"* war historian Lieutenant Allan L Dexter observed in a 1931 newspaper article: *"With a runner, it was merely a question of how long he would last before being wounded or killed."*

By the end of the conflict, four Albion players – Jasper Batey, Charlie Dexter, Charlie Matthews and Bob Whiting – and four former players – Alan Haigh-Brown, Arthur Hulme, Tom Morris and Jimmy Smith – had all made the ultimate sacrifice.

Jasper Batey is buried in the Cambrin Military Cemetery in northern France.

Such was the bond with Brighton & Hove Albion that a parcel of cigarettes was sent by the club to his grieving comrades at the front.

Jasper's three medals were sold at auction in 2004, for £520.

5

Charlie Dexter
(Charles Dexter)
1890-1917
BHAFC 1913-1915
Left Back
Appearances: 36

Derby born Charlie Dexter began his professional football career at Sheffield Wednesday after impressing at Ilkeston Town FC, but was unable to break into the Owl's star-studded team of the time.

Charlie was confined to the reserves before moving to Portsmouth in the close season of 1912.

But he found opportunities at Fratton Park limited, making just 14 appearances across two seasons, and becoming only the second ever Pompey player to be sent off, in one of those games against Northampton Town.

Charlie had just completed his seven-day suspension for the sending off when he joined Brighton & Hove Albion, going onto make the left back spot his own in the 1914-15 season.

His career began to blossom at the Goldstone Ground. Little is known of his abilities as a player, except he was a no-nonsense, tough tackling and hard running full back who formed a good understanding with left half Jasper Batey, who played directly in front of him.

He became good friends with Batey and lived at 6 Montgomery Street, just off Sackville Road in Hove - less than half a mile from the Goldstone Ground.

A neighbour reported that Charlie would often *"run all the way from his front door to the ground"* as part of his own fitness regime. And *"he always had time to smile and say hello to anyone who recognised him... he was a real gent."* he added.

Charlie started 36 of the first 37 games of the campaign before enlisting as a private in the Footballers' Battalion (17th Service Battalion) of the Middlesex Regiment in April 1915.

Ironically, second-in-command of the unit was former Albion half back Frank Buckley. At the time of Charlie's enlistment, he was a lieutenant, but was later promoted to major and given full charge. On 10th March 2015, a match was staged at the Goldstone Ground against the Footballer's Battalion XI, in which Charlie played. Though being heavily outranked, Albion won 2-0

A snapshot of life in the battalion is provided by this extract in a letter from Albion goalkeeper Bob Whiting to Albert Underwood, the club secretary at Brighton & Hove Albion, dated 7th December 1915: *"There are only five of us (from the Brighton & Hove Albion team) out here doing our bit - myself, Booth, Tyler, Woodhouse, and Dexter, and they are very pleased to hear from you, and told me to tell you they are going on fine.*

"I daresay it has been rotten not having or seeing any football. There is plenty out here, and we are receiving challenges every minute of the day. But we are too good for them all.

"They are trying to pick a team out of the whole Army out here to play us, so it will be a big match, though I think we are certain winners."

Charlie enjoyed the camaraderie of fellow footballers before he fought on the Somme and suffered badly from being gassed in the trenches and was invalided home.

He spent several months in hospitals in Exeter and Torquay before he was medically discharged from the Army on grounds of his ill health on 10th April 1916.

More than 35,000 patients from the World War One trenches were treated in Devon's Red Cross temporary war hospitals between 1914 and 1919.

The hospitals were the first line of medical and surgical care for wounded or critically ill soldiers, taking patients direct from ambulance trains from Southampton.

Patients were treated for all sorts of conditions including the effects of gassing, wounds caused by shells or bullets, loss of limbs, eye injuries and illnesses ranging from mumps to trench fever and tuberculosis. The hospitals were equipped with operating theatres, x-ray units, and an electrical treatment unit, and were staffed by local consultant medical and trained nursing staff as well as by hundreds of Red Cross volunteers.

But septic poisoning took hold, either from external wounds or from the damage to his lungs, and Charlie died just over a year later aged 24, on 27th June 1917.

The *Ashbourne Telegraph* reported his death on 6th July 1917:
"A sportsman of some repute was reported to have succumbed to 'failing health' after being injured in France.

"Charles Dexter, of Derby, who had played football for Ripley, Ilkeston, Sheffield Wednesday, Portsmouth and Brighton and Hove had joined the Sportsman's Battalion of the Middlesex Regiment, but was invalided home after about six months in France with 'septic poisoning'.

"Dexter, who was also described as being "a cricketer of no mean order" had been discharged from the army and died aged 27."

By the time of the Armistice on 11th November 1918, the use of chemical weapons such as chlorine, phosgene, and mustard gas had resulted in more than 1.3 million casualties and approximately 90,000 deaths. The physical effects of gas were agonising, and it remained a pervasive psychological weapon. Although only three per cent of gas casualties proved immediately fatal, hundreds of thousands of ex-soldiers continued to suffer for years after the war. Many, like Charlie, suffered as their lungs decomposed, often causing sepsis of the blood they were supposed to oxygenate.

His parents George and Harriet Dexter of the Crewton part of Derby attended his funeral at Nottingham Road Cemetery.

6

Bert Longstaff
(Albert Edward Longstaff)
1885-1970
BHAFC 1906-1922
Outside/Inside Right
Appearances: 443
Goals: 86

During the first 30 years of the 20th century, Albert Edward Longstaff was a household name in Brighton and across the south of England.

Born in 1885, in Shoreham-by-Sea of parents John and Sarah and one of four brothers and two sisters, he lived for a short while at the family home at Queens Place near the railway station, before moving to their more permanent home in Victoria Road.

His father was an agricultural engine driver experienced in steam ploughing who later used his knowledge to become a traction engine agent for Shoreham and the surrounding area.

While living at Queens Place, the Longstaff family were next door neighbours of Shoreham FC manager and secretary Oswald Ball who recognised Albert's footballing abilities from a young age, and perhaps encouraged him (and his brother Harvey) with a view to enlisting him in the town's team.

Oswald was also a teacher and became headmaster at Ham Road school in 1901. He may have been there earlier as a teacher when Albert was a pupil. After junior school at Ham Road, Albert followed his brothers to the fee-paying York Place Intermediate

School in Brighton – and he would have travelled to Brighton daily in the company of other boys from Shoreham.

Albert played initially for Shoreham Excelsior, a now defunct club, before progressing to Shoreham FC Reserves and then to the town's First XI who played their matches at the Oxen Field. He was just 17 when he first played for Shoreham in the West Sussex Senior League in season 1902-1903, the year that they first won the Sussex Senior Cup.

By now Albert, or Bert as he became known, was gaining the interest of the professional clubs as well as the Sussex County selectors. This soon attracted the attention of the mighty Tottenham Hotspur who wanted to take him to White Hart Lane, a move blocked by his mum who told him he had to remain at home close to his family.

But the 1905-1906 season brought Shoreham and Bert's greatest honours when they won a county treble by taking the Sussex Senior Cup, the Royal Ulster Rifles Charity Cup, and the West Sussex League championship.

The success soon brought fresh interest from the professional clubs and by the next season (1906-1907) Bert signed as an amateur with Brighton & Hove Albion, who were then in the Southern League.

He became a professional player with the Albion the following year. In the early part of the 20th century, the Southern League was more of a force in English football and almost on a par with the Football League itself.

Initially used as an inside right, Bert was quickly recognised to be most effective on the right wing where his accurate crosses tormented defences for nearly 16 years… he rapidly became a favourite with Albion fans. He was a successful goal scorer but his crosses from the wing to his inside forwards particularly resulted in many goals for the club.

During the 1910-1911 season, Brighton were drawn in the FA Cup against Leeds United (then Leeds City) in the second division of the Football League.

A report of this match provides a glimpse of Bert in action:
"Although City were unhappy about the Brighton opening goal, they could have

no complaints about the overall result. Brighton started brightly and before five minutes had elapsed Bert Longstaff crossed from the goal-line, with Leeds complaining the ball had gone out of play, but Harry Bromage could only parry the cross and Bill 'Bullet' Jones had the rebound in the net in a flash.

"City were on level terms five minutes before the interval after some brilliant work by Billy McLeod. He had already tested the Brighton Goalkeeper, Bob Whiting, on several occasions, and he tried to lob the ball over the keeper's head and, after it hit the bar, Hugh Roberts was on hand to rifle the ball home from the rebound.

"City, however, failed to build on that goal and after sixty-five minutes they fell behind again.

"Bert Longstaff found himself in lots of space on the right and from his accurate cross, Bill Bullet Jones lived up to his nickname to head his, and Brighton's, second goal as Bromage unavailingly could only get his fingertips to it. It was Bert Longstaff, once again, that created Brighton's third and best goal.

"The tiring Leeds defence failed to hold him from making another searching run down the flank and he sent over a teasing centre for Jimmy Smith to power in a great header for the killer third goal, in a 3-1 victory. Leeds finished well beaten by a much fitter, cleverer and more organized side."

Bert was now performing at what many believe to have been his best and in much the same way as his performances helped his former club to achieve their treble, the Albion's similar success in the 1909-1910 season was due largely to his influence when they carried off the Southern League title, the Southern Charity Cup and the FA Charity Shield.

The Charity Shield was competed for between the champions of the Football League and Southern League and the winners were nearly always from the former.

As told in chapter three, Aston Villa were Brighton's opponents that day and the match was played in front of 13,000 spectators at Chelsea's ground, Stamford Bridge. Brighton started well and were the more impressive of the two teams until nearer the end of the first half when Villa started to take control.

In the second half, Villa continued to press but Brighton easily contained the pressure and only two long distance shots were made at their goal.

35

But then the Longstaff magic came into play. On 72 minutes, Bert crossed the ball which Villa failed to clear. Bill Hastings took possession of it and passed to Charlie Webb who *"dribbled round two defenders before hitting a rising shot into the net."*

In winning this match Brighton effectively became the footballing champions of England.

The outbreak of World War One bought an interruption to Bert's and most other footballer's careers but he returned to the Albion again when the war ended, and the football leagues recommenced their competitions.

Bert was a prize capture for the Albion when he returned to the Goldstone Ground in the summer of 1919 and helped many of his pre-war playing colleagues helping renovate the ground.

Despite his age (34 in 1919), he continued in the first team after the war and in the season 1920-1921 he played for the Albion in the newly formed Division Three South of the Football League that included such clubs as West Ham, Portsmouth, Southampton, and Crystal Palace.

His pace and skill caught out many opposition full backs. Indeed, Bert holds the distinction of being in the first XI for the very first game for the Albion in the Football League on 28th August 1920, when he was selected as inside right alongside centre forward Jack Doran and inside left Zacky March.

But this was to be his last season as a professional.

During his time at the Albion, Bert earned himself two benefit (testimonial) matches. The first was in 1913 when the opponents were Portsmouth. A crowd attendance of 2,000 earned him £135-3s-0d, equivalent to about £16,000 in 2021.

Unusually, his second benefit in 1923 was after he had left the club in a match against Merthyr Town (then a Division Three South club like Brighton) when the gate was 5,000. This, however, was a joint benefit with another player so that the shared amount would have been a little over what he had earned in 1913.

Bert made 443 appearances for the Albion during which he scored 86 goals thereby becoming the only Brighton player to hold for many years both records for aggregate appearances and goals.

Bert (second left front row) in Shoreham's treble winning side of 1905-1906

Once his Albion career came to an end in 1922, Bert went back to Shoreham where he continued to contribute to the success of one of the county's best non-league sides of the era.

In 1924, Bert secured permission from the Football Association to revert to amateur status and re-joined Shoreham then in the Sussex County League for his remaining playing years and appeared for them in the 1925 Sussex Senior Cup Final aged 39.

After retiring from football, Bert and his wife Marguerite moved to Freshfield Road in Brighton, and ran a beach kiosk on Hove seafront south of the bowling greens.

Maureen Abbott was a child in the 1960s and she and her family lived two doors away from the Longstaffs in Freshfield Road.

"They were a lovely couple who I believe were childless but that may be wrong," she said.

"They certainly made a fuss of me and my friend and Aunty Madge, as we called her, would take us with her for the day where we could play on the beach and help serve in the shop.

"Uncle Bert never came with us and I don't know how he spent his time, but he was quite elderly.

"We moved away from Freshfield Road in 1970 having been there for 10 years and that is such a precious memory of our time there."

Bert died the same year that Maureen's family moved away from Freshfield Road at the good age of 84. Marguerite passed away five years later.

An Albion great and a great of Sussex football in general.

7

Tommy Cook
(Thomas Edwin Reed Cook)
1901-1950
BHAFC 1921-1930
Centre Forward
Appearances: 209
Goals: 123

**For the sheer number of goals
scored Tommy Cook will
always remain top of any list of
Albion legends.**

He was also rather good at
cricket!

Tommy was a true son of
Sussex and a real *Boy's Own*
sporting hero. But his life was sadly also a real Greek tragedy.

Tommy Cook was born in 1901 at 30 South Street in Cuckfield,
where his parents Alfred and Eliza ran a sweet shop. He soon
showed promise at school level in both football and cricket, where
he enjoyed success with the village teams. Such were his skills as a
footballer that he was only 12 when he started playing for Cuckfield
Football Club.

During World War One, aged just 16, Tommy enlisted in the
Royal Navy as a boy seaman. He served on the mine sweeper, HMS
Glow Worm and it was while the vessel was in the sea off northern
Russia that he won a medal after diving into the icy waters at
Archangel harbour to rescue a shipmate.

While at secondary school in Brighton, Tommy had been noticed
during a casual match on the Marine recreation ground at Hove by
Albert Underwood, Brighton & Hove Albion's secretary. Word was

passed on to manager Charlie Webb. So, whenever Tommy was on shore leave, he played for Albion reserves.

But towards the last months of the war, Webb was taken as a prisoner of war in Germany. Nevertheless, Tommy had made an impression.

On returning to civilian life, Tommy attended the Crystal Palace School of Engineering and eventually qualified as a structural engineer. And before obtaining his passing out papers, he worked as a fitter for Southdown bus company and kept fit by playing part-time for Cuckfield. He then signed amateur forms for the Albion in the late summer of 1921 and had a cricket trial with Sussex before being invited to play for the county. He became one of Sussex's finest ever batsmen, scoring more than 20,000 runs in a 15-year career, including hitting 1,000 runs a season on 10 occasions.

Indeed, Tommy preferred cricket to soccer and only narrowly missed playing for England in both sports.

In the early 1930s, as a forcing batsman, he was given an England trial. He was truly an all-round sportsman,

His mum Eliza Cook was Tommy's greatest supporter. Once when he made a spectacular catch, she jumped up and shouted at the top of her voice: *"I'm his mother!"*

Tommy had played only one game for Cuckfield 2nd XI when the call came to turn out for Sussex the following Saturday.

The skipper, Arthur Gilligan, required him to bowl. *"But I don't bowl,"* said Tommy Cook. *"You jolly well will bowl,"* replied Gilligan, and soon the new boy was taking the first of 80 wickets which he captured for the club. But it was as a batsman that he made his mark.

After signing amateur forms with the Albion, Tommy became a regular in the first team the following season, initially as a half back before moving into the forward line and beginning a record-breaking run of goal-scoring for the club that has not been matched in peacetime football since, ending with 123 goals in 209 league and FA Cup matches between 1922 and 1929.

After playing friendly games in 1921-1922, Tommy proceeded to his first full League season with the Albion.

Following the opening three matches, Webb gave him his chance, and it was on his third appearance that Tommy scored his first hat trick at home to Gillingham. It was the first of an avalanche that included eight hat tricks.

In September 1922, Tommy signed professional forms and 16 matches after opening his account Tommy lined up for the first of three memorable FA Cup-ties against the famous Corinthians.

Albion could hardly believe their good fortune in getting such a plum draw and a record 23,642 crowd paying £1,923 saw a 1-1 draw. Perhaps for the first time on the ground, a film was taken of the match and shown in cinemas throughout the south of England.

Crystal Palace, home of the Corinthians, was the setting of the replay. The entire Albion club caught the 11 o'clock train from Brighton while two specials carried an estimated 4,000 supporters travelling on cheap tickets.

Seven minutes from half-time Tommy Cook drove Albion ahead with a searing shot but Corinthians equalised, and it stayed 1-1 after extra time.

The second replay was set for Stamford Bridge on the Monday. The attendance of 43,760 reflected how the battles had caught the imagination of the public and Tommy was feted when he scored the only goal, and the quality of his play alerted the England selectors.

An historic dinner at the Café Royal in Regent Street was held after the match, given jointly by the clubs in commemoration of one of the most sporting cup-ties ever played.

Both clubs were invited to a West End show, but as the Albion were committed to returning by the 10 o'clock train, the invitation was declined. At Brighton station, fans gained every vantage point and the players were mobbed as they made for the Hove platform. A total of 76,702, paying £5,609 had seen the three matches and Albion prepared for the visit of West Ham.

Charlie Webb always maintained that his side were lucky to draw 1-1 against the Corinthians, and that was due to Tommy Cook's equaliser. The replay saw Tommy shifted to inside left but he could not find the net again and one solitary goal sent West Ham through.

Seasons came and went and 1923-1924 will be best remembered for the Albion's second round hammering of Everton when Tommy scored a hat trick in the 5-2 triumph. A Goldstone record crowd of 27,450 witnessed the win.

Tommy went on to end the campaign with a return of 25 goals following Webb's inspired decision to turn him from an inside left into a centre forward.

Albion were playing in the Third Division South when his exploits in front of goal earned him a call-up to the England team in 1925. Even though he was playing in the third tier of the English game, Tommy's prodigious feats could not be ignored.

Tommy Cook remained the only Albion player to make the full England side until Peter Ward 55 years later. His cap came in February 1925 in a Home International against Wales at Swansea's old Vetch Field ground, a game which England won 2-1.

That gives some idea of his stature in the game, yet he had less than 10 seasons as a Brighton player.

He was placed on the transfer list in May 1930, with the asking price reduced in August. He joined Southern League side Northfleet on 30th September 1930 and then Bristol Rovers on 6th October 1931, initially on a month's trial. Tommy retired in June 1933 to concentrate on his cricket. He finally retired from his sporting career completely at the age of 36.

Tommy moved to South Africa the following year and coached cricket in Transvaal, playing against the MCC in 1938, and became a publican.

During World War Two, he was badly burned in an air crash in 1943 while serving as a corporal with the South African Air Force. He was thrown from the wreckage and spent six months recovering in hospital - the rest of the crew perished in the flames. His son Roger later said Tommy never recovered from that traumatic experience. Other friends say the crash brought about a fundamental change in his personality. Tommy had sustained injuries that meant hospitalisation for six months and that had plunged him into deep depression.

After the war ended, in 1947, Tommy returned to manage the Albion and suffered the indignity of losing his job when the side had only three wins in 17 games.

By 1948 he had returned to cricket by coaching the boys at Radley College but images of that burning aircraft and the screams of his pals haunted him in nightmares.

He was struggling physically too after developing bronchitis and on 15th January 1950 - just a month short of his 49th birthday - he took an overdose of sleeping tablets and died in his sleep at his home in Cuckfield.

In 2020, a new gravestone was dedicated to his memory at Cuckfield Cemetery. Albion fan Phil Dennett, whose grandfather played for the Albion, decided to get the new memorial stone laid on Tommy's grave after seeing the worn-out state of its headstone.

Tommy Cook's grave at Cuckfield Cemetery

The Albion agreed to pay for the silver inscription and local funeral directors Gallaghers donated the granite tablet, as well as tidying up the weather-beaten headstone.

"Tommy was a unique Sussex sportsman in that no-one else has excelled at two professional sports to his level. The tablet acknowledges his superb achievement. He deserves to be remembered in this way," said Phil.

8

Hugh Vallance
(Hugh Baird Vallance)
1905-1973
BHAFC 1929-1930
Centre Forward
Appearances: 50
Goals: 34

Hugh Vallance was only a one season wonder for Brighton & Hove Albion, but what a wonder he was!

Wolverhampton born Hugh was the complete centre forward and the first Albion player to score 30 goals in a season.

But he stayed for only one season.

Nobody has ever discovered why Hugh Vallance, who has now been dead for nearly 50 years, suddenly disappeared at the height of his fame. He took his secret to the grave.

The sketchy circumstances of his overnight flit after the first seven games of the 1930-1931 season, and after breaking all goal scoring records the season before, gave rise to huge speculation over what might have happened.

The club said nothing except to confirm that his contract had been terminated for what was enigmatically described a *"serious misdemeanour."*

Another player, Irish international Jack Curran, was also kicked out at the same time so, presumably, they had acted together when breaking club rules.

But what rules, and why the hurry to see them off the premises?

There were rumours that Hugh had an eye for the girls, but with Curran also being shown the door, that theory doesn't suggest there was a breaking of the pretty strict moral code of the day. Nor would there be the slightest foundation in suspecting the pair were in a gay relationship together.

The most likely explanation is that the players had been caught drinking while under express orders to stay away from the booze... and not for the first time.

Yet it was a drastic measure for the directors to take.

Scandal cropped up again shortly after their departure, when another popular player made the Mayor of Hove's daughter pregnant and was given leave of absence while the furore died down.

The 1929-1930 season had seen a new-look Brighton & Hove Albion side enjoy a much-improved campaign to finish fifth in Division Three South. Not only were league performances good, but there was also a remarkable run in the FA Cup in which the Albion eliminated two top-flight opponents on the way to a fifth round exit, the furthest that the club had ever progressed in the competition.

Following the 15th placed finish of 1928-1929, Charlie Webb had undertaken a mass rebuilding of his squad over the summer prior to the season kicking off. A number of seasoned players said goodbye to the Goldstone Ground, most notably record scorer Tommy Cook who left to take up a cricket coaching post in South Africa. Regular goalkeeper Reg Williams retired, as did Jack Jenkins while Wally Little and Jimmy Hopkins moved on to Clapton Orient and Aldershot respectively.

Coming in, Webb secured the signings of Harry Marsden from Nottingham Forest, Geordie Nicol from Manchester United, Harold Sly from Gillingham, Potter Smith from Cardiff City, Dave Walker from Walsall and most notably Hugh Vallance from Queens Park Rangers, who had started as an amateur with Aston Villa.

Most of the new arrivals made a good impression, but none more so than Hugh who after only being a reserve at QPR, became the first Brighton player to score 30 league goals in a season.

Nobody would break that barrier again until Peter Ward's record-setting 36 in the 1976-1977 season, 47 years later.

Yet Hugh's remarkable, though short-lived career at Brighton, showed no sign of taking off while he was at Villa. The former guardsman played only in the reserves and shortly went to QPR. He didn't fare much better there and had played just one League game before arriving at the Goldstone in the spring of 1929.

But Charlie Webb had seen something in the player and soon gave Hugh his chance and, in the same way Peter Ward would later derive both service and inspiration from Ian Mellor, Hugh quickly became part of a deadly duo with Dan Kirkwood.

Indeed, Hugh's partnership with Dan Kirkwood was pivotal to the Albion's success. Kirkwood himself hit 28 league goals for a total of 31 in all competitions.

Meanwhile, Hugh grabbed four hat-tricks before Christmas! He also notched twice in the FA Cup run to just finish ahead of his strike partner on 32 in all competitions to take the top scorer accolade.

With such firepower at their disposal, it was no surprise that Brighton's total of 87 goals was the most that they had managed in a single season. The Goldstone faithful witnessed some big score lines from a rampant Albion. Norwich City were beaten 6-3 on 7th September 1929, Fulham 5-0 on 21st December 1929, and Torquay United 5-0 on 8th February 1930.

The Albion scored 4 on five separate occasions while an 8-2 win at bottom side Merthyr Town on 1st February 1930 is the Albion's club-record away win to this day.

When it was adding-up time, Hugh Vallance had 30 League goals in 37 outings and Kirkwood knocked in 28 in 40. However, despite the sacks of goals, Brighton could do no better than finish fifth and 18 points behind Plymouth. Losing seven out of the last 10 games accounted for the disappointing finish.

And over the course of just one season Hugh became an icon... and a Brighton & Hove Albion legend.

Although the season ended without tangible reward for Albion in the League, Vallance and Kirkwood were very much top dogs. All told, the two forwards netted 63 goals.

But the next season began badly with just two wins out of nine games; Hugh's magical touch deserted him. Just two goals in seven matches was a poor return by a player from whom so much was expected.

Jack Curran, a left back, played in the first four games and Hugh's farewell, although he might not have known it at the time, was on 20th September 1930 when Albion lost 3-1 at Torquay.

Geordie Nicol, who had lost his place on Hugh's arrival, returned to the side and Albion pulled themselves together to finish fourth.

So, what became of Hugh after his mysterious departure from the Albion?

He tried his luck in the comparative obscurity of the Birmingham League with Worcester City.

But less than six months later he was an Evesham player. Something, or somebody, attracted him back south and he signed at the beginning of the 1930-1931 season for Tunbridge Wells Rangers.

His move to Gillingham later that year meant Albion were entitled to a fee and £500 was settled.

If Gillingham thought Hugh was going to recapture the sensational form he had displayed at Brighton, they were disappointed. While seven goals in 13 outings wasn't bad, it was not enough to impress the directors at Priestfield, and he was released a few months later and returned to non-League with Kidderminster Harriers.

By now, Hugh had decidedly itchy feet. It was not common then for players to ply their trade on the continent but that was his next berth. He played for Nimes and then moved to Basle in France and Switzerland.

By 1934-1935 he was back at Gillingham again with three goals in five appearances and at the age of 30, he chucked in professional football and joined the RAF.

He died in Birmingham in 1973 aged 68 - four years before Peter Ward beat his record with 32 Third Division goals.

Record goal scorer Peter Ward meets Hugh Vallance's son Brian before a game against Stoke City in 1977

It was therefore appropriate that after Wardy beat that record with a goal against Swindon in May 1977, the club arranged for him to meet Hugh's son Brian Vallance before the newly promoted Albion's away fixture against Stoke City at the Victoria Ground in October that year.

But the mystery of why Hugh departed the Goldstone Ground so suddenly 47 years earlier had died with him.

9

Ernie *Tug* Wilson
(Ernest Wilson)
1899-1956
BHAFC 1922- 1936
Outside Left
Appearances: 566
Goals: 71

South Yorkshire born Ernie Wilson is a true legend of the Goldstone Ground after making a record 566 appearances for the Albion.

Playing as a left winger Ernie – better known as Tug – was almost ever present for the club for most of an amazing 14 seasons between 1922 and 1936 – primarily in the Third Division South.

Ernie was born in Beighton, Sheffield, and went to school in the nearby village of Swallownest in the borough of Rotherham.

The little winger was rejected by his home team Sheffield Wednesday as a teenager for *"being too small"* (he was 5 feet 6 inches in his stocking feet) and subsequently spent World War One working as an essential worker for the war effort at the city's famous Silverwood Colliery.

Ernie played football for the colliery's works team. He also played for Beighton Recreation, and for Midland League club Denaby United in Doncaster.

In May 1922, Ernie had a trial with Brighton & Hove Albion in a charity cup match against Reading, then signed professional terms the following August. He made his full Albion debut on Saturday 21st October 1922 in a 2-1 home win against Brentford.

But he had to wait until the following February to score his first goal for the club, against Watford in a 2-1 victory at Vicarage Road.

Tug scored one other goal that season… the winner against Charlton in a 1-0 victory at the Valley on 16th April 1923.

By the start of the following season, Ernie had taken over from Jimmy Jones at outside left and was undisputed first choice for the next 12 years… he missed just 29 games for the Albion over that time.

He was described in the **Daily Mirror** as *"very quick"* and *"with the ball at his feet he could embarrass any full back with his trickery"*.

On 28th January 1928, a gate of just 4,494 was registered at the Goldstone Ground for the visit of Crystal Palace. The attendance was well below the Albion's average crowd of around 7,500. The home side ran out 4-2 winners with Tug Wilson grabbing a brace.

On Saturday 10th March 1928, after just six years with the club, Tug enjoyed the first of two benefit matches and netted just over £326 from the Third Division South game against Gillingham at the Goldstone Ground, in front of a crowd of 7,860. That benefit in 1928 would be worth about £20,600 in 2021.

Five years later, aged 34 and still giving his all, Ernie was part of a Brighton team in January 1933 who beat the mighty Chelsea 2-1 in the third round of the FA Cup. Arthur Attwood and reliable Tug scored the two Albion goals.

One report of the game by the **Daily Mirror** said: *"The poor Chelsea defence seemed mesmerised by Tug Wilson's quick touches and his uncanny sense of how to take the ball to the by-line or into the penalty area."*

Ernie's almost telepathic relationship with most of the Albion's centre forwards of his time at the club made him invaluable as a provider of goals rather than as a scorer.

He was key to the Albion's successful FA Cup run in the 1929-1930 season, providing goals for Kirkwood, Vallance and Dutton. He only missed one game that season of 41 fixtures.

But it was during Ernie's later seasons at the Goldstone when he really found his scoring boots – presumably because he was asked to cut inside rather than running himself ragged along the touchline.

Ernie (front row far right) in the Albion's successful 1930-1931 squad

In the three seasons between 1931 and 1934 he scored 25 goals.

Overall he scored 71 goals in his time with Brighton & Hove Albion and even put his cricket skills to good use with a couple of appearances for Sussex second XI.

Described by those who watched him as being full of deft feints and swerves and with an unmatched ability to produce beautifully flighted crosses, few have had an Albion career as impressive as the man who was working down a Yorkshire coal pit when the Albion came calling.

Indeed, it was Ernie's physical fitness and consistent high-quality displays which gave him the edge over other pretenders for the left wing berth for more than a decade.

In 1935-1936, Ernie finally lost his place to Bert Stephens, and retired from professional football at the end of the season, aged 37.

In hindsight, it is ironic that the Albion's appearance record holder was being replaced by the club's eventual goal scoring record holder.

Ernie had made 509 Football League appearances, 566 in all first-team competitions, which remains a club record and is never likely to be beaten.

Extremely popular with the Goldstone fans, he qualified for two benefits with the club, which together netted him around £650 – worth about £42,700 today.

He remained in Sussex, playing football for Vernon Athletic in the Sussex County League, and went into the bookmaking business in Hove with his friend and former Albion centre half Frank Brett.

Ernest Wilson died while living in an apartment in Portland Road, Hove in 1955 at the relatively young age of 56.

10

Bobby Farrell
(Robert Farrell)
1906-1971
BHAFC 1928-1939
Outside Right
Appearances: 466
Goals: 95

One of the greatest characters to ever grace an Albion shirt, Bobby Farrell, was the real comedian in the team during the 1930s.

He was also a brilliant footballer.

Dundee born Bobby began his football career with junior club Dundee North End before joining Dundee in 1926.

He ended his career some 13 years later as one of Brighton & Hove Albion's top scorers of all time and fourth in all-time appearances for the club.

According to the **Dundee Courier,** the young Farrell was a *"well-built lad"* who could *"fill any position in the forward line, having played in junior circles on the right and left wings with equal success."*

He made four Scottish Division One appearances in his first season and 12 in his second but was given a free transfer at the end of the 1927-1928 season.

Reports of him joining bitter rivals Dundee United proved premature and a trial with English First Division club Portsmouth came to nothing.

In September 1928, on the recommendation of a scout, Bobby signed for the Albion, who were then in the Third Division South.

He soon established himself at outside right in Brighton's first team and continued in place for most of the next 10 years.

The 1932-1933 season was one of the most memorable in Brighton & Hove Albion history thanks to an astonishing FA Cup adventure.

Back in March 1932, club secretary Albert Underwood had forgotten to enter the competition for the following campaign, which meant that if the Albion wanted to take part then, they would have to start with the country's non-league clubs in the qualifying rounds.

What followed was an extraordinary run which started against Sussex County League side Shoreham in the first qualifying round and ended 11 matches later in a fifth round replay against West Ham United.

A crowd of 5,500 supporters turned up for the visit of Shoreham to the Goldstone Ground on Saturday 1st October 1932, intrigued by the prospect of the professionals of the Albion taking on the amateur Musselmen. The result was Brighton's biggest ever win in a competitive fixture as they ran out 12-0 winners with Arthur Attwood netting six, another club record.

The second qualifying round paired the Albion with another County League side, Worthing on Saturday 15th October 1932. The Rebels agreed to switch the game from Woodside Road to the Goldstone so that they might pocket a larger share of a bigger gate receipt and 5,952 were treated to another big Brighton win, this time 7-1.

Southern Amateur League outfit Hastings & St Leonards provided the opposition in the third qualifying round on Saturday 29th October. Hastings declined the Albion's offer to move the game to Hove, instead opting to host at the Pilot Field where a record crowd of 7,723 saw Brighton run out 9-0 winners with Bobby snatching a hat trick.

The Albion's final game of the qualifying competition took place on Saturday 12th November 1932 away against Athenian League side Barnet.

The Bees were one of the best non-league outfits in the country at the time, but Brighton easily swatted them aside at Underhill, winning 4-0 to reach the first round proper.

A trip to Crystal Palace was next on the agenda on Saturday 26th November 1932. Most people would have expected the Albion's run to come to an end at Selhurst Park given that the sides had already met twice in the league with Palace winning 5-0 and 2-1. Brighton had other ideas though and won 2-1.

Two games were then needed in round two, for the Albion to eliminate Division Three North side Wrexham. A 0-0 draw at the Goldstone on Saturday 10th December 1932 was followed by a 3-2 extra time win for Brighton at the Racecourse Ground four days later.

Charlie Webb's men had trailed 2-0 at the break, before launching an incredible second half comeback to eventually win it in the 108th minute, with the winning goal scored by Bobby.

It was described at the time: *"The Albion's superior fitness told in extra time and Bobby Farrell waltzed through the Wrexham defence with 12 minutes left to crash the winning goal."*

The Albion's reward for their efforts over the previous seven games was to draw the mighty Chelsea at home in the third round. The tie took place on Saturday 14th January 1933 and Arthur Attwood scored after just 30 seconds to shock the Division One visitors. Tug Wilson added a second on 65 minutes and although Chelsea pulled one back, Brighton held on for a shock victory.

Bradford Park Avenue came to the Goldstone Ground in the fourth round on Saturday 28th January 1933 and were easily beaten 2-1. Cup hysteria was by now at fever pitch for the visit of West Ham United in the fifth round and a Goldstone crowd of 32,310 packed in for the visit of the Hammers, an attendance record that would stand for the next quarter of a century.

When Reg Wilkinson and Attwood put the Albion 2-0 ahead with 30 minutes on the clock, it looked like Brighton were heading to the quarter finals of the competition for the first time.

But West Ham showed their quality though to level things up with 10 minutes remaining, before running out 1-0 winners in a Wednesday afternoon tie which required extra time.

After nine rounds, 11 matches, two periods of extra time and 43 goals, Brighton's FA Cup run was at an end.

Unsurprisingly, the team's form in Division Three South suffered due to the extra games that the cup adventures foisted upon the fixture list.

The Albion faced a jam-packed run-in with seven games crammed into the final three weeks of the season. Fatigue crept in and they lost the first five of those final seven, including back-to-back 2-1 reversals against eventual champions Brentford.

Bobby Farrell and Potter Smith missed just one match apiece in the bumper 53 game season. Bobby netted 16 goals that season.

He maintained his consistency throughout his time at the Albion and always seemed on target to notch a goal.

Stan Hurst took over his position during the 1938-1939 season, and Bobby retired at the end of that campaign, but he remained on the Albion's books until World War Two ended six years later. After playing his last Brighton game at the age of 35, he maintained a keen interest in the club and rarely missed a home game.

But his humour was never far away. In an interview with a Brighton match programme editor in 1966, Bobby, then aged 60, said: *"It was a great life playing football. Why, I would have played for nothing – and I'm a Scot!*

"I had 13 years with the Albion and they flashed by like 13 minutes," he added.

He then recalled a newspaper sports reporter who asked how he kept so fit during the summer months: *"I told him I walked to Scotland and back – and he printed it!"*

Bobby was also serious about his time at the Goldstone Ground.

"Inside forwards were the hardest working members of a side in my day and generally we worked to a 2-3-5 pattern. But at times the inside men were back in defence, so I suppose we had 3-3-4 and other patterns too," he said.

Bobby Farrell (right) has fun sparring with playing colleague Potter Smith during an Albion training session at the Goldstone Ground

Bobby was only 5 feet 7 inches tall, but he had a knack for heading many goals and used to get up high for crosses. He put this down to constant skipping in training during which he brought his knees up under his chin.

He also praised manager Charlie Webb very highly.

"He did so much for me, and other players," he said. *"He was a shrewd judge of a player as well as a helpful manager and built up a great team spirit."*

And the other side to Bobby was that for much of the 1930s, he spent his summers as 12th man and baggage master for Sussex County Cricket Club.

This extremely popular player then became landlord of the Nevill Hotel public house in Hangleton.

He served in the RAF during World War Two and was still in the licensed trade at the time of his death in 1971, at the age of 65.

11

Jock Davie
(John Davie)
1913-1994
BHAFC 1936-1946
Centre Forward
Appearances: 191
Goals: 120

**Dunfermline born Jock Davie
was a no-nonsense centre
forward who developed a
habit of scoring a lot of
goals… especially against
Chelsea!**

Jock started his career with
Scottish amateur side
Dunfermline Wednesday in Fife,
then played for St Bernard's and progressed with St Johnstone,
Dunfermline, and Hibernian with three Scottish League appearances
in August 1934.

The 5ft 9in and 11st 4lb striker moved south of the border
joining Arsenal in the 1934-1935 season, playing at Highbury with
their nursery club Margate. He helped them to win the Southern
League Central Section and Eastern Section titles as well as the Kent
Senior Cup and Kent Senior Shield with his 37 goals in 1935-1936
and a further 17 goals from 10 appearances between January and
March 1936.

He also appeared for them in a famous 3-1 win over Queens
Park Rangers in the FA Cup on 30th November 1935 and was part
of their team that reached the 3rd Round of the Cup.

His exploits with Margate drew the attention of Brighton scouts
and he signed for the Albion in May 1936, making 89 League

appearances with 39 goals and 14 FA Cup appearances with 18 goals... therefore averaging a goal every two games.

He made 102 wartime appearances for Brighton scoring 81 goals. He also netted two more goals for the Albion in the abortive 1939-1940 season.

In all first team competitions Jock scored 120 goals for Brighton & Hove Albion, putting him third on the all-time goalscoring chart, including eight hat-tricks – although 62 of those goals were scored in the peculiar conditions of wartime.

The figures alone demonstrate Jock's scoring power and he holds the record, alongside Tommy Cook, for the most hat-tricks for the Albion.... starting with three goals against Exeter City in November 1936, followed by three more against Tunbridge Wells a year later and four against South Liverpool in the FA Cup in December 1937.

He led the line in dashing style and was known to complain bitterly if the ball wasn't played to him in the manner which he preferred.

In 1939 at the outbreak of World War Two, he enlisted with the Police Reserve Force and was later an Army PT instructor, reaching the rank of Sergeant. He saw service with many teams during the war, playing for Brighton and scoring 24 goals in 34 games in 1939-1940.

He also guested for a record 19 different clubs: Brentford, Clapton Orient, Reading, Queens Park Rangers, Crystal Palace, Fulham, Millwall, Southampton, Aldershot, Charlton Athletic, Leeds, Chesterfield, Mansfield Town, Nottingham Forest, Notts County, Sunderland and Manchester United. These appearances included a hat-trick AGAINST the Albion while playing for QPR in August 1941.

Jock is still remembered fondly by football historians at Chesterfield and Leeds for his war-time exploits.

During the 1942-1943 season there was no stopping Jock. Apart from the goals he scored for other clubs, he netted 27 times for the Albion, including eight in the two league fixtures with Chelsea.

He also scored 10 goals for Chesterfield in the 1944-1945 season and repeated the feat in the following season of 1945-1946.

One pre-war report in the ***Daily Mirror*** on 2nd September 1937 highlighted Davie's prowess in front of goal in a 3-1 victory against Southend. Under a headline of *Davie Brighton Sharpshooter* it reads:

"Best tryer for Brighton was centre forward Davie who has as many shots as a G-Man. I counted five in one inspired minute and a half. He was unlucky to only score once.

"Brighton's first two goals – a clever piece of opportunism from Davie, who kicked the ball out of Southend goalkeeper Mackenzie's hands, and a perfectly timed drive from Stephens... really rattled Southend."

But it was Jock's continual exploits against the mighty Chelsea which catch any football historian's eyes. The dynamic Davie scored a goal against the Blues in a WWII South fixture at Stamford Bridge on Boxing Day 1939. Brighton lost 3-2 in front of 3,000 fans.

But better was to come! The burly Scot scored a hat trick in an impressive 3-1 Albion victory at Stamford Bridge on 25th October 1941. And he scored five times against Chelsea in an 8-2 wartime victory at the Goldstone Ground on 31st January 1942, despite turning up for the game 10 minutes late!

One report said: *"There was no stopping Davie. Like his physique he barrelled through the Chelsea defence at every opportunity and seemed to have also been instructed to shoot on sight. Rarely have I seen such a deadly display from any centre forward."*

In hindsight it is unfortunate that Jock's best years as a player coincided with the war, for who knows where he would have been in the scoring records if peace had prevailed.

After leaving the Albion in August 1946, aged 33, Jock joined Stockton in the North Eastern League. But he returned to the Football League that December and played out his football career at Barnsley (where he made just six appearances), Kidderminster Harriers and Shrewsbury Town.

Enjoying a more rural lifestyle in gentle Shropshire, Jock settled in Shrewsbury, where he died in 1994, aged 81.

12

Len Darling
(Henry Leonard Darling)
1911-1958
BHAFC 1933-1948
Wing Half
Appearances: 341
Goals: 14

Len Darling stands out for having the third longest career span of any player in the Albion's history - almost 15 years and 341 appearances, just behind Bert Longstaff and Steve Foster.

His appearance record would surely have been higher but for World War Two and the seven-year suspension of the normal Football League.

He was a huge favourite of the Goldstone fans who loved his robust style to break down opposition attacks and set up chances for his own colleagues.

Born and bred in the Medway towns, Len began his football career with Colchester Town and Tufnell Park, but then returned home to Chatham.

As a young Kent county representative, he signed for Gillingham in 1932 in the Football League Third Division South.

But after one season, during which he made 14 league appearances, he then signed for Brighton & Hove Albion in August 1933, where he quickly established himself as a first-team regular in a dynamic wing half role.

Len made 141 league appearances in the pre-war period before serving as an ARP ambulance driver during World War Two, as well as playing for Brighton and as a guest for Bournemouth & Boscombe Athletic in the emergency wartime competitions.

One of those war-time games was one of the strangest – and the shortest – in the Albion's history.

The 1940-1941 season was arguably already the strangest wartime football campaign as Brighton and Southampton were two of 34 clubs from the south of England who took part in a huge Football League South Division. There was no formal fixture list; instead, clubs were responsible for arranging their own games against any willing opponents. The final table was decided on goal average due to no club being able to guarantee they would complete a certain number of games because of the constant disruption brought about by air raids and warnings.

The strange game took place on Saturday 21st September 1940. A week earlier, Southampton's great rivals Portsmouth had been leading 2-1 at the Goldstone when the warning of an incoming air raid went up and play was immediately suspended.

It ended up being the most devastating single raid on the city of Brighton in the entire war. A lone Dornier bomber had become separated from its squadron and with a Spitfire in hot pursuit, the Dornier commander decided to drop all 25 of its 100-pound bombs in a desperate attempt to lose weight and boost the plane's speed and chance of escape.

The bombs rained down on Kemp Town, including two which directly hit the old Odeon Cinema on St George's Road where around 300 people had gathered to watch a matinee showing of a comedy film, *The Ghost Comes Home*.

Some 55 people were killed - four children and two adults in the cinema - and a further 49 in the surrounding areas.

In the aftermath of such horrors, there was an understandable reluctance to go to public spectacles, so a crowd of just 250 turned up to the Goldstone seven days later for the fixture with Southampton.

Those who did were treated to all of 210 seconds of action before the sirens were sounded as the Luftwaffe launched another raid.

But the three-and-a-half-minute match didn't count towards the final league table.

The line-up that day for the shortest match in Albion history was Gordon Mee, Roy Watts, Ted Martin, Stan Risdon, Stan Hickman, Charlie Chase, Joe Wilson, Stan Willemse, Bobby Farrell, Charlie Harman and Len Darling!

At the end of the war, Len played a further 58 Football League matches for the Albion after the resumption of proper competition in 1946.

During his lengthy career with the Albion, Len became a huge crowd favourite of the Albion fans.

Albion die-hard and former youth team winger Charlie Harman will never forget Christmas morning 1940 at Norwich City's Carrow Road ground.

It was the scene of Albion's heaviest League defeat.

But the stigma of losing 18-0 was mitigated by the extraordinary circumstances. Only four of the visiting players in this wartime fiasco were on Brighton's books and two of those were juniors, one of whom was Charlie, then aged 16.

Another game against Watford at the Goldstone on 1st June 1940 also included 16-year-old Charlie Chase, Roy Watts and Bert Austen, both 17, and 18-year-old Stan Hickman.

Charlie said: *"There were some seasoned professionals in the Watford side and one kept kicking lumps out of me.*

"At half-time the backs of my legs were black and blue. Len Darling saw what was happening and warned the player that, if he didn't stop, he'd have him to deal with.

"The second half began much as the first and Len was as good as his word. He caught this player just right and he was carried off."

Brighton's youngsters amazingly held on for a creditable 2-2 draw.

Len retired in April 1947 to qualify as a schoolteacher under the Government's post war training scheme.

Albion players wait for the train at Hove Station for the trip to South Liverpool in the second round of the FA Cup in December 1937. Len Darling is seventh from left.

However, with the Albion struggling during the 1947-1948 season he made a come-back and played a further 21 games before finally turning to his new teaching profession at the age of 36.

As a qualified FA coach Len also coached in schools both before and after the war and acted as trainer to the England youth team.

He died in Felixstowe, Suffolk, in 1958 at the very young age of 47.

13

Bert Stephens
(Herbert James Stephens)
1909-1987
BHAFC 1935-1948
Outside Left
Appearances: 366
Goals: 174

In between the scoring records of the illustrious Tommy Cook and Glenn Murray, Bert Stephens is often the forgotten man... yet this maestro scored more goals for the Albion than both of them!

For a full 13 years, Bert scored goals for Brighton & Hove Albion at a phenomenal rate of one every two games, an incredible feat of marksmanship and consistency, which made him the most prolific goal scorer in the club's history. His record of 174 goals from 366 matches – including wartime tournaments – is 51 more than the next best and a record unlikely to ever be beaten.

When his tally in friendly and reserve team matches is included as well, the total rises to around the 200 mark.

Although many of his 174 goals were scored in the peculiar conditions of wartime emergency football, he had hit 87 goals in four seasons before World War Two broke out in 1939. He may well have gone on to beat Tommy Cook's peacetime mark had the war not intervened.

The most remarkable thing is Bert was not even a centre forward, but a left winger and was never Albion's penalty taker.

Although born in Gillingham, Bert was raised in Ealing in London where he played for St Thomas's FC before graduating to the Ealing Association club in the Southern Amateur League.

While working as a travelling salesman, he appeared in Brentford's reserve team as an amateur before signing professional forms at Griffin Park in February 1931, at the age of 21.

In four years with the Third Division South club, Bert played in their highly successful reserve team that won the London Combination title in 1932 and 1933, and the 1934-1935 London Challenge Cup. But the flying winger made just six appearances for the first team and scored one goal, before his departure at the end of the 1934-1935 season.

Bert joined Charlie Webb's Brighton & Hove Albion in June 1935.

On his arrival at the Goldstone Ground, the now 26-year-old winger was played on the right while club legend Tug Wilson saw out his own extraordinary Albion career on the other flank.

But after seven games, Bert was switched to his favourite wing and never looked back.

He scored four times in four games, including a brace in each of the 5-1 demolition of Northampton Town and the 6-0 thrashing of Cheltenham Town in the winter of 1935. Bert finished the season second only to Alec Law in the scoring charts.

And with Tug Wilson calling it a day at the end of that season, the Albion had already found his natural successor.

Playing a roving role, the highly skilful Bert had the knack of popping up in the right place at the right time scoring 21 goals in the 1935-1936 season and was then Brighton's top scorer in the 1936-1937 season, with 26 goals in all competitions and again in 1938-1939, with 17 goals.

During those seasons, he also hit two hat-tricks and five goals in consecutive games against Bristol City, Torquay and Notts County. This matched a similar feat he achieved the previous season when he scored five goals against Newport County, Exeter City and Bournemouth and Boscombe Athletic inside 14 days.

In fact, Bert was Albion's top scorer in four separate seasons and is one of only two Albion strikers to have hit 20-plus goals in three consecutive seasons (Albert Mundy 1954-1955 to 1956-1957 is the other).

One report in the **Daily Mirror** described Bert's exploits on the football field as *"unstoppable"*. It went on to say: *"Brighton's talisman has a habit of always being on the end of a pass, and through his own skilful play, able to score a goal at any time in the game."*

After competitive football was suspended in 1939 due to the outbreak of World War Two, Bert remained with the Albion. He served with the National Fire Service and represented them several times in the Inter-Services Cup.

He notched another four hat-tricks during the wartime emergency fixtures and played as centre forward and inside forward on a few occasions.

One of the most remarkable games ever seen at the Goldstone Ground on 29th December 1945 was a regulation fixture against Swindon Town. On the half-hour, the Albion's Charlie Longdon knocked himself unconscious on the perimeter fencing and took no further part. Swindon immediately took the lead, but 10-man Albion fought back well to lead 3-1 at half-time.

But further misfortune was to follow... after the interval. Joe Wilson limped off injured and Jimmy Watson spent the rest of the game as a passenger on the wing. Effectively down to eight men, the Albion succumbed to Swindon pressure and the score was 3-3 with just three minutes left. With Swindon pressing for a winner, Bert broke away and hit Albion's fourth. At the final whistle, the crowd spilled onto the pitch to acclaim the remarkable victory and the more remarkable goal machine Bert Stephens.

Bert had spent most of the wartime games in his familiar number 11 shirt until the resumption of regular League football in 1946.

In his last two seasons with the Albion, he swapped flanks and played the remainder of his games as a right winger with the younger Wally Hanlon on the left.

No longer the devastating and quick winger he had been before the war, Bert played his last senior match in November 1947 at the age of 38 and hung up his boots the following year.

In a report in the **Evening Argus** he was regarded as: *"the most prolific goal scorer in the entire history of Brighton & Hove Albion."*

During 1948-1949 and along with Len Darling, Stan Risdon, Joe Wilson and Ernie Marriott, Bert was granted a benefit.

But such was the austerity of the post war years that the income of three testimonial matches had to be shared between five players who had given a total of 68 years' service to the club.

Herbert James Stephens died in Thanet, in his home county of Kent, in August 1987, aged 78... a true Albion legend.

14

Stan Willemse
(Stanley Bernard Willemse)
1924-2011
BHAFC 1940-1949
Left Back
Appearances: 110
Goals: 6

Famed throughout the Football League for the ferocity of his tackling, Brighton born Stan Willemse was arguably the best player to ever wear an Albion number 3 shirt.

The tall, hard tackling left back even drew praise from England winger Tom Finney as the hardest opponent he had ever faced.

Stan served as a Royal Marine commando during World War Two and after shining at schoolboy level, joined his home-town Brighton & Hove Albion. He spent three seasons at the Goldstone Ground helping the club rebuild in the post war years.

He had already made his first-team entrance as a 16-year-old in a wartime competition in 1940, making him one of the youngest debutants in the history of the club.

But Stan's first senior games were as an inside left during a quartet of FA Cup encounters early in 1946.

That summer he signed professional forms, and soon after he was converted to left back, taking over from Freddie Green. He became a permanent fixture in the number 3 shirt, excelling even as Brighton finished bottom of the Third Division South in the 1947-

1948 season, then helping them rise to sixth place in the table a season later.

It is reported that: *"Willemse tackled like a runaway tank and was the rock on which so many illustrious flankmen foundered."*

Although his uncompromising play earned him a reputation as a hard man, Stan won a host of honours to demonstrate that he possessed a good deal of quality in addition to his fearsome presence.

He was a staunch defender, but he could also pass the ball and quickly became a fan's favourite.

His consistency attracted the attention of top-flight clubs and in July 1949 he was transferred to Chelsea for £6,500, the cash helping to pay for the rebuilding of the South Stand.

Unthinkable in today's climate, most of the locally based players were employed by the club's builders during the close season, thus going on to perform in front of a stand they had helped to erect. Stan was delighted that his fee - the highest ever received by the Albion at the time - had proved so useful to a club which always retained his affection, and he scratched his initials into the wet concrete footing of the new stand.

Henry Wood, a former England Youth international, who played for the Albion's A Team and Reserves during the 1940s and 1950s, has painful memories of former marine Stan.

"He was a hard and very good player, but he nearly killed me!" he recalls.

"It was the 1947-1948 season and I was 16 and told to carry the kit up to Arsenal for a Wednesday Reserve game.

"I was not expecting to play, but when we got there I was suddenly told "You're playing this afternoon at left half". I was already exhausted from carrying the kit, but I knuckled down… it was a dream to play at Highbury and this was my first Reserve game.

"Anyway, Stan was at left back right behind me and he cleared a ball at such power that it hit me in the back and knocked me flying… those old leather balls were heavy.

"As I lay on the grass, Stan just shouted: "Get up and play." When I later took my jersey off, I had a huge purple bruise on my back. Stan just laughed.

"That man was tough!"

Stan took a little longer to make his mark at Stamford Bridge, at first finding himself in the shadow of veteran Billy Hughes before the Welsh international was injured.

Stan seized his opportunity, impressing in several lengthy spells for Billy Birrell's strugglers, though it was not until the arrival of Ted Drake as manager in 1952 that he claimed a regular berth.

Having survived the major changes instituted by the new boss, the tall, powerful defender began to thrive. Effective in the air and an accurate passer as well as being unceremoniously forceful, he became a favourite with the Bridge faithful and played a telling part in Chelsea's remarkable transformation from relegation battlers to champions in 1955.

Stan only missed six games during that League title winning season, partnering John Harris and then Peter Sillett.

But as befitting a former Royal Marine who survived a shrapnel wound at Dunkirk, he was not a man to be carried away by sporting triumph, even cutting short his celebrations on the day the crown was confirmed by a home victory over Sheffield Wednesday so that he might watch his greyhound *Bandit* run at Brighton.

Although Stan never earned a full international cap, he played for England B against Switzerland in 1953 and for the Football League against the Scottish League in 1954, then represented London twice in a new European competition, the Inter-Cities Fairs Cup in 1955.

After making 221 senior appearances for the Londoners, Stan was judged to be *"surplus to requirements"* and was sold to Leyton Orient for £4,500 in June 1956, but not before featuring, albeit almost indiscernibly, in one of the most famous of all football photographs. As he hurled himself into a typical high-velocity challenge on Tom Finney at a saturated Stamford Bridge, the defender was virtually submerged in spray while the *Preston Plumber* somehow managed to retain his balance. That was no mean feat given the identity of his opponent, and the resultant image was truly memorable and immortalised in a fountain statue outside Preston's Deepdale ground.

Stan serving customers while landlord at The Eagle pub in Brighton

Years later when Finney was asked to name the most formidable opponent he had faced, his reply was instant and unequivocal. The great man's verdict went to Stan Willemse, who he described as a pacey, immensely brawny athlete yet also a footballer of poise and considerable quality.

Chelsea club historian Rick Glanville summed him up: *"Stan was tall for a full back in those days, at a shade under 5ft 11in, and as hard as nails in the tackle with a powerful left boot. He never flinched, despite facing brilliant outside rights every week."*

Big Stan also did well for Orient, who were newly promoted to the second tier. His experience was hugely valuable as he helped them to consolidate over two seasons making 59 appearances before he retired in May 1958.

After retiring he took over *The Eagle* public house in Gloucester Road in Brighton before running a betting shop in Southwick. He then became a security officer for London University before retiring to Hove.

But his memory was captured many years later when Stan was in his seventies.

72

Former Albion physio Malcolm Stuart explains: *"Towards the end of our time at the Goldstone the press were often in and out of the building talking to old players about their Brighton memories.*

"One particular day we had a tea break for the injured lads, so I went to make a drink in the players' lounge.

"Imagine my surprise and delight that waiting to be interviewed in the lounge were John McNichol and Stan Willemse.

"I asked if they would like a tea and asked one of the younger players to make it. I had a lovely 20-minute chat with them both.

"Then as I walked back to the gym the young lad who made the tea asked who the two old geezers were, my reply was two old players who were club legends and both just happened to have something he would never have in league championship medals, having both won them with Chelsea.

"The poor lad did look a little sheepish… but only a little," he added.

Stan Willemse died at the Bramber Nursing Home in Peacehaven on 5th August 2011 at the age of 86.

15

Harry Baldwin
(Harold Baldwin)
1920-2010
BHAFC 1939-1952
Goalkeeper
Appearances: 215

Brummie boy Harry Baldwin was an exceptional and consistent goalkeeper for Brighton & Hove Albion and had an amazing knack for saving penalties.
And until his death in 2010, Harry was the last survivor of the Albion's post war team of 1945-1946.

The underlying theme of Harry's life was luck. Good luck and bags of it. His first slice came as a member of the Erdington Schools' side in his native Birmingham.

"In 1936, I was asked if I would like a trial with Sutton Town who played in the Birmingham League. I was 15 and jumped at the chance," he told the **Evening Argus** in a 2001 interview.

"When I turned up they said I was a bit small for a goalkeeper and that a bigger lad was also being tried out and would I play wing half instead?

"Okay, I said, happy to get a game. But early on the keeper was injured and I took his place and saved everything that came at me and I was signed."

Events happened quickly after that. A month later Harry was spotted by a West Brom scout. Without more ado, he went to the Hawthorns as an amateur and made his First Division debut at 17, by which time he had grown to 5ft 9in… ironically the same height as arguably Brighton's greatest goalkeeper Brian Powney.

That baptism was a local derby with Birmingham City before a 45,000 crowd during Easter 1938 and West Brom won 4-3.

He kept his place for the remaining four matches of the season but was unable to help West Brom retain their top-flight status.

Young Harry turned professional, but broke his collarbone, never regained his place, and was released at the end of the season.

He moved on to the Goldstone Ground, on the recommendation of former West Brom and England inside forward Eddie Sandford, a nephew of the Albion's assistant trainer Bill *Bullet* Jones.

But Harry played just one league match for Brighton before competitive football was abandoned for the duration of World War Two. He served in the Royal Navy during the war but was medically discharged. After recovering, he made guest appearances in the wartime competitions for clubs including Nottingham Forest and Northampton Town.

He then returned to Brighton & Hove Albion and for the next seven seasons, Baldwin shared the goalkeeper position with Jack Ball, and took his appearance total to 183 in first-team competitions.

Despite his lack of height, he was particularly adept at saving penalties. In the 1947-1948 season, he saved seven penalties out of nine he faced, including five in succession, the sequence eventually stretching to 12 out of 16.

Inevitably he was dubbed Albion's Penalty King and, when the spot-stopping was at its height, Baldwin would be playfully teased by left back and local boy Stan Willemse: *"I'll give 'em away Harry, and you save 'em. Right?"*

However, it is unlikely there was much skylarking towards the end of that particular season when Albion finished bottom and had to apply for re-election.

The post war years were hardly a palace of fun with food rationing and rebuilding of communities flattened by German bombs. Austere Britain was all about picking up the pieces after six years of war and the life of a professional footballer offered opportunities of job satisfaction denied to most other returning ex-servicemen.

Harry Baldwin and his fellow pros had a lot of catching up to do and Harry resumed playing football after being medically discharged from the Royal Navy.

But Charlie Webb's spies were out and Albion's manager went to Birmingham and obtained Baldwin's signature.

Initially, Gordon Mee was preferred as keeper but, on 2nd September, the day before Britain declared war on Germany, Harry played his first Albion game in a 3-3 draw at Bristol City.

The fleet was already at its stations and very soon Baldwin volunteered for the Royal Navy hoping to be a physical training (PT) instructor. Instead, he was trained as a signaller. At the completion of his course, he was put on draft for HMS Trinidad, a new light cruiser.

But before joining the ship's company, Harry was selected to play for the Southern Command against the RAF. HMS Trinidad was sunk on her maiden voyage and Harry thanked his lucky stars that because of the invitation match, he wasn't on that ill-fated departure from Devonport.

Instead, the war came to Harry and the inhabitants of the naval base. He was badly shaken in an air raid on Plymouth and spent six weeks in hospital, with his nerves shattered.

He was barely able to walk for six months and felt so bad that he had given up all hope of playing football again.

No longer up to the fitness standards required, Harry returned to civilian life and joined the workforce at an engineering factory in Birmingham and it was there he met his future wife Rose. A whirlwind courtship followed and in three months they were married.

Two years after hospitalisation Harry felt fit enough to play again and guested for Nottingham Forest, Northampton Town and Worcester City.

At the end of the war Burnley expressed an interest but Harry returned to Brighton. Charlie Webb had kept the home fires burning and put Jack Ball in for the first three games of the 1945-1946 season after which Harry took over.

Albion competed in the Southern Section of Division Three, there being no promotion or relegations as football prepared for a resumption of full-scale League competition the following year.

Then business as usual signs went up all over the country and league players welcomed a jump of £3 in wages to £12 a week.

Harry got the nod for the first nine games then Ball took over the jersey for the rest of the season and so the friendly rivalry went on. They were firm friends and, fittingly, they shared a benefit in 1950-1951.

When Don Welsh took over as manager in 1947, he soon stopped Harry commuting from Birmingham.

"I used to catch a train at 9am getting to Hove at 1.25, play, and then race to catch the 5.25 back to London to be back home by midnight," Harry recalled.

"Don Welsh insisted that I stayed overnight and then made it a condition that I moved to Brighton.

"The club fixed Rose and myself up with a house in Southwick and we lived there for five years," he added.

After leaving the Albion in 1952, Harry moved on to an engineering job in Northampton. He continued his football career with Kettering Town of the Southern League but returned to the Football League in 1953 with Walsall.

After 18 months and 37 appearances, he moved to Wellington Town where a severe head injury ended his career. Diving at the feet of an oncoming opponent, he almost suffered the loss of his left eye, needed 32 stitches in his face and had a cracked skull into the bargain. So, aged 35, Harry directed his skills to the machine tools business and became director of three companies, travelling the world as sales director.

"Life has been very kind to me. I've been lucky," he said in 2001.

Harry Baldwin died in Northampton in 2010 at the ripe old age of 90.

16

Jack Ball
(John Albert Ball)
1923-1999
BHAFC 1940-1953
Goalkeeper
Appearances: 164

Local lad Jack Ball was quite literally an Albion *one of our own* and lived and died in his beloved East Sussex.
Jack was born in Brighton where he attended Brighton Intermediate School and he joined Brighton & Hove Albion from Vernon Athletic in 1940 as a 17-year-old amateur.

He turned professional three years later.

While many players had their careers ruined by World War Two, Jack Ball's flourished during the seven emergency seasons of the conflict.

Thrust into the first team at the age of 18 in December 1941, he went on to serve the club for another 13 years and enjoyed a benefit in 1950-1951.

The tall keeper had impressed the management enough to become a regular between the posts in the 1942-1943 season and signed as a professional in February 1943.

A month later he was called into the RAF but he continued to play for the club during the war years, whenever his duties allowed.

Arguably and ironically during that period, Jack will be best remembered for a game he never even played in.

When Watford visited the Goldstone Ground in the final game of the 1942-1943 season on Saturday 10th April, Jack's absence was the talk of the town.

The Football League South competition had finished some two months earlier with the Albion in a respectable 12th place out of 18.

But the Football League South Cup which had been played in the six weeks since the end of the regular campaign had been a complete disaster. Brighton sat bottom of their group with just one point from a possible 15 and having conceded 22 times in five games.

"Brighton's outstanding player that season was 19-year-old goalkeeper Jack Ball," was a contemporary report.

"He had already played a couple of times for the first team since making his debut against Queens Park Rangers in 1941, but he found himself thrown in at the deep end four games into the season when regular number one Gordon Mee's duties as a Police Reserve saw him called away from Sussex."

Jack played 29 times, earning himself a professional contract with the Albion in February that year.

A month later, on the eve of a game against Watford game, he was called into the RAF, which left the Albion with a bit of a conundrum.

Brighton boss Charlie Webb only found out the 11th hour that he would be without Ball's services. The only thing that Webb could do was ask his outfield players if anybody would be happy to volunteer to go in goal.

It was popular right back and captain Stan Ridson who found himself taking on the unenviable job, and it became even more unenviable when the Albion came in at the break with Ridson having conceded five times.

Webb had seen enough of Ridson's efforts in goal, and so inside right Ernie Reid took over.

Remarkably, Reid went onto record a clean sheet in the second half, much to Webb's delight.

Jack was meanwhile miles away helping the war efforts and unaware of the crisis back at the Goldstone.

When the war finished, and competitive football resumed, he made his full professional debut in the Third Division South in October 1946.

But he broke his wrist a year later, losing his place to Harry Baldwin, and the two shared the position until 1952 when Baldwin left the club.

Jack himself left in 1953 after he lost his first team place to Harry Medhurst.

He joined Hastings United of the Southern League and helped them reach the third round of the FA Cup in both 1953-1954 and 1954-1955 and remained on their books until the early 1960s.

He is today regarded as a club legend at the Arrows.

The Albion's official historian Tim Carder says Jack was an exceptional sportsman: *"Blessed with a wonderful pair of hands he was also a useful performer at cricket, golf, snooker and billiards."*

In 1958, Jack opened a sweet shop in Abinger Road in Portslade saying at the time that *"sweets always helped keep team-mates happy at the Goldstone Ground."*

He said that he was being retained by Hastings United on a part-time basis, but he needed to look for *"a new enterprise after football"*.

He soon got a taste of the retail trade and many people remember his second-hand and swap shop at Edward Street in Brighton. It became widely known as an Aladdin's Cave full of guitars, ice skates, telescopes and lots more.

But his history as Albion's goalkeeper for 13 years remained a matter of conjecture for many of his customers.

David Eldridge recalls: *"I remember buying some roller skates from his shop as a young lad. And I thought that Jack had once played in goal for the Albion, but guessed it was just a rumour he put about to aid business."*

Tim Sargeant added: *"I used to buy all sorts of stuff from him in the 1950s especially old radios that I tried to make work or took to bits for the parts, wireless being my hobby."*

Kevin Bushby added: *"My dad and I looked in Jack Ball's place every time we had our hair cut at Derek's Barber shop, right near Jack's. If there was any Scalextric stuff in there, my dad bought it for me.*

"I had one set which was huge, with about 25 cars, and bridges, and buildings, all from Jack Balls!

Martin Scrace added: *"When I was young I'd go scrumping from apple trees in Jack's garden in Florence Road… such happy days!"*

Jack continued living in Hove and died in Brighton in 1999 aged 76.

17

Johnny McNicol
(John McNichol)
1925-2007
BHAFC 1948-1952
Inside Forward
Appearances: 165
Goals: 39

Johnny McNichol was a prince among inside forwards and a true Brighton & Hove Albion legend, but he did not make his League debut until the age of 23.

Then he went on to notch more than 550 first team appearances for the Albion, Chelsea and Crystal Palace and was considered one of the finest and most respected forwards of his generation.

Kilmarnock born Johnny was one of the most influential players to ever have donned an Albion shirt and was the brains of the side during the late 1940s and early 1950s. He was admired by all those who watched him play.

When Johnny held sway at the Goldstone from 1948 to 1952, he played 165 games, scored 39 goals and assisted in many more.

During World War Two Johnny served with the Fleet Air Arm and came to Newcastle's attention with Scottish non-league club Hurlford United.

As a part-timer at Newcastle United, Johnny only left St James' Park because the manager and he couldn't agree whether he should be paid £8 or £7 when it was time to renew his contract.

At the time, Johnny, a trained motor mechanic, was earning outside the game and the manager thought this justified offering him a lower wage.

After two years in the North East of England he moved to the South East to play for Brighton. Despite his lack of first team experience, the club set a then record fee of £5,000 (equivalent to £180,000 today) before the start of the 1948-1949 season to bring him to the Goldstone Ground.

Brighton & Hove Albion were a small club compared to Newcastle, who at the time would regularly attract attendances of over 40,000 and at times even over 50,000. The Albion's average attendances were much lower than the reported 15,000 Newcastle attracted to a pre-season friendly between the reserve team and the first team back in 1946 that formed a part of Johnny's trial at the club.

Whilst at the Albion, Johnny continued to work as a mechanic, this time at a local garage which was situated conveniently close to the Goldstone Ground.

It is not a surprise given that at Brighton, in no small part due to the clubs relatively lowly status, he earned a £10 signing-on fee and a weekly wage of £12 (equivalent to a £22,000 a year salary today), in what were tough post-war economic conditions.

His arrival heralded a great improvement in the Albion's fortunes, and he was leading goal scorer in two of his four seasons at the Goldstone.

Johnny's ball-playing style was first evident in a typically tough Third Division South battle with Swindon on 21st August 1948.

Brighton had to apply for re-election the previous season after finishing bottom of the Football league, but fresh players, including Johnny McNichol, created renewed interest and the gate was 21,500.

He settled in gradually with just two goals from 33 starts and only nine were good enough to make him top scorer the following campaign.

The club finished sixth in the division in Johnny's first season and eighth, despite having no regular goal scorer – Johnny's nine goals made him top scorer in 1949-1950.

The next year, Johnny played in all the Albion's games, the only player so to do, and again finished as top scorer for the season, this time with 14 goals.

According to Brighton's official club historian Tim Carder: *"He had a superb season with a brand of play which won him the reputation as the finest inside forward in the Third Division.*

"Long-serving supporters are of the general opinion that the talented Scot was the finest inside forward to have played for the club since the war.

"While celebrated as a football craftsman and visionary, he also backed his skill and perception up with a fierce shot and an eye for goal, scoring at an admirable rate of almost a goal every fourth game."

After Billy Lane made him club captain, Johnny scored 14 goals in the 1951-1952 season as the Albion narrowly failed to mount a successful challenge to Plymouth Argyle for the title.

He was again the star of the side and *"was thought by many to be the most stylish inside forward to play for the Albion"*.

That season, Johnny scored a hat-trick against eventual runners-up Reading, which caught the eye of Chelsea manager Ted Drake.

Shortly before the next season started, he became Drake's first signing for his new club, Chelsea, at a fee of £12,000 plus Jimmy Leadbetter, a club record fee received for Albion.

Johnny went on to make more than 200 appearances for the pensioners and was a key member of the team that brought the First Division Championship trophy to Stamford Bridge in 1955.

Later at Crystal Palace, Johnny McNichol was captain for six years adapting to full back without turning a hair.

He didn't miss a game between March 1958 and August 1962.

Under his captaincy after three seasons in the bottom division, Palace achieved their first promotion for 40 years back to the third tier.

Johnny was still a first team regular after promotion, but he retired during the 1962-1963 season after a fractured cheekbone and broken jaw.

All the time he kept his house near the Goldstone Ground and bought a newsagent's shop in Newtown Road. After getting the paper boys on their rounds he would catch the 8.15am from Hove station and be at Stamford Bridge by 10am in time for training.

Johnny enjoys a centenary celebration lunch Withdean Stadium in 2001

When his playing career at Palace ended, Johnny had four seasons as player-manager of Tunbridge Wells Rangers in the Southern League and returned to Selhurst Park for 12 years on the fund-raising side.

Former Albion chairman Dick Knight says Johnny McNichol was his *"all-time favourite Albion player"*. He went on to praise him saying: *"He was brilliant, mesmerising. He would show the ball to a defender, nutmeg him, go either way, and he was a goal scorer.*

"He was the brains of the team and had an incredible touch on the ball... I think he was one of the greatest players the Albion has ever had."

Dick goes on to say that his favourite game was a record drubbing of Newport County in April 1951, with a 4.30pm kick off at the Goldstone Ground. The early kick-off was because floodlights had not yet been installed.

"It was pouring with rain, but McNichol absolutely turned it on," he recalls. *"We won that game 9-1 with Johnny scoring four, making the other five,"* added Dick.

Whilst at Chelsea, Johnny again combined his football with another second job. But rather than staying in the auto-mechanics industry, he bought and worked at his own newsagents in Brighton.

This meant that despite signing for Chelsea he continued to live in Brighton commuting to London on the train, something that didn't go down well with manager Ted Drake and that Johnny admitted that: *"Ted Drake and I had words about my shop".*

In total he made 202 appearances for Chelsea between 1952 and 1958, scoring 66 goals.

He later played for Crystal Palace for a five-year spell before working in their fundraising department. Johnny also owned and ran a newsagents in Croydon while still living in his house near the Goldstone Ground.

He then once again crossed the footballing divide and worked for Brighton in a similar fundraising role to that of Crystal Palace between 1979 and 1992 before retiring.

Johnny McNichol died from a stroke the age of 81 on 17th March 2007.

It says a lot of Johnny that at all three clubs where he spent most of his career, he is still considered a club legend.

18

Jack Mansell
(John Mansell)
1927-2016
BHAFC 1948-1952
Left Back
Appearances: 122
Goals: 11

**Better known as a coach and
manager in his later years,
Salford born Jack Mansell was
one of the most cultured full
backs to ever play for the
Albion.**

Jack joined Brighton & Hove
Albion on a lengthy trial in 1948,
having previously been an
amateur on Manchester United's books.

Jack came to the Goldstone Ground in early 1949 for a lengthy
trial period as a winger and made his first team debut on the left
wing against Southend United in February that year and signed
professional forms in March.

However, it was after switching to left back that he became a
regular in the side.

He went on to play 122 games for Brighton scoring 11 goals and
made the number 3 shirt his own.

Blessed with good pace, Jack was a hard tackler and possessed a
fierce shot. So much so that he was called upon to take penalties.

Always interested in the tactical side of the game, he earned his
preliminary FA coaching badge in 1951 and the full badge the
following year.

He coached county league side Littlehampton while still playing for the Albion.

Henry Wood remembers him well: *"Jacky was a very good player indeed, and well-liked by everybody."*

It was always going to be difficult for Albion to hold on to a player of his class and in October 1952 he joined First Division Cardiff City for a £15,000 fee.

Less than a year later, he switched to Portsmouth for £23,000 and went on to win two England B caps, represented the Football League on two occasions and be elected for two FA tours of South Africa. He also played in the first ever Football League staged under floodlights, a 2-0 home defeat by Newcastle United in 1956.

After his playing career was cut short in February 1959 by a bout of appendicitis, Jack, with his FA badges in his pocket, embarked on a coaching and management career, initially as player-manager with Sussex County League side Eastbourne United and later as manager at Littlehampton. He nearly became Albion manager, but the job was given to George Curtis ahead of him in 1961 and he was an applicant again when Archie Macaulay was appointed in 1963.

He joined the coaching staff at Sheffield Wednesday. Then in early April 1964, he became interim manager after the sacking of Vic Buckingham.

He coached many clubs, with his longest spell being at Reading and he had experience overseas with the likes of Blauw-Wit Amsterdam, Heracles, Boston Beacons, Maccabi Haifa and the Israel national football team.

A keen cricketer, Jack spent his retirement in Seaford. He died on 19th March 2016 at the ripe old age of 88.

A couple of years before his death, football writer Steve Ringwood caught up with the former Albion legend. These are a few snippets of his lengthy interview with the great man:

"It was late summer 2013, and we were in the sitting room of a well-ordered flat, tucked away in the quiet Sussex town of Seaford. Jack and Moira Mansell had been retired on the south coast for more than 20 years.

After retiring from playing, Jack was a highly successful football manager and coach

"Entering through their front door, there was nothing to suggest what had been before, how they'd lived their lives. As it turned out they'd managed in seven different countries across three continents over nearly a quarter of a century, and when they spoke it was always WE, they took on each new role together, wherever they went.

"Despite his Lancashire roots, as a player Jack Mansell spent the majority of his career on the south coast of England.

"It was during those early years at Brighton that he took his first coaching steps, attending the fledgling FA summer courses at Lilleshall.

"Jack had opened a coaching school whilst at Brighton working with local children and operating in the basement of the King Alfred Centre on Hove seafront.

"As a player he would often stay on after training to work with team-mates, and management just seemed like a natural step.

"It was something I seemed to enjoy doing when I was playing", he recalled, "it wasn't a question of intending to, I just went into it".

"At that time clubs from all over the world would contact the English FA requesting assistance with coaching or filling managerial vacancies.

"Jack had experience of coaching overseas, having travelled during previous close seasons to South Africa and Bermuda, and, by that stage a trusted staff coach, was now in a position to take advantage of these opportunities.

"I think we were pretty adventurous", says Jack, "anything that came up, we looked at it and if it sounded interesting we went".

"This sense of adventure led to spells in Holland, the United States and Greece; punctuated by periods in charge of Rotherham United and Reading.

"We've moved house about 37 times", recalled Moira.

"I asked Jack how he approached a new role overseas, but his philosophy was uncomplicated; he always started with the players.

"Experience had shown him that you knew what you were looking for in terms of a player's standards, the way he looks, the way he lives, the way he seems".

19

Jess Willard

(Cecil Thomas Willard)
1924-2005
BHAFC 1946-1953
Wing Half
Appearances: 202
Goals: 24

Chichester born Jess Willard is one of a small group of footballers who ended up playing for both Brighton & Hove Albion and Crystal Palace.

Jess attended the Lancastrian School in his West Sussex home town of Chichester and at the age of 14 went to work at Shippams, filling jars with various sandwich pastes.

He also boxed in his youth for the local boys' club and acquired the nickname Jess after the famous US World Heavyweight boxing champion Jess Myron Willard, otherwise known as the Pottawatomie Giant. The nickname stuck and Jess harboured dreams of being a professional boxer.

Although unbeaten in all his teenage encounters as a light-heavyweight, and in RAF bouts, other matters overtook Jess who, as a member of the ATC, hankered after graduating to an air crew on call-up.

In the early years of World War Two, minus some teeth and with a better-than-average soccer pedigree, he joined the RAF as an NCO (non-commissioned officer) and was drafted to fight in the far East against the Japanese.

He played for Sussex and South of England Boys and had the odd representative match for the RAF during training.

As a Warrant Officer, Jess was a wireless operator/air gunner on B24 Liberator bombers with a crew of three Aussies and three Brits. Each raid must have seemed like the last for any crash in the jungle could only end with either a mercifully quick death or mutilation if found by the enemy.

Back home in Sussex, football was quickly becoming his first love.

A wing half or inside forward with a huge capacity for non-stop running, Jess had no difficulty on demob in captaining Chichester City to victory in the Sussex Senior Cup.

He soon gained a full county cap and late in 1946 was asked to the Goldstone for a trial with the reserves.

"I remember well Charlie Webb signing me. Everybody called him Mr Webb because he was a perfect gentleman," he said in an interview with the **Evening Argus** in 2001.

"I had half a dozen games or so in the first team as an amateur and then Mr Webb put me on professional forms. After my first game I reported back to him and he asked what expenses I had incurred.

"I told Mr Webb the truth that it had cost me three shillings to get to and from the ground and he gave me six. I thought this is a bit of all right. I was later approached by Portsmouth, but I had to turn them down as Brighton had got in first."

Jess impressed sufficiently to be included in the first team, and with seven League outings as an amateur under his belt, he signed as a 23-year-old professional in June 1947.

Usually remembered as a dynamic, attacking wing half, Jess had joined the club as a forward and turned out in all numbers from 7 to 11, before settling into the number 4 shirt.

Despite the harrowing experiences and responsibilities of flying against the Japanese during the war, Jess was still a very young man.

He and his new wife Kay, who had served in the WAAF, set up home in a club flat in Sackville Road. But all the time Jess commuted from Chichester he felt acutely aware of his rookie status.

"I was on the bus travelling to my first game and I overheard two chaps discussing the team and saying there was an amateur named Willard playing. I just sat there cringing," he told the **Evening Argus.**

But in 1947 manager Charlie Webb, and Tommy Cook, his right-hand man, departed from the Goldstone Ground and Don Welsh took over as manager. Slowly but surely, Albion extricated themselves from a series of difficulties both on and off the pitch and Jess settled down as a key player.

The most he received in wages was £12 a week and a £2 win bonus. He and Kay got by and during the summer he and other players did odd jobs around the ground for cash in hand.

Jess also made scale models of aircraft at a local shop and the extra money was put by for holidays.

Henry Wood who played for the Albion's A Team and Reserves during the 1940s and 50s, remembers Jess Willard fondly.

"He was a very likeable lad... a real local boy, who was born, lived and died in Chichester. And a real hard worker too," he recalled.

Not long after his testimonial in May 1952, Jess, Billy Reed, Jack Mansell and Jack Ball were all placed on the transfer list and Jess joined Crystal Palace in 1953 for a fee of about £1,000.

He went on to make 46 appearances from 1953-1955 for Palace.

"But they signed me with a gammy leg and I had 18 months before giving up playing," he later recalled.

"George Smith was the manager and he asked me to take the youth team and shortly after I was made first team coach. I got on well with him as I had with Don Welsh.

"George was a real man and once whacked one of his players who was asking for it and he went on to manage Portsmouth. I had 20 years at Palace, but I always regard Brighton as my club. It is the first result I look for."

After his retirement from playing, Jess became a coach and trainer, first managing the youth team and serving as first team coach at Crystal Palace, then later working as trainer at Brentford and presiding over one match as caretaker manager in January 1975.

After a lifetime in football, Jess joined Securicor security services and in retirement lived in Turners Hill Park for 11 years.

Before the Goldstone was demolished in 1997, he and his wife Kay went for a last look.

"It was a terrible feeling knowing that the old place would be turned into something else. Us wives used to have a tea-room in the South Stand and the friendships we built up will never be forgotten," said Kay.

Cecil Thomas Frederick Willard died aged 81 on 6ʰ May 2005 in his home town of Chichester.

20

Billy Reed
(William George Reed)
1928-2003
BHAFC 1948-1953
Outside Right
Appearances: 132
Goals: 37

**Rhondda born Welsh
international winger Billy
Reed became something of a
star with Brighton & Hove
Albion in the post war years.**

From the famous coal mining
South Wales valley Billy began
his football career with local side
Rhondda Transport FC.

He joined Cardiff City in July 1947 after winning two caps for
Wales at amateur level and moved to the Albion a year later in
August 1948 as the club began rebuilding after the ravages of World
War Two.

As an industrious and speedy outside right he became the club's
top scorer in the 1951-1952 with 19 goals when he played in every
one of 47 matches that season – quite some achievement for a
winger.

He also developed an excellent understanding with Johnny
McNichol and inside right Ken Bennett as they turned provider and
scorer for each other.

This was Billy Lane's first full campaign as boss. He had been
appointed Albion manager before the start of the season – having
been caretaker boss since March, following Don Welsh's departure

to Liverpool – and he immediately won popularity with the fans by reintroducing the traditional blue and white striped shirts.

He also adopted an all-out attacking style by employing the traditional five forwards and brought in new players including Jimmy Sirrell from Bradford Park Avenue and Paddy McIlvenny from Cardiff City.

Billy - a former Welsh schoolboy and amateur international - was already established as part of that forward line and but he had only eight goals to his name over the previous three seasons.

He was soon to gel with his new colleagues and became a prolific goal scorer as well as a fast-raiding winger.

Albion kicked off the 1951-1952 season with a 5-1 victory over Colchester United at the Goldstone, in which Billy scored one goal and provided two more for Ken Bennett. This was followed by away wins at Torquay and Millwall, which took the side to the top of the Division Three table.

Then a 4-1 win at Reading on 22nd September started a run of 15 games with just one defeat. It also saw the side return to the top of the table at Christmas with back-to-back wins against Crystal Palace.

Albion kept in promotion contention with some fantastic performances until April, including a 5-0 win against Southend United which saw Billy Reed score twice.

And the on-fire winger also netted another two goals in a 4-0 win against Swindon Town at the Goldstone, where once again he also turned provider for Bennett, and did the same in a 4-2 home win against Aldershot.

Sadly, a five-game winless run brought an end to the side's title hopes and it was Plymouth who were crowned champions.

Albion finished fifth in the table, but the fans had flocked back to the Goldstone to watch a side that scored 87 goals that season, equalling the previous best in 1929-1930.

Billy had scored 19 league goals with Ken Bennett on 18. Skipper McNichol was the star of the side, while left half Glen Wilson, full-back Jack Mansell, and right half Jess Willard all caught the eye.

Henry Wood said: *"I liked him, but he was a shy lad. He came from the South Wales valleys and I think it took him a bit of time to adjust which showed in his first two seasons at the Goldstone.*

"Homesickness was often there among boys who were miles away from where they'd grown up, but once he settled, he really played well."

Billy scored a further 10 goals in 29 appearances in the 1952-1953 season before a falling out with management after requesting a move on several occasions.

He eventually joined Ipswich Town for a fee of £1,750 in July 1953. It proved to be an excellent move for Billy, and he became a bit of a club legend for the Suffolk club, staring as they won the Third Division South title in 1953-1954 and 1956-1957. He made 155 appearances for Ipswich, scoring 43 goals.

He was also the first player to be capped by his country while playing for Ipswich Town, earning his two caps for Wales against Scotland and Yugoslavia.

Ipswich fan and family relation Matt Catherall said: *"My Great Uncle Billy was part of the Ipswich Town side that faced Manchester United in their last home game before the Munich Air Disaster, playing against the Busby Babes. He was some player."*

In February 1958, at the age of 30, Billy moved back to Wales and joined Swansea Town for a £3,000 fee. But he only made eight league appearances for the club before being forced into retirement.

He later played in minor football with Worcester City, Abergavenny Thursday, Cairau, Milford Haven and Ferndale Athletic

After retiring from football, Billy worked for Ashland (UK) Chemicals, and was later a local government officer. He also coached local youngsters and did some scouting work for Dave Bowen, manager of the Welsh national side.

Billy Reed died in January 2003, aged 75 after a short illness.

21

Jimmy Sirrel
(James Sirrel)
1922-2008
BHAFC 1951-54
Inside Forward
Appearances: 55
Goals: 16

Glaswegian Jimmy Sirrel is better known as a manager and will forever be linked with his favourite club Notts County.

But he also left an indelible mark as a player for Brighton & Hove Albion, scoring an impressive 16 goals in just 55 appearances.

As an inside forward Jimmy began his football career with Renfrew Juniors while working as a coppersmith's apprentice near Paisley.

In 1939, aged just 17, he was linked with a move to Chelsea. But he spent World War Two working in shipyards in Cairo (Egypt) and Mombasa (Kenya) before joining Celtic at the conclusion of the war in 1945.

On the fringe of the first team for nearly four years, Jimmy netted four goals in 33 games for the Glasgow club before moving south and signing for Bradford Park Avenue in 1949, but despite his early promise he again failed to get regular first team football, playing only 12 matches.

He was subsequently brought to the Goldstone for a month on trial by new manager Billy Lane in the summer of 1951.

When Jimmy signed for the Albion in August 1951, along with Albert Whetton from Spurs and Paddy McIlvenny from Cardiff City and alongside incumbents Billy Reed, Johnny McNichol and Ken Bennett he helped give Brighton the most attacking and adventurous line-up since the mid-1930s.

Jimmy was also quite the comedian and known as the joker of the Albion's Third Division South side, often playing practical pranks on his team-mates.

He was a strong little player and skilful on the ball, but his lack of pace held him back and subsequently he was in and out of the first team for the next three seasons before signing for Aldershot in 1954.

Two years later his playing career was ended by sciatic nerve problems. He retired from playing and turned his attention to coaching at the age of 34.

As a qualified FA coach, Jimmy found his way to Brentford, where he was eventually appointed manager in 1967, leaving them in November 1969 for Notts County.

Upon taking his new position Jimmy said: *"Ask any kid what he knows about Notts County and he'll tell you they're the oldest football team in the world. By the time I've finished he'll know a lot more."*

From previous managers Jack Wheeler and Billy Gray, Jimmy had inherited a team including Don Masson, David Needham, Bob Worthington and Les Bradd, and his team would become increasingly difficult to beat.

His first season in charge of the Magpies ended with a respectable seventh-place finish after several seasons of struggle on the pitch and financial woes off it.

The following season the County stormed their way to the Fourth Division Championship, without a single defeat at Meadow Lane.

The following season the Magpies excelled again, missing out on a second successive promotion by three points.

But in the 1972-1973 season his team secured second place and promotion into the Second Division.

Jimmy had overseen a transformation of Notts County from Division Four strugglers to a Division Two side in little under four years.

For the next two seasons, the Magpies finished with respectable mid-table positions and looked to be heading that way again during 1975-1976. Jimmy however announced that he was leaving for Sheffield United and was appointed their new manager on 21st October 1975, replacing Ken Furphy.

But his two years at Bramall Lane were not happy ones and in 1977 he returned to his beloved Notts County to achieve promotion to the First Division for the first time since 1926.

This time, he would stay manager until 1982, when he became general manager, the actual managers in succession being: Howard Wilkinson, Larry Lloyd and Richie Barker. None stayed more than a season, and in 1985, Jimmy took over again as manager for a last couple of years.

By then, lack of financial resources had brought Notts County down to Division Two where they lasted just one season before slipping into Division Three.

It was Jimmy Sirrel who had given them their halcyon years. He is forever regarded as a legend of the club, and the County Road Stand at Meadow Lane was named after him in 1994.

And he was never overshadowed by his far more flamboyant and hugely successful next-door neighbour, Brian Clough, at Nottingham Forest. Indeed, they got on well, and Jimmy never showed an ounce of envy of Clough and his achievements.

"We were very friendly," Jimmy recalled.

"He was a bit bombastic about his football," adding, *"I was at his funeral in 2004."*

In 1997, while looking back on his career Jimmy said: *"Brian and I had a few things in common, not least Brighton & Hove Albion.*

"My years with Brighton were some of the happiest in my life and I still have great affection for the club."

As a fellow Glaswegian, Jimmy was said to have been an important influence on another manager far more celebrated than himself, Manchester United's Sir Alex Ferguson.

When Jimmy died in his adopted home of Nottingham in 2008, aged 86, the tributes flooded in.

Top of these was Sir Alex who underlined Jimmy's managerial skills at a club with strict budgetary constraints.

"All I can say is that I'd be confident in Jimmy Sirrel managing a team I supported, and that would be the general opinion from all the managers in the game," said Ferguson.

22

Paddy McIlvenny
(Patrick Dennis
McIlvenny)
1924-2013
BHAFC 1951-1955
Wing Half
Appearances: 60
Goals: 5

**Northern Irish midfielder
Paddy McIlvenny was not
only an Albion legend but
also a top golfer.**

Although an Ulster man, he
sowed his heart forever in his
adopted and beloved Sussex.

Paddy was born in Belfast in
1924 and came from a football-playing family. His father was an
Irish international centre forward with Belfast Distillery, Cardiff
City, Sheffield Wednesday and Shelbourne.

His younger brother Bob played for Bury, Barrow, Southport
and Oldham Athletic.

Paddy was on the books of Distillery as an amateur before
crossing the Irish Sea, together with Bob, to sign for top South
Wales' side Merthyr Tydfil of the Southern League, with whom he
won the 1948-1949 Welsh Cup.

He signed for Cardiff City in 1950, but never made the
breakthrough to their first team, and moved on to Brighton & Hove
Albion a year later, to join Billy Lane's new set of all stars.

When Paddy signed for the Albion in August 1951, he provided
the nucleus of Brighton's first title winning team.

In his first season, he was kept out of the team by the irrepressible Jess Willard, but Paddy became a regular thereafter. An excellent ball-playing attacking half back, he occasionally also played at inside right.

All was going well for Paddy until, in March 1954, a torn knee cartilage effectively ended his Albion career.

In an interview with the **Seagull Love Review** in 2008, Paddy was forthright about his time with the Albion. Like a few other Albion players from the 1950s, Paddy's thoughts about manager Billy Lane weren't very complimentary:

"He wasn't well thought of, although his work record was good," he said bluntly. *He was a crook, everything he did, you looked at and thought, argh, what's he on? What's happening? You were always worried that he was pulling a stroke on you.*

"He tried to cut my wages following the injury and so we couldn't agree terms and I went to Aldershot," he said.

As for his contemporaries as players, Paddy had more pleasant memories. *"Steve Burtenshaw was a very effective player, he was big; and usually big players get a bit cumbersome, but Steve held control,"* he recalled.

"He could play at wing half and he could still tackle well and make a pass and back the pass up.

"Des Tennant was also a lovely bloke. He was hard and he was fat but held the ball well and he could move with it, he was very fast.

"Dave Sexton had great knowledge of football, and he had his own mind about football. In the team he was the number one man when he was out there on the playing pitch.

"At half time, he'd give a little lecture, he spotted things that others didn't.

"Roy Jennings was another lovely player, a centre half, big and strong, and he did his job - he would get up higher than anybody else. He was a good player in his position, a very good player.

"Peter Harburn was underrated. He was a centre forward and it was hard to beat him. He would go forward and whack a player out of his way without any bother at all. Very strong player."

Paddy, second left, after winning the Kent Senior Cup with Dover in 1960

As for playing at the Goldstone Ground, Paddy said: *"The Goldstone pitch was a good pitch. The worst snag was when you got down the bottom, as it sloped from just over the halfway line down to the by-line. Nothing worse than a sloped pitch. The South Stand was taken over by the wives and girlfriends who had their own area.*

"The North stand was noisy, they'd bollock everybody. Unforgiving. They expected a goal with every attack."

Although the Albion offered Paddy a new contract following his knee injury, he was unable to agree terms with an intransigent Billy Lane and joined another Third Division South club, Aldershot, on a free transfer in December 1955.

After 16 league appearances, Paddy returned to the Southern League with Hastings United and skippered the side that lost 2-1 to Notts County in the FA Cup in 1959.

He then played for Dover, and managed Sussex County League side Southwick.

After leaving professional football, Paddy set up and ran a building firm in the Brighton area.

But it is in golf that he is probably best remembered. He was an active golfer for most of his life, captained the Sussex county team in the 1970s, and was a vice-president of the Sussex Golf Union. Among later honours with the small white ball, he won the Sussex seniors championship in 1985, 1986, 1987 and 1993.

Upon his death in March 2013, aged 88, the County Golf Union issued this statement which showed the high regard Paddy was held as an all-round sportsman: *"Paddy died peacefully at Oak Lodge Nursing Home in Burgess Hill where he was well looked after for the past five years.*

"Paddy was born into a large family in Belfast in an era where everyone was "self-made" in their career. He was a gifted athlete and played with distinction for Brighton & Hove Albion before setting up a family construction business.

"At golf Paddy was a household name throughout Sussex and beyond and he was gifted with a wonderful swing and timing to go with it. Allied to a graceful and flawless swing he had a wonderful competitive temperament which saw his name on many honours boards at the highest level of amateur golf.

"Paddy was County Captain from 1972 to 1974 and a Vice President of the County.

"He was an ever present at the Dyke and a great support to junior golfers such as Carl Watts whom he gave great support to as they set out on their golfing careers.

Paddy never ever spoke about his own golf or his successes but was always there to help others.

"For many of our older members the sight of Paddy sitting on the seat above the 7th green made the second shot to the green a lot harder – a nod or a shake of the head, acclimation or no, and boy did you feel proud if you hit a good one in front of the master!

"A poignant footnote for Paddy and his time at the Dyke was when the lockers were changed a few years ago – Paddy's locker when opened contained his clubs and three bags of birdseed for feeding the pheasants on the 13th… that was Paddy."

23

Jimmy Langley
(Ernest James Langley)
1929-2007
BHAFC 1953-1957
Left Back
Appearances: 178
Goals: 16

London born Jimmy Langley was an all-time Albion legend noted for his fast rampaging runs from the left back position and his long throw-ins.

Nicknamed *Rubber Legs* because of his superb tackling, he was a player who excited the fans with his dashes and dribbles up the field, long before the idea or overlapping full backs had been thought of. Indeed, many spectators believed his abilities were wasted at full back and he should have played further forward.

Jimmy started his football career as an amateur, playing for a number of non-league sides in Middlesex whilst still a teenager. He played for Yiewsley FC, in the London Borough of Hillingdon, at the age of 15.

His ability was soon attracting attention and in 1946 he was given his dream move - First Division side Brentford signing him when he was still only 17 years old.

But Jimmy's stay with the Bees did not last long - his height of 5 feet 9 inches apparently counting against him with manager Harry Curtis - and he was soon looking for another club.

As with many youngsters his age, Jimmy was called upon to do National Service and it was while he was still serving in the Army, in the Royal Army Medical Corps, that he joined Billy Lane's Guildford City in 1948. After a season playing with the Southern League side as an amateur, during which they narrowly avoided relegation, Jimmy turned professional in 1949.

His second shot at making it in the Football League was as unhappy as his first as Jimmy made only nine appearances for Leeds during his one season there. Despite scoring on his debut and on two subsequent occasions in his nine appearances on the left wing, manager Frank Buckley preferred to play Leeds stalwart Grenville Hair at Langley's preferred position of left back.

Already a favourite of Brighton & Hove Albion manager Billy Lane, who knew all about him after his time at Guildford, Jimmy was enticed moved to the Goldstone Ground in July 1953.

Immediately winning a regular place in the number 3 shirt, he missed just five games in his time at the Albion and skippered the team for more than two years.

In the 1955-1956 season, he played a big part in the side which finished runners-up in the Third Division South with a record number of goals scored and points gained.

As well as tackling and dribbling, other features of his game were speed of recovery and his incredibly long throw-ins which were as effective as a corner kick.

In many press reports at the time, Jimmy was singled out as the "star" of the game, which was unusual for a full back to get such glory.

In one 4-0 thrashing of Northampton Town, Jimmy was praised for his skill in lobbing in the fourth goal when he noticed the keeper was out of position.

Regularly he and right back Des Tennant were described by the press as the "most venturesome" full backs in the division.

In his autobiography **Mad Man**, former Albion chairman Dick Knight recalls: *"Maurice McLafferty left the club in 1953 and was replaced by Jimmy Langley, who joined us from Leeds United as a left winger. Billy Lane quickly converted him into a defender and became the best left back that ever played for Brighton.*

"He was a wonderful buccaneering player – very speedy, as you'd expect from a former winger – and averaged about 12 goals a season from left back."

In March 1955, Jimmy was chosen to play for the England B team in a 1-1 draw with West Germany at Sheffield. He went on to gain two further B-international caps while at the Albion.

Henry Wood remembers Jimmy fondly.

"He was a hard worker, a good lad, a real team man and fun off the pitch," he said.

"He used to cycle to training sessions and games and leave his bike propped up outside. After one game his bike had disappeared, and he came back into the dressing room asking: "Has anyone seen my bike?"

"Frankie Howard had hidden it on the toilets roof outside… he took it all in good spirit as everyone laughed."

It was only a matter of time before a big club came calling for Jimmy's services and on 1st February 1957, a £12,500 fee took him to Second Division Fulham, where he spent eight years with 323 first-team appearances and 31 goals.

In 1958-1959 he returned to Hove as a record 36,747 crowd packed the Goldstone Ground to see the Albion beat Jimmy Langley and Fulham 3-0.

He is remembered particularly fondly by supporters of the Cottagers for his long service with the club during which he helped them achieve promotion to the First Division during the 1958–1959 season. He is also remembered by QPR fans for featuring in the side which won the Third Division title and beating First Division West Bromwich Albion in the League Cup Final in 1967 and by Guildford City where he remains one of their most successful former players.

Jimmy Langley retired in 1971 and became a coach at Crystal Palace before returning to Hillingdon Borough as a club administrator.

He had one last sojourn in management for Dulwich Hamlet in the latter part of the 1976-1977 season where he strived, ultimately fruitlessly, to prevent their relegation into the Second Division of the Isthmian League.

After his time at Hillingdon Borough FC finished, Jimmy moved into a career in hospitality as a managing steward with overall responsibility for the operation of the club including the bar and premises firstly at West Drayton Royal British Legion and then at Sipson Royal British Legion.

He was a popular person and renowned for the friendly charm that he displayed to everybody that he met.

Perhaps the ultimate accolade however came from Sir Stanley Matthews when he selected Jimmy to be his opposite number in his final league match.

Jimmy's son, Peter Langley, said: *"Dad left to join QPR really to have a rest because he felt his career was coming to an end!*

"He wanted to take it easy and thought being at a team in the third division would be just the kind of relaxing experience he was looking for.

"Instead, he found himself there when they were right on the upswing and that is unquestionably where he experienced his greatest joy as a player, winning the double and getting to play club football at Wembley."

"Us kids were older by the time of the 1967 final so we no longer got forced to go and watch him, but we still went anyway. My sister's hero was Rodney Marsh and watching dad in the same team as him was amazing for her.

"Then when dad was playing for Hillingdon Borough in 1969, they beat Luton Town in the second round of the FA Cup.

"Luton were being managed by Alex Stock and he told dad before the game that if Hillingdon won he would eat his famous Trilby hat.

"After the game, dad saved it from being eaten by claiming it for himself and he always kept it as a memento."

Jimmy Langley died in London in 2007 at the age of 78.

There were many highlights in Jimmy's career but particularly picked out by the press after his death, were his goal for Fulham in the 1962 FA Cup semi-final replay against Burnley, despite his side eventually losing to the Clarets; and his selection for a London XI which lost to Barcelona in the Inter City Fairs Cup final in 1958.

24

Albert Mundy
(Albert Edward Mundy)
1926-1999
BHAFC 1953-1958
Inside Forward
Appearances: 178
Goals: 90

Albert Mundy was a real goal scoring machine for the Albion during the heydays of Billy Lane's attacking sides of the 1950s.

Albert was Brighton's top scorer for three consecutive seasons, from 1954-1955 to 1956-1957, and he stands third only to the immortal Tommy Cook and Glenn Murray in the club's list of peacetime goal scorers.

He is also one of only two players to score more than 20 goals in each of three successive seasons (the other is Bert Stephens).

Albert was born in Gosport, Hampshire and played for his hometown club Gosport Borough Athletic before moving into the Football League with nearby Portsmouth.

He made his debut in March 1951, in a goalless draw at home to Manchester United in the First Division, but despite earning himself a fine reputation, he failed to establish himself as a first team regular and joined Brighton & Hove Albion in November 1953.

An instant success at the Goldstone Ground, the 27-year-old forward became a great favourite and formed an incisive partnership with right winger Dennis Gordon.

Although he was an instinctive finisher, Albert was essentially an inside forward and led the attack only on the odd occasion; his scoring consistency was therefore quite remarkable.

In press reports of the time, Albert Mundy is mentioned more often than any other Albion player. Often these reports were to describe his goals such as a poacher's rebounded shot in a 4-0 thumping of Northampton Town, a lightning-fast snapshot in a 5-1 victory over Norwich City and a brace, including a scrambled winner, in a crucial 3-2 game against promotion rivals Ipswich Town in February 1953.

But it was his first and equalising goal which excited the watching football reporters. The **Daily Mirror** reported: *"Albert Mundy, the Brighton inside right tried an optimistic lob from the left. Goalkeeper Jack Parry misjudged the ball's flight and palmed it into the net."*

Almost two years later in December 1954, in a 5-1 mauling of Norwich City at the Goldstone Albert helped himself to a pair of fine goals including a dazzling inter-pass with Leadbetter straight from the second half kick-off.

"Mundy has such timing and always knows where his team-mates and the opposition goal is," reported the **Evening Argus**, after the game.

In April 1957, Albert scored six goals in the last few games of the season, including a hat-trick in the 8-3 goal feast against Reading in the final home game, which one newspaper heralded as his *"personal triumph"*.

But it was the previous season that his scoring exploits propelled him into national attention. In the 1955-1956 season, fired by the goals of Albert Mundy, Albion were involved in a fascinating three-way promotion battle.

Albion fans were certainly entertained during that season, with the team winning 14 league games in succession at the Goldstone Ground at an average of almost four goals scored per game.

The opening half of the season was a closely fought affair but once we turned into 1956, the title charge became a three-horse race between the Albion, Leyton Orient and Ipswich Town – although Billy Lane's side never actually headed the table at any stage.

Indeed, Albion's attacking style sometimes left them exposed, with surprise defeats suffered at struggling QPR, Newport County and Shrewsbury Town. Six points over Easter did, however, keep the pressure on but a 1-1 draw with the O's at the Goldstone on 18th April, in front of 30,864 fans, followed by a 2-1 defeat at Ipswich the following week ended any title hopes.

The 65-point total and a second-placed finish was the highest the club had ever achieved, likewise the 112 league goals scored. In fact, Albion scored more goals than any other Football League club that season; Albert leading the way with 28 goals, followed by Peter Harburn with 23.

Three times during his five seasons with the club Albert headed the Albion goalscoring charts and scored more than 20 goals in three successive seasons.

Despite contributing 10 goals to the Albion's 1957-1958 campaign, Albert seemed to be slowing down and lost his place to the newly signed Dave Sexton. He left for Aldershot in the February of 1958.

In four seasons at the Goldstone, Albert scored 90 goals (86 in the League) in 178 outings and went on to make 130 appearances for Aldershot.

Playing for Aldershot against Hartlepools United in October 1958, Albert scored a goal after only six seconds - which was at the time the fastest goal ever recorded - in a 3-0 victory.

He went on to play 136 games for the Shots, scoring 13 goals.

In total Albert made 346 appearances in the Football League, scoring 111 goals.

Later he switched to half back, before leaving Aldershot in July 1961 to join a large contingent of ex Albion players in the Southern League at Guildford City.

After several seasons with the Surrey side and at the end of his playing career in 1960 Albert returned to Gosport Borough Athletic as a player-manager in the Hampshire League.

He later drove lorries for his friend and fellow ex-Pompey player Dennis Edwards, who ran a refrigerated food business in the city.

On 11th December 1999, Albert Edward Mundy died at the age of 73 in Portsmouth.

25

Dave Sexton
(David James Sexton)
1930-2012
BHAFC 1957-1958
Inside Forward
Appearances: 53
Goals: 28

Dave Sexton will be most remembered as one of England's most endearing managers, enjoying success with Chelsea, QPR and Manchester United over an unbroken 14 years at the top. This was followed by an even more impressive 15 years as manager of the England U21 teams before becoming the FA's first technical director at the national school at Lilleshall.

Dave was born in Islington, North London, the son of professional boxer Archie Sexton, and started his playing career as a forward with Chelmsford City before joining Luton Town for one season and then West Ham.

He scored 29 goals in 77 appearances in the mid-1950s for the east London club, and it was there that he became immersed in the culture of football coaching.

He was part of a group of young players, including Malcolm Allison, Noel Cantwell, John Bond and Frank O'Farrell, who would spend hours discussing tactics in Cassettari's Cafe opposite West Ham's Upton Park ground. All were destined to become successful football managers.

But first and foremost, Dave was a free scoring inside forward who delighted the Goldstone Ground crowds for two seasons with his play and style.

After stints at Luton, West Ham and Leyton Orient, Dave was already a seasoned professional when Billy Lane brought him to Brighton & Hove Albion for £3,000 in October 1957.

Dave later said: *"Mr Lane was a very affable, quietly spoken bloke who loved attacking football and that suited me down to the ground. We got on very well, he was a striker like me and was interested in boxing and knew my dad Archie, who is joint holder of the British record for knockouts with 78.*

"All the players got on well, but a lot of what we achieved stemmed from the manager's positive approach."

In his time on the south coast, Dave enjoyed a prolific goal scoring spell with 28 goals in his 53 games and helped the club win the Third Division championship in 1958, before injury ruled him out of the climax to the season.

Indeed, his impressive form won him a place in the Third Division southern representative side versus the northern section at Carlisle in March 1958.

Blessed with excellent ball skills, Dave was the brains behind the attack and could control the pace of any game with his ease of distribution.

He appeared in all three inside forward positions while with the Albion but was transferred to Crystal Palace in May 1959.

He then suffered knee problems and was forced into retirement from playing in January 1962, at the age of 31.

Soon after leaving Selhurst Park, Dave was appointed assistant coach at Chelsea by the flamboyant new manager Tommy Docherty – the start of a tremendous new career for the quiet, thoughtful Londoner.

And any disappointment at having to hang up his boots would have been quickly overshadowed by his managerial achievements.

The highs of his accomplishments included steering Chelsea to FA Cup (1970) and European Cup Winners Cup (1971) triumphs.

With three different clubs he managed the teams to the runners-up spot in the First Division. First with Chelsea (1970-1971), then

Queens Park Rangers (1975-1976) and finally with Manchester United (1979-1980).

He was the antithesis of the outspoken blunt football manager. A modest and deep-thinking man, he was one of the most influential and progressive coaches of his generation and brought tremendous success to the two London clubs he managed,

His deportment was a contrast to his Chelsea team, which including swaggering party boys, such as Peter Osgood and Alan Hudson, and the tough-tackling Ron Chopper Harris.

Yet Dave was embraced by players and supporters for advocating a mixture of neat passing and attacking flair backed up with steely ball-winners.

He was a student of Rinus Michels and Dutch total football, a fluid and highly technical system in which all 10 of a team's outfield players can switch positions quickly to maximise space on the field. He would sometimes fly to Holland at his own expense to watch games.

At QPR he instilled in the side a discipline and aesthetic that was ahead of its time, emphasising the importance of diet and fitness, and video analysis using footage that he had painstakingly edited himself.

He also had a very successful period as coach of the England Under-21 side, and won the UEFA Under 21s Championship twice, in 1982 and 1984.

He also wrote a book on coaching a football team for coaches of all levels called *Tackle Soccer*.

A resident of Hove for many years, Dave Sexton later lived in Kenilworth in Warwickshire, where in 2008 he was commemorated with a new commercial building in the town centre, named Sexton House.

He ended his full-time managerial career at Coventry in 1983 but continued his England Under-21 coaching in a part-time capacity.

In 2001, he attended Brighton & Hove Albion's Centenary Evening of Legends at the Brighton Centre and said that winning the Division Three title with the Albion was the highlight of his then glittering 51-year career in football.

"It was my biggest highlight as a player and the most satisfying time of my career when Brighton won the title," he said.

"You enjoy being a player the most. As a manager or coach you are responsible for everything, you are never free.

"But as a player you haven't got those worries. You can just go out, work hard and express yourself and with the Brighton team that year that's what I did.

"The free-scoring, positive approach was such a wonderful experience. It was the first time I'd won anything. It was tremendous."

Dave says he scored the best and most important goal of his career for the Albion as they closed in on the title with four matches to go at Port Vale. It turned him from villain into hero.

He said: *"I remember it well. It was dramatic. We were losing, had a penalty which I scuffed it and the goalkeeper saved. I looked around at the players' faces. Their look of disappointment is one I'll never forget. It was an awful feeling.*

"But I made up for it by getting an equaliser. It was a bullet header from a rocket cross by Frankie Howard who, with Dennis Gordon, supplied a lot of my goals by whizzing down the wing to provide a fantastic service.

"The sense of relief I felt is still with me now because we really needed that point to keep on track for the title.

"But there was a down-side because I had gone for the ball with the centre half. I ended up underneath him, crumpled up on the floor with ligament damage and missed the last three games. My replacement Adrian Thorne, though, came in and scored five goals in our final game against Watford."

Dave and his team-mates suffered when they kicked off in the Second Division the following season, suffering a 9-0 reverse at Middlesbrough.

He recalled the trials and tribulations of goalkeeper Dave Hollins, brother of Swansea manager John, who played for him at Chelsea.

"I was rooming with Dave up there and gave him all the talk," he said.

"Middlesbrough were a good side, but I told him to treat it like any other game. Poor fellow. Nine of the goals were his fault and Brian Clough got five.

"We then lost 5-0 to Liverpool. It wasn't the best of starts but we managed to pull things around and ended up mid-table."

Dave at the Albion centenary reunion in 2001

Ever a dapper dresser he said: *"There were a lot of baggy shorts around in those days. But when I was at West Ham we were all struck by the Hungarian's short shorts as well as their fantastic football in 1953.*

"So when I got to Brighton I cut my shorts in a similar style."

It was during his second and final season that Dave got involved in coaching with the help of his former West Ham pal George Petchey, who went on to coach the Albion.

He said: *"It was George who got me on my first couple of practical coaching courses in Brighton and it all grew from there.*

"Ron Greenwood, who I knew from Hove, was a big influence too and he appointed me England under-21 manager in 1977. He was a very studious football man."

He added: *"I love it at Brighton. When I retire I'll move back down here like a shot."*

Dave Sexton died in November 2012 aged 82, after battling dementia for many years.

The tributes to him were fulsome and for many, he was a *"gentleman"* both as a coach and as a player.

"Anyone who was ever coached by Dave would be able to tell you what a good man he was, but not only that, what a great coach in particular he was," said Football Association director of football development, Sir Trevor Brooking.

Paul Gunn, the grandson of legendary Sussex bookmaker George Gunn said: *"Dave was lovely and an absolute gentleman."*

John Ansbro said he had played against Dave in a Jimmy Hill's XI in 1971: *"He was there with Mel Hopkins, George Cohen, Ray Crawford and Brian Powney. He was an utter gentleman and always had time to chat."*

Steve Whiting was at school with Dave's son David and would often stay at their house in Hove.

"Dave would always make time for a chat. He was a true gent, as was Denis Foreman who lived near to us," he added.

26

Frankie Howard
(Francis Henry Howard)
1931-2007
BHAFC 1950-1959
Outside Left
Appearances: 219
Goals: 31

Titter ye not, Frankie Howard was a larger-than-life comedian and a hugely loved legend of Brighton & Hove Albion.

For 43 of his 76 years, Frankie devoted his life to the services of one club, first as a player and then as groundsman par excellence from 1962 to 1993.

Frankie was the most loved Albion player of the side that brought enjoyment and success to the Albion during the 1950s.

He is remembered not only as a fast left winger who could electrify a game but also as a comedian who could make the whole dressing room laugh. After all, how many modern players would get away with smuggling a whole bag of beer into a prison for a friendly game of football?

Acton born Frankie first came to the Goldstone Ground as a teenage trialist with Guildford City and was offered professional terms in May 1950.

To obtain Frankie's signature, Albion manager Billy Lane used a workman's cradle to winch himself up to the roof of the Cumberland Hotel. Frankie was in the building trade and working there. Billy's haste came after suddenly discovering that Spurs were interested in the young winger.

A chunky little player, he was one of the fastest wingers to have ever worn an Albion shirt, and was a noted sprinter for Polytechnic Harriers in his youth. Yet strangely, he was rejected for National Service because he had flat feet!

His early career with the Albion came in fits and starts, but an injury to Doug Keene gave Frankie his chance but it was not until 1954-1955 that he became a regular in the team and he formed a brilliant partnership with Denis Foreman on the left wing.

They, and the entire team, sparkled in the 1957-1958 promotion season and Denis recalled: *"Frankie always put a smile on your face and he and Don Bates were like the Morecambe and Wise of the team."*

Frankie was at his best during that season, missing only five games.

But in March 1959, he tore knee ligaments while playing for the reserves which resulted in his premature retirement nine months later at the age of 28.

Such was his popularity, a place was found for him on staff and in 1962 he was appointed groundsman.

Soon afterwards Frankie took a job in the building industry, but with the Albion in his blood he returned as groundsman in 1965.

Henry Wood, a former Albion player remembers Frankie with great fondness.

"We got on quite well together as he lived nearby," he recalls.

"He was always the life of the party and a real leader and very well known locally.

"There was one time he got up a team to go and play at Ford Open Prison. But before we left he wanted £1 from every player and he wouldn't explain why.

"When the coach got to the prison we had to park outside and carry the kit bag and everything through the gates. All the prisoners lined up and cheered and shouted: "Hello Frank".

"Then anytime a prison officer tried to move our kit bag, Frank would shout "Leave that kit bag alone!"

"We then found out that the bag was full of beer... that's what the £1 subs was for!

"Anyway, the game was refereed by the prison's PTI chap. Sometime in the second half one of the prisoners hacked Frank down. Suddenly other prisoners were running onto the pitch to give the guy what for… that's an indication how popular he was."

Albion fans from the 1950s remember Frankie with similar affection.

Ian McKechnie said: *"I recall the glory days of Frankie Howard making those wonderful bursts down the left wing.*

"I remember going to one mid-week game at the Goldstone at that time when there were 34,000 present. Frankie and that team were wonderful inspirations to young football fans."

Albion supporter John Hewitt has fond and funny memories when Frankie was groundsman at the Goldstone.

"The Albion were going to be on TV, and Frankie came down to us at George Freeman Builders Merchants in Conway Street to buy some green emulsion paint," he recalls.

"He wanted to paint the brown bare bits in the South East corner of the pitch so it looked good on TV!

"He was such a fantastic character."

Junior groundsman Jon Hill added: *"Frankie was the nicest man I ever knew. I worked helping him on the ground.*

"The paint story was very true as I had that to do as one of my jobs. However, I am sure the TV was in those days were black and white," he laughed.

Former Goldstone Ground ball boy Tim Bennett recalls: *"Frankie was fearsome to us ball boys. I got a proper clip around the ear from him for trying to dodge divot duties. Mind you, his attention to that pitch paid off… it was a better playing surface than Falmer and one of the best pitches in any of the divisions."*

Albion FA Cup Final player Gary Stevens added: *"I never saw Frankie play. However, as groundsman at the Goldstone he was totally dedicated. Us apprentices would often help repair the divots in the days after a game. Heaven help you if you didn't do it to Frankie's high standards!"*

Frankie was fiercely protective of the pitch.

Albion fan Kit Morgan recalled: *"As a young kid, I remember wandering into the Goldstone one day after school and walking down the North West terrace towards the pitch.*

"Frankie spotted me and shouted in no uncertain terms to clear off. Needless to say, I made a rapid exit."

Vaughan Woolley, who was an apprentice player at the Goldstone Ground between 1975 and 1978, has sharp memories of Frankie as the groundsman.

"The club's preparations for match days were very meticulous and structured, and everything was planned to a very high standard," he recalls.

"But my dream of being a professional footballer became a nightmare one Saturday. I was snuggly tucked up in my warm bed when my landlady said: "Glen Wilson has called and you need to get down to the ground as fast as you can".

"The weather had been terrible all week, it had rained continuously. That Saturday morning was no different and having managed to drag myself out of bed I made my way to the ground.

"On arriving Glen just said: Report to Frankie Howard.

"Frankie just handed me a pitch-fork and us apprentices that lived local spent the next three to four hours forking the pitch to drain away the rainwater.

"I just recall being soaking wet and very cold. I know the game went ahead though I have no recollection of who played that day... I just wanted to get warm and dry."

Albion legend Peter Ward said Frankie was: *"Already a proper legend long before I arrived at the club... everyone loved him.*

"At evening or winter games when it was cold Frankie would wait until before the players entered the tunnel and give every one of us a tot of whisky saying "that will warm you up".

"When we came in at half time the empty whisky bottle was in the bin after Frankie had drunk his tot!"

It was not just as a player and groundsman that Frankie worked on Albion's behalf.

Former manager Archie Macaulay asked him to run the rule over Barrie Rees playing in a reserves match for Everton before he signed for Brighton in January 1965.

Archie explained that he should pay at the turnstiles in case Everton, thinking that Albion were interested, would put up the asking price.

It was as a perfectionist groundsman that Frankie is remembered by many at the Goldstone Ground

When Frankie asked for the rail fare Archie replied: *"Don't worry Frank, you've got plenty."*

It was the same Archie who ordered Frankie to pull the floodlights switch when Albion were in danger of losing. But a late equaliser stayed his hand.

The club awarded him two testimonials and one shared.

"The happiest days of his life was being in the promotion team. Perhaps I'm getting old, but there was something about those days that is missing today," he told the **Evening Argus** chief sportswriter John Vinicombe.

"I think it is respect. There was altogether more respect shown then by people to one another and not just in football. It all went out of the window. Why, I don't know but they were marvellous days, marvellous."

But Frankie's loyalty to the club he loved was rewarded by being kicked in the teeth by a regime that betrayed their public by selling the Goldstone Ground.

It took a lot to anger an irrepressibly cheerful soul like Frankie. But the arch prankster of the dressing room was devastated at being made redundant in 1993, after more than 28 years in the job.

Frankie's world was in turmoil as he recalled that fateful day. *"Bellotti didn't mess about and came straight out with it. I had been made redundant and would finish that day and I was getting three months money in lieu. Only a few minutes earlier Greg Stanley had given me a wave and said Hello Frankie, how are you today?"* Frankie told John Vinicombe.

While this undoubtedly clouded Frankie's later years, he is best remembered as a player and custodian of what was one of the finest pitches in the country.

It broke his heart to see it cluttered by what he described as a load of sheds. He steadfastly refused even to pass by along Old Shoreham Road.

Frankie died after a short illness on 11th October 2007, at the age of 76.

Albion's players wore black armbands during their 1-0 victory away at Port Vale following his death and dedicated the result to him.

Friends, family and more than 50 former players packed into the chapel at Woodvale Crematorium in Bear Road, Brighton, for his funeral service.

Around 150 people attended the service, with another 100 waiting outside the chapel. A true testament to Frankie's legendary status at the club he loved.

27

Des Tennant
(Desmond Tennant)
1925-2009
BHAFC 1948-1959
Right Back
Appearances: 424
Goals: 47

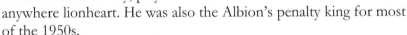

Several Brighton players down the years have been known as *The Tank* for the power of their play, but Des Tennant was the true original.

Few, if any, Albion players of his era set the pulses racing more than the stocky, play-anywhere lionheart. He was also the Albion's penalty king for most of the 1950s.

He signed from Barry Town in the summer of 1948, as a 22-year-old, and made a whopping 424 appearances for the club.

Des was born in Aberdare, South Wales and attended the town's Boys' Grammar School, where he played both football and rugby. He began his football career as a junior with Cardiff City, when he was capped by Wales at youth level.

He went on to make 31 appearances in the Southern League for nearby Barry Town.

Then when their player-manager Les Jones came to the Goldstone in 1948, he brought with him the Welsh side's 22-year-old utility player, Des Tennant. Although Jones' stay in Sussex was brief, his protégé was a huge success.

Des was signed by Brighton & Hove Albion and made his Football League debut at right half early in the 1948-1949 season.

Although primarily right back, he played in a variety of positions, turning out in the numbers 2, 4, 6, 7, 9 and 11 shirts, and while utilised as a right winger and inside right, he was the club's top scorer in his first season with 11 goals in all competitions.

But when manager Billy Lane converted him to right back at the start of the 1951-1952 season, Des made the position his own, although he spent most of the 1955-56 and 1956-57 seasons at right half.

Indeed, in the 1955-1956 season the Albion only conceded 50 goals in 46 matches and the half back line of Tennant, Whitfield and Wilson was reckoned by many as the best in the division.

But it was at full back where Des was most at home.

Weighing in at nearly 13 stone, he possessed a fierce tackle, which made him the scourge of many left wingers… hence his nickname!

One Albion supporter recalls: *"I remember many opposition players bouncing off him and ending up on the ground when trying to shoulder charge him.*

"In the days when I first watched the Albion he played right back but wasn't afraid to take the ball forward as a winger which was unusual in those days as the two full backs normally didn't venture beyond the half-way line."

His marauding forays down the touchline made him a favourite at the Goldstone.

Former BBC Grandstand presenter and Albion fan Des Lynam, in his autobiography, referred to the *"other Des"* as *"a favourite player of mine."*

Indeed, along with the Jimmy Langley at left back, the pair formed a formidable attacking and defensive partnership.

But no matter what position he was played in, Des was an automatic choice for the Albion for 10 years. And surprisingly for a natural defender, he often caught the headlines for some spectacular goals.

In a 2-0 league win in 1953 against Leyton Orient, the ***Daily Mirror*** reported: *"Brighton owe much of their success to full back Tennant,* *who scored from a magnificent 40 yards free kick, having defended brilliantly in the early stages of the match."*

The following season in December 1954 he was a goal hero again in a 5-1 demolition of Norwich City at the Goldstone Ground.

This time the **Daily Mirror** reported: *"Norwich were only one down at half-time. Chief danger to their goal came from Brighton's venturesome full backs, Des Tennant and Jimmy Langley.*

"It was Tennant in fact, who opened the scoring in the eighth minute. He took the ball 70 yards to the goal-line and scored with a shot from a fantastic angle."

Des was also captain for three seasons, including in 1953-1954 when Brighton were runners-up in Division Three South. Unfortunately, in those days, only the champions were promoted.

He was later described as a *"very important player"* in his 35 appearances in the Brighton team promoted to the Second Division for the first time in 1958.

Henry Wood thought highly of Des: *"He was with us for years and was a really good lad and could play on the right wing or as right back.*

"He came from Wales but he quickly mingled with everybody and always gave 100% and stayed in Sussex when he stopped playing."

Des enjoyed a benefit match against second division Brentford at the Goldstone in May 1954, and 3,500 fans turned up to pay their tribute. Four years later, after a decade of service to the Albion, he was presented with a writing bureau.

By the time he retired in 1959, having lost his place to Tommy Bisset, he had played 424 matches and scored 47 goals in all competitions, 23 of which were penalties – an all-time Albion penalty record bettered only by Wally Little.

He then joined the coaching staff at the club. In 1962 he became chief scout at the club and worked in the Goldstone office for a while before taking a post with the ambulance service.

Des became landlord of the Allen Arms pub in Lewes Road, Brighton in 1965. But he returned to South Wales the following year with his wife Eileen.

**Des was reunited with playing friends
at an Albion centenary event in 2001**

Des settled in his wife's hometown of Glynneath where he
became a prominent member of the local choir and golf club.

During his football career he played in many celebrity sides and
pitted his skills against the likes of Sean Connery, Des O'Connor
and Tommy Steele.

Des and Eileen had three children and five grandchildren. His
son, Warren, skippered the Brighton Boys and was on Chelsea's
staff as a youngster.

In later life Des suffered from motor neurone disease (MND)
and Parkinson's disease, and died in January 2009, surrounded by
his family, at the age of 83.

After his death his niece, Gillian Marsh said: *"My uncle was a
wonderful character who loved life and valued his family and friends above all
else."*

28

Glen Wilson
(Glenton Edward Wilson)
1929-2005
BHAFC 1949-1960
Left Half
Appearances: 436
Goals: 28

**Glenton Edward Wilson was
a Brighton & Hove Albion
legend in almost every way
you might care to use the
word.**

Glen, as he was known to
everyone, had the unique
distinction of leading Albion
into the Second Division for
the first time.

It was the highlight of a playing career that could, and should,
have gone further but for his reluctance to leave the Goldstone. The
Albion's resolute captain, who led by selfless example, stayed rather
than try his luck when big clubs came calling for his signature.

He instead spent half a lifetime in the cause of the Albion: 12
years as a highly respected and popular player followed by 18 years
in a variety of roles from trainer and kit man to caretaker manager.

Glen was born in 1929 in Winlaton, in County Durham. He
attended High Spen Senior School and was capped by England at
schoolboy level during World War Two.

He joined Newcastle United in 1945 but was soon called up for
National Service with the REME based at Bordon Camp in
Hampshire. While there, he guested for nearby Farnham Town
against Albion's A Team in 1948.

He impressed Brighton player-coach Jack Dugnolle, who recommended him to Albion manager Don Welsh.

After playing for the A team himself, the 20-year-old Glen signed professional forms at the Goldstone Ground in September 1949. His older brother Joe had recently come to the end of a long-playing career with the Albion and was on the coaching staff.

Fellow Albion A Team player Henry Wood said: *"I got on really well with Glen as a player. He had just come out of the Army and he was a really hard boy."*

Glen made his senior debut at inside left later that month, but his true vocation was at left half and he quickly became a regular in the side during the 1950-1951 season and remained a regular for the next 10 years.

Glen brought his whiplash tackle and stamina in midfield and was the driving force of various Albion sides during the 1950s and was rated by many as the finest wing half in the Third Division.

He was rated highly enough to represent the Third Division South three times in the annual fixture against the Northern Section and attracted interest from the likes of Arsenal and Aston Villa.

He also played for a Football Combination XI in a 6-1 defeat of the Dutch national team in 1956.

Consistent and as hard as nails, he was a virtual stranger to the treatment room. His inspirational captaincy spanned the best part of three seasons and for as many campaigns he was ever-present.

Glen's tough no-nonsense approach took no prisoners on the football pitch.

"I remember a game at Swindon," recalled one Albion fan.

"All through the game he and one Swindon player were giving each other physical stick. Glen was seemingly the only one to be punished with a string of free kicks against him. Towards the end of the game he was booked.

"Just after the final whistle the Swindon player held out a hand to Glen with a broad grin on his face.

"Glen stepped forward and delivered a beautiful left hook and left the guy flat on his back. He then walked down the tunnel leaving a hell of a commotion behind him."

Glen was at his best when he captained the Albion to the 1957-1958 Third Division South title.

The title was secured in front of a 31,038 crowd with a remarkable 6-0 victory against Watford at the Goldstone, with five of the goals scored by 20-year-old reserve forward Adrian Thorne.

The **Daily Mirror** at the time hailed the win with a banner headline: *Brighton up with a Six Goal Rush*, and continued: *"This stocky, local boy scored FIVE of the six goals that rocketed Brighton into the Second Division for the first time after thirty-eight years in the Third Division wilderness….. skipper Glen Wilson scored the other goal from a penalty for handling by right back Bobby Bell in the thirty-fifth minute."*

Albion supporter Ray Eggleton recalls Glen Wilson's involvement: *"My biggest memory of Glen is from the Watford game on 20th April 1958 and Adrian Thorne scoring a hat-trick inside four minutes early in the game, securing us promotion. Then we were awarded a penalty and captain Glen took the ball to score number 4.*

"Adrian scored the 5th before half-time. He scored his 5th and Albion's 6th at the end but could have had all six if Glen had allowed him to take the penalty. Always thought that was mean of Glen but he was professional."

Fellow Albion fan Bill Spencer added: *"Glen was my brother-in-law and I was there that Wednesday night. When I asked him why he didn't let Thorne take the penalty, he said "I was captain and it was my responsibility to get us promoted and in a position to not get beaten."*

Four months later, Glen was still leading the side in the club's first ever game in Football League Division Two away to Middlesbrough on 23rd August 1958.

It was the antithesis to the Watford game and a total disaster as the home team ran out 9-0 winners at Ayresome Park – a record defeat for the Albion, with future Brighton manager Brian Clough scoring five of the goals.

Apparently after the final whistle, Glen knocked on the referee's dressing room door and asked to touch the ball, because he hadn't managed it during the entire 90 minutes of play!

Years later, Glen recalled the incident: *"I never touched the ball once in the match and got sunburnt. So, I said to the referee: I didn't touch the ball during the game, could I touch it now… thankfully the ref saw the funny side."*

But Glen was not finished and he played on for two seasons in the Second Division and still grabbed the headlines for consistently dominating displays.

In October 1959, he led Brighton to an amazing 5-4 victory away at Bristol Rovers. One newspaper report summarised: *"Brighton's win was due as much to their attacking wing halves, Glen Wilson and John Bertolini as to their forwards. They were the strength behind their fighting victory."*

Just eight months later and aged 30, Glen hung up his Albion boots and joined Exeter City as player-manager in June 1960.

But the Devon club struggled both on and off the pitch, and Glen's tenure with the struggling Grecians lasted less than two seasons.

He and wife Joan returned to Brighton and took over the Flying Dutchman pub in Elm Grove on Lewes Road. but the lure of football was too great and he returned to the Goldstone in 1966.

After 436 appearances, placing Glen sixth in Albion's all-time list, he went on to do the backroom jobs of coach, trainer, physio and kitman. He was briefly caretaker manager for two games in October 1973 following the sacking of Pat Saward.

Charles Wright, who was an Albion Youth goalkeeper in the early 1970s recalls: *"I was a Brighton Youth player for two seasons, before I joined Hastings United. Glen was the youth team coach. He was great with us kids and always had stories to tell, gave us a lot of verbal encouragement and advice and taught us tricks which the old players used (some maybe not always within the spirit of the game).*

"He was a very warm, kind guy, although as tough as nails when it came to football."

Sammy Morgan, an Albion centre forward in the mid-1970s, said that when Glen was the club physio he left him on a treatment table for 10 minutes wired up to a heat treatment machine. The only thing was that Glen had forgotten to turn it on.

But upon his return he asked Sammy if he felt better for it. Sammy wholeheartedly agreed and got down from the table and did a little jig to demonstrate.

Apparently during this time Glen's massages were delivered in a very zealous manner. The players nicknamed him *Boston* after *The Boston Strangler*.

Vaughan Woolley, an apprentice at the Goldstone Ground between 1975 and 1978, has many memories of Glen.

"My first job after signing an apprenticeship contract with Ken Calver, the club secretary in the summer pre-season in 1975, was to report to Glen Wilson who was primary overseer of the apprentices," he said.

"Glen was also the club physio and kit man. In his role he would be the go-to guy for all those cuts, bumps and bruises and ailing limbs typical of the trade.

"He would also make sure the kit that the first team played in was laid out neatly in the dressing room.

"Underneath the old main stand there was the board room, a referee's room, boot room, home and away changing rooms, a small but perfectly functional gymnasium, and the physio room where Glen was often to be found.

"I immediately experienced Glen as very stern and somewhat frightening to a raw 16-year-old kid from Derby.

"He had a fierce assertiveness which meant there was no messing around and if you stepped over the line you paid the price.

"Issues arose when: the tea was not ready in time when the players finished training; the match boots, training boots and flats (trainers) were not cleaned and polished to a good standard; the training kit was not dried or cleaned correctly; the changing rooms not mopped and disinfected to the right standard, or simply not pulling your weight.

"All would be worthy of the Glen Wilson wrath.

"There was one occasion when another apprentice and I had stepped over the line so we had to face the dreaded '4-3-2-1' punishment.

"This was a running exercise around the Goldstone pitch. Glen with his stopwatch would set you off at the halfway line adjacent to the old players, tunnel. The objective was to run four times round the pitch in five minutes.

"Then a thirty second break to get your breath back was followed by three times round in three minutes thirty, a thirty second recovery. Then two laps in two minutes twenty and a final lap in one minute.

"Now, this had to be completed within the times otherwise you would be ordered to repeat until you completed it to Glen's satisfaction.

"Possibly the worst punishment us apprentices faced was on one occasion the day following the misdemeanour, Glen, with a smile on his face, handed each of us a toothbrush.

"We spent the next three hours on our hands and knees scrubbing the sinks, showers, urinals and toilet basins until they were spotlessly clean.

"The worst of it was that it resulted in us not getting away from the ground until around four o'clock, thus missing our bread pudding and pint of milk across the road at Wagg's Cafe and our afternoon pitch n' putt on the sea front.

Glen had his own mannerisms which made us chuckle and we would imitate him when he wasn't there.

"He would walk the corridors beneath the old west stand and would hum a tuneless ditty, clicking his fingers together repeatedly as he went on his jobs, with a 'la la la' as he went.

Glen was also partial to the odd flutter on the horses. He claimed that he was good friends with the local and great racehorse trainer Josh Gifford.

"Glen would say "Josh had just phoned with a tip for a horse running that afternoon" but he would never tell you which horse he had the tip on.

"Perhaps he was concerned that our apprentice twenty pence each way might affect the horse's starting odds!

"But Glen did show at times a softer side to his personality.

"I had several injuries and setbacks during my time with the Albion as all players did.

"I recall having to see a specialist at The Sussex University Hospital and Glen went with me to see the doctor.

"He was always kind with me and reassuring that all would be well, as a young lad I very much warmed to that.

"I'm not saying that Glen was a 'father figure' but when you are a young kid and 200 miles from your parents, his compassion went down well with me.

"On another occasion during a Youth Team game at the Goldstone Ground I was injured when shooting for goal caught the defender's studs on my ankle.

"I was in terrific pain," recalled Vaughan.

"Glen raced onto the pitch, then gave me a piggyback back to the physio room to treat my injury. I was in agony and unable to put weight onto my foot.

"Glen took me home to my lodgings for which I was truly grateful.

"I had experienced different sides to him that helped me understand the man really as a caring and standards driven person.

"In many older Albion fans' eyes Glen is a legend, and probably more so to me, I never saw him play football for Brighton.

Glen was tough as both a player, a physio and a coach

"What I did experience in my three years at the club was a person whose commitment to excellence and to the club was paramount and foremost in his expectations of how he should operate."

Glen was a widely popular member of the Albion backroom staff until a cost-cutting exercise ended his career in May 1986, during acrimonious times at the Goldstone Ground.

During his years at the Goldstone Ground, Glen had been a player, youth and reserve team coach, trainer, physio, kit man, assistant manager and caretaker manager. But the club he served in so many ways for most of his adult life, treated him appallingly.

In 1999, Glen recalled: *"After 34 years as part of the club, I was sacked in 15 seconds. The directors were more worried about me handing in the keys than anything else."*

So, what price loyalty after a lifetime of dedicated service?

Not a lot when measured in terms of a £7,000 redundancy pay-out, especially when he spent about half that in legal fees.

Years later after Dick Knight's takeover of the club, Glen jokingly said: *"I haven't yet been a gateman, so I'm going to ask Dick to let me man the gate for one match, so I can say I've done everything."*

Glen remained living in his adopted home of Brighton and later became a porter at the University of Sussex.

He died in November 2005, following a heart attack aged 76.

29

John Shepherd
(John Herbert Shepherd)
1932-2018
BHAFC 1958-1960
Centre Forward
Appearances: 45
Goals: 19

**John Shepherd was one of the
best known and most
respected people in Sussex
football, and more than 60
years since he last wore an
Albion shirt, he is still
remembered as a true legend
of the Goldstone Ground.**

Indeed, after he died in 2018, two dozen former Albion and Southwick (another club where he is considered a legend) players turned out to play a friendly match in his honour.

Kensington born John played professional football for Millwall, Gillingham and Brighton & Hove Albion between 1952 and 1961.

But it may not have been that way at all.

In 1951, John contracted polio while undertaking his National Service in the RAF. It was feared he would not walk again, but he made a full recovery and signed professional forms for Millwall on 6th October 1952.

As a strong, bustling centre forward he made his first team debut on 25th October 1952 away at Leyton Orient where he scored a record four goals. He became known as a *"hat trick specialist",* and in his first season with Millwall he scored a hat-trick in a 4-1 win against Barrow in the 2nd round of the FA Cup to earn a 3rd round tie against Manchester United.

He finished top scorer with 21 goals (15 League and 6 FA Cup) in his first season. He was also Millwall's top scorer with 25 League and Cup goals in the 1956-1957 season, during which they had a memorable FA Cup run beating First Division Newcastle United in the fourth round.

John Shepherd remains Millwall's top FA Cup goal scorer with 15 goals in 17 games and is their sixth highest ever goal scorer.

In June 1958, John, then aged 26, was signed by Albion manager Billy Lane for a fee of £2,250 to lead the attack in the club's first season in League Division Two.

Despite the Albion's disastrous start to the season – a 9-0 defeat at Middlesbrough, he repaid Billy Lane's trust and ended the season as the Albion's top scorer with 18 goals in 36 League appearances.

Indeed, the *Evening Argus's* lead story at the time of his signing was that the Albion had signed a powerful and proven forward.

"He should make a very useful acquisition to the Goldstone Ground staff," wrote Jack Arlidge.

"Big, black-haired Shepherd can play at centre, inside or wing forward. He knows the way to goal and his height and weight make him a formidable opponent."

John is remembered fondly by many fans of the time.

Robert Rogerson said: *"John Shepherd had supremely strong neck muscles and great timing. Some of the goals I saw his scored with his head were among the hardest hit balls I remember, fairly whizzing into the net."*

John had been given a club owned flat in a large Victorian property in Walsingham Road, just a stone's throw from Hove seafront, where he, his wife Esther and his family seemed settled.

The house was in fact divided into two flats and their neighbours in the ground floor flat were Albion full-back Des Tennant and his wife Eileen and two children. The two families would become life-long friends.

But after losing his automatic place, John only played for another season for the Albion before transferring to Gillingham in 1960.

John scores against Sheffield United at the Goldstone in March 1959

Although he enjoyed playing at Gillingham under the managership of Harry Barratt, he later said moving there was the biggest mistake of his career and he wished he had stayed on to fight for his first team place at Brighton.

John then played semi-professional football at Ashford Town (Kent), Margate and Tunbridge Wells, before going on to become player-manager at Southwick FC who were struggling in Sussex County League Division Two at the time.

He led them to promotion to Division One, and in 1968 led them to victory against Athenian League Horsham in the Sussex Senior Cup Final, played at the Goldstone Ground, for the first time in the club's history.

The following season Southwick were Division One Champions.

The fans' favourite later returned to the Goldstone as a scout and youth coach, where he founded the club's first-ever youth team in 1976, in collaboration with Alan Mullery and Mick Fogden.

In total, John spent almost 30 years with the Albion as both a player and coach, working with numerous managers, including Mullery, Brian Clough and Jimmy Melia.

He also spent time as manager of Lancing and Sussex, before he had two spells back at Southwick as joint manager with his son, Dominic… a former Albion trainee.

In September 1993 John was honoured with a testimonial dinner at Hove Town Hall.

In January 2013, his daughter - Julie Ryan - released a biography about her father entitled *In and out of the Lion's Den: Poverty, War and Football*.

In 2014, John Shepherd was presented with an award from the Sussex FA recognising his services to Sussex football over the years.

John also struck up an almost paternal friendship with Albion legend Teddy Maybank, who was almost 24 years his junior.

Julie explains: *"Both Londoners, dad and Teddy Maybank became good friends after Ted signed for Brighton in November 1977 for a club record fee.*

"Fans had high expectations of Maybank, but when he did not start scoring regularly and his form was blighted by injury, he received a lot of stick from the terraces.

"Dad, who was on the coaching staff at that time, realised what a miserable time Teddy was having and made a point of offering him encouragement and became a mentor to him, which was appreciated and never forgotten by Teddy. They remained friends until dad's death."

She added: *"Away from football, dad was a real family man and all the grandchildren and great-grandchildren loved him to bits."*

Following his death in June 2018, after a long battle with Parkinson's Disease, both Brighton & Hove Albion and Southwick honoured the popular footballer. In October 2018, a crowd of around 350 turned out to support a friendly game between the two clubs with all proceeds in aid of Parkinson's Disease research.

The players included Steve Foster, John Byrne, Paul Rogers, Ian Chapman, Charlie Oatway, Stuart Tuck and Adam Hinshelwood. Former Seagulls stars Dean Wilkins and Chris Ramsey were also in attendance, along with ex-Albion chairman Dick Knight.

Before the match kicked off, the John Shepherd Stand was officially unveiled at Old Barn Way by Sussex FA chairman Mathew Major and Sussex FA board member Tony Kybett.

The match finished 4-4. Dominic Shepherd was among the scorers for Brighton - netting against his son, and John's grandson Lewis.

John enjoys a coffee and a chat with his great friend and former Albion striker Teddy Maybank

Two of John's other grandsons, Dan Porter and Greg Ryan, were both on target for Southwick.

In the matchday programme, many tributes were paid.

Former Brighton player and manager Dean Wilkins said: *"John was one of those guys, who, when you met for the first time, you formed an instant bond with.*

"We had many conversations in the players' lounge after I'd played. I really enjoyed the advice he offered because of the level of individual detail. John got me thinking about my game and I'd take that advice into the following week's training.

"John had a way of putting things across that was totally engaging. A kind-hearted lovely man."

Gary Stevens, who played for Brighton from 1979 to 1983, wrote: *"Many people played an important part in my football career and John Shepherd was certainly among them.*

"To understand how influential John was, I include the following, amongst a few others, in that very same category; my father, Alan Mullery and Sir Bobby Robson."

He went on to add: *"John regularly offered advice, encouragement and support when I moved into the Seagulls first team and likewise when I transferred to Spurs and playing for England.*

"He always had my best interests at heart, one of his great qualities as a man."

Both John and his old friend and former Albion player, Jimmy Collins, were commemorated at Brighton's first home match of the 2018-2019 season against Manchester United, when the players and crowd all joined together to give a minute's applause in appreciation for their contributions to the club.

30

Denis Foreman
(Denis Joseph Foreman)
1933-2016
BHAFC 1952-1961
Inside Forward
Appearances: 219
Goals: 63

**Some of the racist treatment
meted out from the
Goldstone Ground terraces
for one Albion legend may
make a lot of readers of this
book wince in shame.**

Yet everyone who came to
know Denis Foreman say he
was one of the *"nicest"* and most
"talented" and *"self-effacing"* men to ever grace a sports field.

Denis Joseph Foreman, a cricketer and footballer from Athlone,
Cape Town, made a name for himself in England in 1952.

He was the first black South African to play first-class cricket in
England.

Denis played 219 games for Brighton & Hove Albion, and
cricket for Sussex for 15 years.

But the strange thing is that before he took the boat from South
Africa to Southampton, he played three first-class matches for
Western Province as a so-called *"honorary white"*, such was the overt
racism of the time.

This was in 1951, when the infamous apartheid legislation had
not been fully implemented in parts of South Africa.

"Nobody made a fuss," remembers Ronnie Delport, who played in
the same Western Province team as Denis, although there was the
odd crude comment about *"a touch of the tar brush"*.

A product of the Hibernian club of Cape Town, Denis was working for the post office in his native city when Leeds United and Glasgow Celtic both made overtures for his signature. But both deals fell through.

Instead, he came to the Goldstone Ground as a 19-year-old triallist in February 1952 on the recommendation of his compatriot Dirk Kemp, the former Liverpool goalkeeper, who had guested for the Albion during World War Two.

Denis performed well during his trial period, and after signing professional forms in March 1952, broke into the first team at outside left the following October to the exclusion of Frankie Howard, the winger with whom he was to form a great partnership and friendship.

On his arrival at Southampton Docks to sign for the Albion Denis was carrying three cricket bats, parting gifts from friends in Cape Town.

Concerned manager Billy Lane asked: *"You do realise that we're a football club?"*

Lane needn't have worried. Placid and popular, Denis excelled in both sporting spheres.

Wearing the number 10 or 11 shirt, he became a fine inside left or outside left and an essential part of the 1958 title winning side netting 10 goals in 37 matches that season for a rampant Brighton – including an impressive brace in vital 4-2 win against Millwall during the final run-in.

Denis was a hugely popular member of the exciting attacking Albion sides of the era. With his natural ball control and distribution, he created many goal opportunities for his colleagues.

He also had a happy knack of scoring important goals, including one in an impressive 3-2 away victory at high-flying Ipswich Town in 1954 and another in an even more impressive 8-3 win against Reading in 1957.

In 1954, Denis was selected for an FA XI versus Oxford University, and two years later in March 1956 played for a team of Anglo-Springboks against Scotland at Ibrox.

Denis was a tough midfielder who also scored many goals for the Albion

An injury in the 1958-1959 season kept him out for a long spell. Denis's first team outings subsequently diminished and he was released in the summer of 1962 to join Hastings United for a season in the Southern League.

That was followed by spells as player-coach with Wigmore Athletic and Steyning Town in the Sussex County League.

His team-mates at the Goldstone remember him as: *"A nice, quiet, lovely chap."*

Normally he would only depart from his quietness only when he was laughing at Frankie Howard's antics or telling anecdotes about Don Bates, who also combined football with Brighton and cricket for Sussex, and who needed spectacles - only he couldn't wear them playing football.

When Bates was granted a benefit year, he gave Denis the takings from one of his benefit matches.

They were nice little earners, on a Sunday afternoon in a Sussex town or village, and Denis made enough to buy a house and settle in England - and to keep playing for Hove Montefiore CC.

Don Bates later recalled: *"Denis was a vital part of both the Brighton and Sussex teams during my time. Reliable, honest, quietly funny and a real friend."*

First and foremost, Denis Foreman loved cricket and played for Sussex from 1952 to 1967.

He appeared in 130 first-class matches as a right-handed batsman who bowled occasional off-breaks – he took nine wickets and had best figures of 4-64. He was also a safe pair of hands in the field with 124 catches.

He was eventually capped for his country in 1966.

After his retirement from first class cricket in 1967, he was appointed sports master at Seaford College in Petworth in 1968. He joined the staff at Shoreham Grammar School in 1974 where he was an *"inspirational PE teacher"* until 1995.

He left his mark on many pupils and is remembered as a *"kind, tolerant and gentle man"*.

Albion fan and former Shoreham Grammar student Adrian Gibbs recalls: *"Denis was my PE teacher in the early and mid-1990s.*

"He organised and took a few of us on a "field trip" to the Goldstone Ground. It was my first BHAFC game and I was hooked ever since that day.

"He was a great teacher and a great man with some brilliant stories," he added.

But he also had a harder side.

Albion supporter Dave Wilcock remembers when he was younger and playing cricket against Denis's son, who played for Lancing Manor.

"I was bowling and peppered him with bouncers, but he smashed me all around the ground. I got annoyed and spent three overs trying to get the ball past his nose.

"Anyway, I also played Sunday football very badly. One game sometime later I was tarting about in midfield and a voice sharply said: "Hey I remember you!" It was Denis.

"Suddenly I felt a draft of wind and I was taken out from behind and ended up in a heap. Took me a year to recover.

"The nasty bugger," he laughed.

Denis with his great friend and former Albion striker John Shepherd

Denis died in August 2016 at the age of 83 after a long illness.

Albion centre forward, John Shepherd's daughter Julie Ryan said his passing was a traumatic moment.

"Dad and Denis Foreman remained great friends after their playing days were over, both living close to each other in Portslade, which had become home to several players from that era," said Julie.

"During dad's final years, his former Albion team-mates began to pass away and it was normally Denis Foreman who was the bearer of the sad news and would phone around all the surviving players.

"Unsurprisingly, there was a sense of impending doom each time John's wife, Esther, announced that Denis was on the telephone for him.

"Sadly, the phone calls finally stopped in July 2016 when Denis himself died."

A memorial page set up following Denis's death is full of tender and funny memories of him as a teacher and mentor.

One former Shoreham Grammar School student wrote: *"A great sportsman, great character, genuinely funny to be around and was an absolute gent. May we all forever stay off his cricket pitch!"*

"He taught me how to stand tall against the bullies during our football match and then slide tackle them with the ball, not conceding any fouls!"

31

Billy Lane
(William Henry Lane)
1904-1985
BHAFC 1951-1961
Manager

There can be few football managers so loved by the supporters and media and so disliked by many of his players.

Yes, Albion legend Billy Lane was that manager!

As a player Billy played for more than a dozen clubs, but as a manager he will be perpetually linked with just one: Brighton & Hove Albion.

After playing for the London City Mission, Gnome Athletic and Park Avondale, Tottenham born William Lane joined Spurs as an 18-year-old in 1922 for the first time but left the club without appearing in a senior match.

He went on to play for Summerstown and Barnet before re-joining Tottenham after a spell with the club's nursery team Northfleet United.

Billy went on to feature in 36 matches and found the net on 12 occasions between 1924 and 1926.

His time with Spurs came to an end after manager Peter McWilliam dropped him after Billy kicked the ball into the crowd after having a goal disallowed in a match against Preston North End.

The incident ended Billy's chances of an international call-up and a longer Tottenham career.

After leaving White Hart Lane, he appeared for Leicester City, Reading and Brentford.

Despite his excellent form for the Bees, Billy was transfer-listed by manager Harry Curtis, who needed the money from his sale to fund the transfer of other players.

He signed for Watford in 1932 and the following year scored a hat-trick in the Football League in under three minutes against Clapton Orient, then a record.

Billy featured in a total of 136 matches for Watford and went on to have spells at Bristol City, Clapton Orient and finally Gravesend United.

In 1945, after serving as an Army PT instructor during World War Two, Billy turned down the manager's job at Clapton Orient to return to Brentford as a coach under Harry Curtis. He remained with the Bees before going into management with Guildford City.

After Brighton had survived a re-election vote in 1948 at the hands of its fellow Football League members, Don Welsh's Albion side vindicated their support with top half finishes in the Third Division South in the following two seasons.

And aside from a 13th place finish in 1951, a season disturbed when Don Welsh left part way through to take the Liverpool job, the club stayed in the top half of the table and continued their never-ending pursuit for promotion to the second tier.

With Welsh's sudden departure, Billy Lane was put in caretaker charge of the Albion.

Then on Wednesday 18th April, with the season drawing to a close, Billy oversaw a 9-1 win against Newport County, setting a club record for the biggest ever league victory in Brighton's history.

It was a result that ultimately helped convince the Brighton board to give Billy the manager's job on a permanent basis.

This proved to be a very prudent decision, as seven years later, he became the first manager to lead the Albion into the second tier of English football when lifting the Division Three South title at the end of the 1957-1958 season.

What made the hammering of Newport more impressive was that under Welsh, the Albion were known for their defensive football. Welsh's final match in charge took place on Saturday 10th March 1951 and saw Exeter City beaten 4-1 at the Goldstone.

But it was only the second time in two years that the Albion had scored more than three goals in a game.

Welsh had barely cleared his desk and packed up his things for the move to Anfield when Billy had begun to radically alter Brighton's style of play.

The newly installed caretaker boss had initially been appointed as assistant to Welsh in the summer of 1950.

During his playing days, Billy was a dashing centre forward and he wanted his team to play with the same purpose and flair that had characterised his own game.

He was told by the Brighton board that he had the job until such time as a successor could be found. With the Albion sitting 17th in the table at the time, untroubled by either promotion race or relegation battle, Billy was not about to let the opportunity pass him by. His message to the players was simply *"go out and enjoy yourself."* And they did.

His first game in charge saw Brighton blow away Northampton Town 5-1 at the Goldstone. Word quickly got around that if you headed over to Hove for an Albion home game with Billy at the helm, you were likely to see a lot of goals.

Attendances duly rose. For the 9-1 humbling of Newport, Brighton pulled in a crowd of 12,114 on a Wednesday. That was a 25 percent increase on the 8,305 who had turned out for Welsh's final game in charge, which took place in the much more friendly timeslot of Saturday afternoon.

The Newport match was Billy's seventh in charge. He had lost just once, a 3-1 defeat at Southend United.

Despite this upturn in results and the goals that had been flowing since his appointment, nobody could have predicted what was to happen on that record-breaking evening against Newport.

One report from the game said: *"Not for many seasons has there been quite the measure of enthusiasm as witnessed as Newport County were thrashed 9-1."*

The result felt like a turning point for the Albion, especially as County were no slouches. In fact, Newport would finish above Brighton in the table despite the 9-1 defeat.

But in typical Albion style, they followed up their now club-record league win by going down 2-1 away at Leyton Orient three days later.

Following the back-to-earth-with-a-bump defeat against Orient, Brighton won two and lost two of their final four matches.

The last game of the 1950-1951 season resulted in another of those 'typical Brighton' moments as the Albion ended the campaign with a 3-0 away defeat against... Newport!

The Albion finished the season in 13th spot and the board had over 50 applicants for the position of manager. After much deliberation, Billy Lane was eventually confirmed as the successful candidate.

With Billy now at the helm on a permanent basis, attendances continued to rise, and goals continued to flow throughout the 1951-1952 season.

The Albion were now embarking on an unprecedented period of success, culminating in the winning of the Division Three South title in 1958 at the 31st attempt.

For this was a different Albion to Welsh's defence-minded teams. Under Billy Lane, Brighton became an entertaining and attacking side, scoring goals a plenty and caring less about conceding a few at the other end.

The club scored more than 80 goals in all bar one season between 1951-1952 and 1957-1958, and in 1955-1956 scored a club record of 112 goals in a Football League campaign.

So there was plenty to keep the fans happy as Billy built probably the best and most entertaining Albion team up to that date.

With the Third Division South and North combining to form national third and fourth divisions the following season, continuing the club's run of top half-finishes was a minimal expectation to avoid an effective demotion.

But this was one worry they would not have as the 1957-1958 season progressed. The team started the season as they meant to go on, with six wins in the first seven games putting the club top of the table.

But four defeats in a row including a 5-0 defeat to Southampton meant the club lost top spot to Plymouth, another trend starting as it meant to go on.

Nonetheless, despite the emphasis being on attack and evidence of the occasional defensive lapse, this wasn't a team without defensive quality. But much as had been the case since Billy Lane took charge, this was a team all about its ability to score goals.

And it was forwards Peter Harburn and Dave Sexton who were the stars, tying for Albion top scorer that season with 20 goals each.

With the help of their in-form forwards, Albion's free scoring team recovered from a run of four consecutive defeats and continued to rack up the wins, with six coming in the next eight games. They were scoring for fun again, twice or more in all except one of those games and were back at the top of the league.

Two successive 5-2 home wins over Colchester and then Gillingham followed and left the club top ahead of a draw with Swindon on Christmas Day and four points clear of the chasing pack.

Come the climax to the season, a win or a draw against Watford would secure promotion to the second tier as Third Division South champions for the first time in Brighton's history. This was a huge game for the club, one which some workplaces and schools closed to allow people to attend the game. A crowd of 31,308 (with thousands more who wanted to attend locked outside) cheered the team on to a historic victory.

Unlike the rest of the season, there was no jeopardy here.

The first Albion roar occurred when reserve striker Adrian Thorn scored his first of his five goals that night, and the team were 5-0 up by half time.

Billy and the Brighton & Hove Albion Third Division champions in 1958

Brighton ultimately ran out 6-0 winners to win the club's first championship and secure its first promotion since joining the Football League. After 38 years as a Third Division South club Brighton & Hove Albion had finally done it.

But if this season ended with a fairy tale story, the next season started with a horror story as the Albion lost 9-0 to Middlesbrough on the opening day, with Brian Clough scoring five, the club's biggest ever defeat in peacetime.

However, under Billy Lane's assured leadership the team found its feet and bounced back to finish a respectable 12th in its first season in the second tier.

Billy continued to manage the club in the Second Division and stabilised the club at that level over the following three seasons.

But with the Albion fighting against relegation during the 1960-1961 season Billy came under pressure from the board. But rather than be pushed, he jumped, resigning at the end of the season which saw the club finish five places above the drop.

When he left the Goldstone Ground in 1961, Billy was heralded by many as the club's greatest ever manager.

After a short stint with Gravesend & Northfleet FC, Billy became a scout for Arsenal and later returned to Brighton & Hove Albion in a similar role. He was still working for Albion at the time of his death in 1985, aged 81.

A devout churchman and occasional lay preacher Billy remained well-respected by many. Former Albion player and trainer Glen Wilson remembered him well.

"He would always keep tabs on every player. He knew everything that was going on, he knew every policeman in the town," he said.

"I remember when I was courting, I went into a pub one night to get 10 cigarettes, I never had a drink in there – I was straight in and out.

"The next morning, he had me in the office, knowing I had been in the pub, and thinking I had been drinking. He was a super guy all round."

But it was not all roses and smiles from those who played under him. Former Albion reserve player Henry Wood said many players did not like Billy Lane.

"He had an off-hand way about him and would often walk right past you without even acknowledging you even existed," he said.

"He was a Londoner but was not good with the locals… either players or fans. I never warmed to him as a manager."

Another Albion player from the 1950s added: *"None of us players liked Billy much. He was arrogant and full of his own self-importance. If the spotlight wasn't on him, he'd sulk into his office and not talk to anyone."*

In an interview in 2008, Brighton wing half Paddy McIlvenny did not hold back when talking about his former manager.

"Nobody liked him. He was a bastard," he said.

"Billy Lane was a bad man as far as looking after players and things, he was always pulling strokes that suited him. He was a poor manager."

But more than 35 years after his death Billy Lane, remains on results and team flair alone one of the Albion's most successful managers.

32

Roy Jennings
(Roy Thomas Jennings)
1931-2016
BHAFC 1952-1964
Centre Half
Appearances: 297
Goals: 22

**Every successful team needs
a rock in defence, and there
could not have been a more
solid rock in the Albion's
history than 6ft 1in
powerhouse Roy Jennings.**
Indeed, Roy was a king pin
in Billy Lane's successful sides
of the 1950s and helped the
Albion settle after they were promoted to the Second Division in
1958. But it took him several seasons to settle after signing at the
Goldstone Ground in May 1952.

Born in Swindon, Roy initially played for his home club and then
Southampton as an amateur before doing his National Service in the
RAF. While at Swindon he also represented Wiltshire and England
Youth.

He signed for Brighton & Hove Albion on the recommendation
of chief scout Ted Nash as soon as he was released from his
National Service.

Former Albion chairman Dick Knight remembers Roy's signing
well as he ended up lodging at Dick's home in Fairway Crescent,
Portslade when he first joined the Albion.

Dick explains in his book ***Mad Man***: *"When Roy and Maurice McLafferty came as lodgers I was moved out of my bedroom, but of course I didn't mind if it was for two Albion players.*

"At 14 I was open to hero-worship. I quickly got on speaking terms with Maurice, but Roy was different – a young lad just starting out and not much older than me and had less to say for himself.

"Years later when I was chairman, I met Roy and asked him if he remembered his digs in Fairway Crescent and he said: "Yes, of course I do. How's your wife?" I answered: "No, that was my mum – I was the kid hanging on your every word at meal-times."

"I told him I was nervous in his presence and he said: "So was I. I'd never been away from home before."

Roy initially played for the first six years at Brighton as a full back before Billy Lane saw his potential to play in the centre of defence.

He was then a revelation when in 1958, in the Albion's first season in Division Two, he switched to centre half in place of Ken Whitfield and the hard as nails defender made the position his own.

He became a great crowd favourite even after the Albion were relegated back to the Third Division in 1962, while he was club skipper.

Dominant in the air, hard in the tackle, and a penalty specialist, he missed just nine games over the next four and half seasons until 1963-1964 when he moved to left back to allow the young Norman Gall into the side.

A measure of Roy's popularity at the Goldstone is when he was dropped in September 1962 in favour of Gall, the decision resulted in angry crowd demonstrations, chants of *"we want Jennings"* and Roy's swift reinstatement.

But it could have turned out quite differently.

The Albion's first ever match in Division Two was a disaster when the Albion were thumped 9-0 at Middlesbrough. Boro also won the return fixture at the Goldstone 4-6.

Three years later in 1961, the Brighton line-up was much changed, but the club had survived and were still competing in the Second Division. And Roy Jennings leading from the back was the tough-tackling stalwart of the side.

One Albion fan, Bert Jackson, described Roy as *"The hardest centre back I have ever seen in a Brighton shirt. Sometimes you could see his heart pumping between the stripes because he worked so hard."*

In the December 1961 issue of **Charles Buchan's Football Monthly**, Roy gave an interesting interview looking back on the previous few years.

"It doesn't seem three years since Brighton won the old Third Division South championship and promotion to the Second Division," he said.

"Yet we are now in our fourth season as a Second Division club – and I am the only survivor of the side which won a championship medal in 1958.

"I made the bare 14 appearances needed to earn a medal. I was mainly a full back in those days and Brighton were well off in that department.

"All the other stalwarts of our Third Division days have moved on… Jim Langley, Eric Gill, Glen Wilson, Denis Gordon, Peter Harburn, Frankie Howard and co.

"Billy Lane, who steered us to promotion and whose powers of persuasion had so much to do with my joining Brighton, has also gone. The place doesn't seem the same without him.

"When we won promotion some people said we would be out of our depth in the Second Division. When we took two early beatings from Middlesbrough it seemed as though the critics were right.

"But we recovered and more than held our place in the higher grade.

"The Second Division is the toughest one from which to gain promotion. Each season there seem to be about four top-class sides challenging, with the rest cutting each other's throats week by week.

"For the last three years I have been the regular centre half and now I am club skipper.

"One of my most memorable games in our first season in the Second Division was a Boxing Day meeting with the then League leaders, Fulham, in 1958.

"Their visit drew a record Goldstone Road crowd of 36,747, with receipts of £4,376.

"We beat them 3-0, Johnny Haynes and all, and I shut out centre forward Maurice Cook out of the game," he added.

Roy pictured while living in Crawley

Indeed, the **Sunday Pictorial** report at the time stated: *"Haynes was controlled and Graham Leggat was rarely in the picture thanks to Brighton's resolute defending… Fulham had a pretty thin time."*

Sadly, after a four-year stay in the Second Division, Brighton finished bottom at the end of the 1961-1962 season and were relegated.

Roy was eventually given a free transfer at the end of the 1963-1964 season and joined Crawley Town, where he eventually became player-manager.

He had made 297 appearances for Brighton, scoring 22 times (13 of which were from the spot).

And he was well-loved at Crawley Town too.

Reds fan Mick Fox said: *"Roy came to Crawley towards the end of his career and he made an enduring impression on us supporters and also his team-mates, not to mention those opposing forwards unlucky enough to feel the force of a Jennings' tackle.*

"I remember watching Roy in his first full season in 1964-1965. He was a no-nonsense centre back who looked as if he had spent a career battling rugged centre forwards in the days when the physical side of the game was significantly more evident than today.

"Roy rarely missed a game from the 1964-1965 season through to the end of his playing days in the 1968-1969 campaign when he made just a few appearances.

"That last season, when Roy had taken over as player-manager, was probably his greatest achievement, coming as it did the year after an underachieving but expensive squad which finished 5th from bottom in the Southern League.

"We therefore feared the worst when budget cuts were announced due to overspending, but with Roy as manager he steered us to a remarkable first ever promotion to the Premier Division.

"Those of us who watched Roy play in the 1960s will remember his toughness but also his uncanny ability to score penalties into either corner of the net without seemingly striking the ball with any force at all.

"And this was in the days when he was often taking penalties in the notorious Town Meadow mud. Roy was the best penalty taker I have ever seen and this allied to his achievements as manager make Roy one of our all-time greats in my eyes."

After retiring from football, Roy remained in Crawley, and became a partner in an accountancy firm, was active in the local community, and served as a magistrate.

Roy Jennings died on 21st October 2016, at the age of 84.

33

Barrie Rees
(Barrie Gwyn Rees)
1944-1965
BHAFC 1965
Right Half
Appearances: 12
Goals: 1

One of the Albion's most skilful players was an apprentice plumber who only played 12 first team games, and never lived to see his 22nd birthday.

Barrie Rees showed tremendous potential when he came into the Brighton & Hove Albion first team after joining from Everton in January 1965.

Born and raised in Rhyl, North Wales, Barrie was originally a centre forward and had represented Wales as a schoolboy before joining the Goodison ground staff, where he signed professional forms in September 1961, aged 17.

Barrie was discovered by Everton's North Wales region scout, Fred Bennett. Barrie played representative school football and went on to play for Wales schoolboys. He was playing for Rhyl in the Cheshire League, before he joined Everton at the age of 17 and serving an apprenticeship as a plumber, as many did at that time. Everton even bought his plumbing tools for him.

Barrie represented the Everton A & B teams before progressing through the reserves into the first team.

His debut came in a 4-2 defeat by West Ham United in October 1963, in which Barrie scored. He made his home debut against

Birmingham City five months later, when he found the net again in a 3-2 victory.

He played his last game that season four days later at Bramall Lane, Sheffield in a 0-0 draw and had also played in the infamous Battle of Goodison game against Leeds United in November 1964, which saw a player sent off in the fourth minute for a chest high tackle, fans warned for spitting at players and for the first time in an English league match, a referee walked off the pitch because of violent play.

After just three appearances leading the Everton attack and one at right back, he was then picked as a reserve for the Wales U23 team, before he came to the attention of Brighton.

When Archie Macaulay despatched Joe Wilson to watch Barrie in Everton reserves, he acted on the strong recommendation of his experienced and trustworthy scout.

Joe had more than one look, as a fee of just under £10,000 was being asked and in those days that was a big sum for Brighton. But Archie and Joe were no doubt that this would be a brilliant signing.

"We should have liked to have had further reports on him, but other clubs are interested, and we shall have to move in quickly" said Macauley at the time. *"Now if he wants to come, we shall sign him."*

Making his debut at right half in a 3-1 home defeat of Crewe Alexandria, Barrie quickly impressed, and his half back partnership with Norman Gall and Dave Turner seemed to form the backbone of an exciting Albion team.

In less than three months, Barrie made 12 first team appearances. He gained instant acclaim from Albion supporters and, most importantly, won the wholesale admiration of his new colleagues.

A tall, stylish player and blessed with two good feet, height, balance and a natural instinct to go forward, he was the complete half back.

Fellow Welshman Mel Hopkins helped him settle in, and he slotted in as if he had a couple of hundred games behind him. It was not long before some of the older hands were looking to him to set an example.

In the lowest division in the Football League, the class of Barrie Rees shone through, particularly in the way he made time for himself by acute positioning. Soon he had rivals wondering how on earth Everton had let him go.

The club had not long brought the First Division championship to Goodison so perhaps Catterick thought he had sufficient strength and that Rees would be better off pursuing his career elsewhere.

And it should not be forgotten that Macaulay was a most astute negotiator and Barrie had no qualms about stepping down in class. Like most players kicking their heels in a second team outfit he wanted first team football and with Albion he got it from day one.

The young Welshman settled well into life at the Goldstone and was becoming a crowd favourite for his attacking style of play. Quiet off the pitch, Barrie loved ten-pin bowling; and to get him back to his parents in Rhyl, he bought a Mini off his colleague Bobby Baxter.

Macaulay knew he had uncovered a diamond and there was no question of Rees being rough-cut. In his 12 games Albion won eight, lost two and drew twice.

The most goals conceded in any one match of that period was the 4-4 humdinger on a stormy Goldstone night with Chester. It was one of the most entertaining games many fans had ever and notable for Barrie's one and only goal.

John Vinicombe, in the **Evening Argus**, called it: *"A feast of football skill"*.

From early February 1965, the Albion bandwagon rolled on and soon Bobby Smith had recovered from injury to regain his place and increase the vital ingredient of competition for places.

With the arrival of Barrie Rees, the side had bags of strength and that counted for much where the physical element was so important. Barrie shirked nothing, but they were all put to the test in the fiery furnace of Rochdale.

Norman Gall was sent off after a dust-up with Bert Lister and a hail of missiles descended on the Albion team when the oldest spectator complained that Gall had smacked him on the nose. He was in fact an innocent victim. Gall aimed a retaliatory punch at Lister close to the touchline, missed, and hit an innocent elderly man.

Meanwhile goalkeeper Brian Powney was hit with a dart from the crowd while team-mates were struck by coins and washers and Barrie ducked to avoid a china cup. Amid all the mayhem, the new boy maintained a cool and dignified presence.

Albion's next game, at home to Southport on 26th March, was played on a Friday to avoid clashing with the Grand National and there were close on 20,000 at the Goldstone to see them win 3-1 and take second spot for the first time.

With no further game for five days there was time to relax and Barrie took himself off to his lodgings in Wordsworth Street after the Southport game and set his alarm for an early start next morning.

Before first light he was in his Mini and en-route on a 300-mile journey to Rhyl and a reunion with his parents. It was to be no ordinary visit as, earlier in the week, Barrie's uncle had won £28,000 (worth £468,000 today) on the football pools.

Nobody knows what happened on the journey. But it was confirmed that at 8.45am Barrie, who was travelling alone, was in collision with a lorry at the junction of the A5 and the Ashby-Nuneaton road in Warwickshire. He died at the local Manor Hospital shortly afterwards.

When told the news Archie Macaulay cried openly. Only a few hours earlier he had congratulated Barrie on yet another superb performance. When word quickly spread all supporters went into mourning. Team-mates could not believe the news at first.

The club immediately put out a public statement which read:

"The death of Barrie Rees was a dreadful shock to us all. Our sorrow, however, cannot be compared to the grief of his parents. To lose a 21-year-old son in such tragic circumstances is almost too much to bear and our heartfelt condolences go out to Mr and Mrs Rees in Rhyl.

"Barrie had been an Albion player for only a short time... but in the space of those short weeks he quickly established himself as a player of undoubted promise and became a firm favourite at the Goldstone.

His style and flair for the attacking wing half role made him a key man and he went from strength to strength with every game. His loss to the Albion is irreplaceable at present."

**Barrie signs for the Albion in 1965 as manager
Archie Macaulay looks on**

Only a couple of weeks earlier and returning from Torquay after
a hard-fought single goal win, they had seen the generous side of
Barrie's nature.

A coming-of-age present, a box of cigars, went to his team who
all lit up on the coach ride back home cracking jokes and larking
about the way teams and well-wishers do when there is good cause
for celebration.

Former Albion chairman Dick Knight remembers Barrie with
fondness.

In his autobiography **Mad Man**, he writes: *"Barrie Rees, is in my
opinion one of Brighton's classiest ever players. An attacking midfield player and
a wonderful passer of the ball, you immediately sensed he was something special.*

165

At 21, he had a big future ahead of him. When he was tragically killed in a car crash it took a long time for the club, the players and the fans to get over it.

"He'd only played 12 games, but everyone who saw Barrie Rees play knew we had lost an outstanding young talent."

Barrie remains a legend of the Goldstone Ground and a reminder of what might have been.

34

Bobby Smith
(Robert Alfred Smith)
1933-2010
BHAFC 1964-1965
Centre Forward
Appearances: 33
Goals: 20

George Best, Jim Baxter, Paul Merson, Jimmy Greaves and Paul Gascoigne all have two things in common... all five were football geniuses; and each of their lives were crippled by either alcohol or gambling addiction.
Add to that list the name of England and Brighton & Hove Albion legend Bobby Smith.

Bobby was born in Lingdale in Cleveland and was spotted by Chelsea when playing for Redcar Boys' Club. Chelsea brought him to London as a 16-year-old, making him a full professional at age 17, in 1950.

He scored 23 League goals in 74 appearances, and seven FA Cup goals in 12 appearances.

He was part of the 1954-1955 Chelsea side that won the First Division.

Despite the fact he never really became established as a regular with Chelsea between 1950 and 1955, Tottenham Hotspur paid £18,000 for his transfer in December 1955.

Initially used by Spurs at inside left, Bobby was soon moved to his ideal position of centre forward. There his strength, his right-footed shooting and his ability in the air, despite a relative lack of height – he stood 5ft 9in, and in his prime weighed 12st 10lb – quickly made him a formidable striker.

The following season brought 18 League goals, and in 1957-1958 he equalled, with his 36 goals, the club record established by Ted Harper in 1930-1931.

Bobby became an integral part of Bill Nicholson's famous double winning Tottenham team of 1960-1961. He was top scorer with 33 goals scored in 43 games, including the first of the two goals in the 1961 FA Cup Final.

The team also went on to retain the FA Cup in 1962 (Bobby scored in the Final again) and won the 1963 European Cup Winners' Cup. He is one of Spurs' all-time top goal scorers, second only to Jimmy Greaves, with 208 goals and he scored in 317 senior matches, including 12 hat-tricks.

The sad irony is the first legal betting shops in the UK were opened in May 1961, the very week that Bobby enjoyed his Wembley glory.

What few people knew is that Bobby was addicted to gambling, and betting shops became like his second home for most of his adult life.

When Tottenham were checking out of their hotel after the away leg of their European Cup first round tie against Feyenoord in 1961-1962, Bill Nicholson called a meeting of the players to say: *"Our telephone bill is 10 times what we expected. Somebody has taken liberties calling home."*

Bobby snapped back: *"All right, all right. Keep your hair on. I'll pay it when I get home."*

Nobody had known that Bobby had been on the phone throughout the trip to his bookie in London.

For England, Bobby played those 15 times with the impressive scoring record of 13 goals, first appearing in October 1960 against Northern Ireland in Belfast, when he scored the first goal in a 5-2 win.

Later in the month, he scored twice against Spain in a 4-2 victory at Wembley.

Bobby signing autographs for eager young Albion fans

Alf Ramsey favoured him at first when he took over the team in 1962, and Bobby took part in Ramsey's first successful European tour in 1963, scoring England's second goal against Czechslovakia in Bratislava in a 4-2 victory.

The following October he led the England attack in a match against the Rest of the World at Wembley, providing the pass from which right winger Terry Paine scored in a 2-1 win.

His last cap came barely a month later, again at Wembley, when he scored once in England's 8-3 defeat of Northern Ireland.

But the following year things went cataclysmically wrong, when Spurs took exception to a series of newspaper articles published by Bobby, and transfer listed their former star.

Even so, 31-year-old Bobby's surprise transfer to Brighton & Hove Albion in the summer of 1964 for a fee of just £5,000 was a shock to the whole footballing world.

Local newspaper and radio journalist Ian Hart sheds some light on the surprise transfer:

"Like most footballers of that time, Bobby enjoyed a fag and a drink. Unfortunately, he also liked a bet, correction, he loved a bet, the only problem was he wasn't very good at it.

"The level of his gambling debts had allegedly reached a point where the then Spurs boss Bill Nicholson felt that with Smith past his best on the pitch, his problems off of it might have a detrimental effect at White Hart Lane.

"Legendary local bookmaker George Gunn was aware of this situation and, along with the Brighton board, managed to broker a deal which saw Smith's extensive gambling debts paid off as part of his transfer to Brighton."

An article in **Charles Buchan's Football Monthly** in July 1964 recounts what happened: *In the history of British football there has seldom, if ever, been such a sudden plummet as that of Bobby Smith.*

Seven months ago, he was centre forward of England and Spurs. He had been Spurs' leader when they won the League and Cup double in 1960-1961. In that season he equalled the 1896-97 record of WC Athersmith of Aston Villa, by winning all honours available.

Yet suddenly, last season, he was sold to Brighton for a reported fee of £5,000. This is his story…

"People stop me in the street and ask me about it," said Bobby… "If Spurs let you go for only £5,000 there must be something wrong somewhere… you must have had an argument or something."

"I've lived in that atmosphere long enough now to be past wondering, but there's something I want to say right away…

"Every time I turn out for Brighton next season I will be determined to show Bill Nicholson how wrong he was to let me go… to show him and Spurs that there is a lot of the old Bobby Smith fire left — and that it is going to be used to help Brighton bid for better things.

"Brighton and the Fourth Division are a challenge to me. I could have gone to bigger clubs, could have stayed in London, could still be in the First Division with Fulham.

"I gave Tottenham nine years of loyal, all-out service, but come the new season I aim to bang them in with Brighton. I still can!

"I've been told I'm in for a tough time; that I will suffer plenty of knocks; that the football in the Fourth Division is too crude to suit me... But I can take care of myself in this new sphere.

"As to the standard of play I'll just have to wait and see, but I know there will be a lot of football from Brighton with a manager like Archie Macaulay in charge of us.

"When I think of the £5,000 Brighton paid for me, I know I should be glad it was so low because it made it easy for me to move.

"I read that Brighton's return for getting me is already beginning to show with increased season-ticket sales. That pleases me.

"It pleases because it shows the interest is being heightened. It is certain that a successful Brighton side would mean gates many Second Division clubs would envy.

"So, I'm really looking forward to having a go with them. I know quite well that what I have been, and what I have done, will not cut any ice next season. To everybody I shall be Bobby Smith, just starting again – for Brighton."

Perhaps unsurprisingly, given his pedigree and positive attitude, Bobby Smith was a phenomenal success in the 1964-1965 season.

Considering the last home game at the Goldstone Ground the previous season had attracted under 9,000, the box office value of Bobby Smith was incredible. Some 20,058 packed into the Goldstone to watch Bobby score twice in a 3-1 win over Barrow on the opening day of the campaign.

In all, he hit 20 goals in just 33 games and his swashbuckling style and deft touch also helped five other players reach double figures.

In the end, Brighton won the Fourth Division Championship in style, scoring 102 League goals.

Despite the successful first season, the good times were not to last.

Manager Archie Macaulay hit the roof and suspended Bobby for two weeks when the centre forward reported for pre-season training in July 1965 weighing 15st 9lb! Bobby had last weighed 12st 9lb in the spring of 1964, according to Tottenham's records.

Then, controversial articles for a Sunday newspaper led Bobby to be transfer-listed and, finally, sacked from the club in October 1965.

Nevertheless, his presence and amazing contribution to the Championship season, with a buzzing Goldstone filled to the rafters, is remembered as one of the highlights of supporting the Albion in the 1960s.

Like so many British football stars, Bobby was a victim of his times. The iniquitous maximum-wage system existed until 1961 – then at £20 – by which point Bobby had only a few years' of playing football left. Gambling was perhaps one way be thought he could boost his income.

Albion fan Philip Dennett recalls: *"I was working in a bankruptcy office as a kid when Bobby Smith came in to sort out his debts. I had to escort him to see someone. I couldn't believe it. My hero had fallen from grace."*

Bobby drifted into non-League football with Hastings United where crowds flocked to see him play as he netted 11 goals in 19 games; but, even there, he fell foul of the administration, with two suspensions for missing training.

He had a trial with Leyton Orient in 1967, and another with Banbury United, a non-League club, in the summer of 1968, but his playing career came to an early end.

He became a painter and decorator and drove a minicab before the crippling injuries he had collected on the football field finally caught up with him, not helped by a fall through a manhole that damaged his already wrecked legs. He had to take a disability pension after suffering heart problems and having a hip replacement.

It would have been handy if he could have sold his League championship and FA Cup winners' medals from 1961 and 1962, but in 1999 they were stolen from his house and he had the heartache of hearing how the 1961 Cup medal had turned up at an auction and sold for £11,200.

Bobby played in the soccer slave era. His rewards were excruciating physical pain and poverty in the pocket.

But in March 1994, as a guest of the club, for a routine match against York City, Bobby received a hero's welcome from the crowd at the Goldstone.

Simon Todd, who watched the Albion for more than 40 years, said: *"Bobby was a hustling, bustling, burly centre forward. He was undoubtedly Brighton's best-ever signing at the time."*

Former Albion chairman Dick Knight expressed his joy and delight at the move of the England striker to the south coast: *"In May 1964, Brighton made one of its best-ever moves, in terms of publicity, by signing Bobby Smith from Tottenham Hotspur, who had been playing centre forward for England at Wembley only six months earlier.*

"I was amazed and tremendously excited and… there was huge anticipation that the England centre forward was coming to play for us.

"There were six gates of over 20,000 – in the Fourth Division – and we won the league with a total of 102 goals. Smith scored 19 of them!"

Fellow Albion die-hard Steve Harrington recalls one memorable meeting with Bobby – long after he retired from playing - when the Albion held a legends' race day at Brighton racecourse.

"It was a fairly warm April day, and Bobby had recently had a double hip operation funded by Spurs. He had fallen on hard times," explained Steve.

"I was lucky enough to spend some time having a chat about his playing days. One story stuck with me as an autograph collector.

"Bobby told me that there was a young thinly clad youngster waiting outside a hotel when the Spurs team stayed in Chester.

"It was a freezing cold day, and this lad approached Bobby for a signature, as he walked to the team bus. A quick signature and Bobby asked where the lad had come from.

"Liverpool was the reply.

"Christ that's a long way. How did you get here?" asked Bobby.

"Hitched a lift was the response. Bobby was shocked and asked why he had come such a long way.

"The lad explained: "to get your autograph as no one at school has it.

"How do you propose to get home? asked Bobby.

"Same way I got here replied the lad.

"Bobby then looked at me and said he told the lad: "Here's some notes… now get a bus home and something to eat."

"Legend is an understatement," added Steve.

"He was a remarkable human being too."

Bobby Smith died on 18th September 2010, following a short illness at a hospital in Enfield, London.

His name remains etched as a legend of Brighton & Hove Albion.

35

Bill Cassidy
(William Pitt Cassidy)
1940-1995
BHAFC 1962-1967
Left Half/Inside Left
Appearances: 129
Goals: 30

Hamilton born Bill Cassidy will always be remembered as one of the all-time great characters and comedians of the Goldstone Ground.

Bill did not need a script to lighten periods of gloom in the dressing room. He had a natural flair for the comic and the unexpected.

When he played the fool or cracked a joke, it did more for morale than a torrent of invective from manager Archie Macaulay. Flagging spirits soared when Bill was up to his pranks.

He was also a highly versatile player on the pitch who wore the number 3, 6, 7, 8, 9 and 10 shirts in his five seasons with the Albion as part of a 20-year career which spanned 12 clubs in England, Scotland and the USA.

On the staff of Glasgow Rangers as a teenager, Bill joined Rotherham United on a free transfer in August 1961.

When Albion manager George Curtis paid around £6,000 for his services in November 1962, the big hard tackling and constant running Scot was initially played at left half but soon proved himself to be a true utility player.

Immediately showing a willingness to go for goal, he scored some crucial goals when Albion won the 4th Division championship in 1964-1965, a season when he is specially remembered for his dogged determination for each game.

Being a good pro, Bill took his football very seriously but was blessed with an intuitive knack of relieving tension by a timely joke or prank.

One high point of Bill's self-appointed role as court jester had the Goldstone crowd roaring with laughter in a match against Darlington. As the referee called for a ball he thought had gone into touch, Bill, grinning broadly, waddled around like a pregnant duck with it stuffed up his shirt. The referee saw the funny side, so did the players and spectators on what had been a drab and featureless game.

Macaulay, a fellow Scot, valued the joker in his pack. He knew full well that a happy dressing room can often be the launch pad of a successful side. This proved to be the case in the 1964-1965 Fourth Division championship campaign when Bill's 10 goals in 24 games proved a good ratio amid so much competition for places.

He played every game as though it was the cup final. The highly charged 90 minutes that he put in either at wing half, inside forward or occasionally centre forward, were particularly effective in the lower divisions where the need to fight for the right to play was paramount.

Bill also knew that he had to make up for lack of pace by extra physical effort. A tackle from him did not contain an option of coming back for more although there was not a bad bone in his body and a joke was never very far away from a stream of Scottish invective.

For five years at the Goldstone, inside forward Jimmy Collins and Bill Cassidy were inseparable and a double act both on the pitch and in the dressing room.

When Collins and Cassidy were starting to settle down there were further new faces at the club - Allan Jackson from Bury, who played up front, and right winger George Waites from Orient.

But former manager George Curtis's formula to bring in youth at every level failed and Albion were staring relegation in the face in early spring of 1963. Not surprisingly Curtis parted company with the club in February. Joe Wilson took over as caretaker manager before Archie Macaulay agreed to accept the challenge after resigning from West Brom.

There were eight games remaining when Archie arrived, and the Albion were hanging just above the relegation zone. Northampton, who went on to win the championship, virtually sealed Albion's fate with a 5-0 thrashing.

This first of three Easter games plunged Albion into the bottom four from which they were unable to escape.

There was no truth in a persistent rumour that Archie viewed relegation pragmatically, but it was a fact that the next season meant he could not do worse.

In that first season, Bill Cassidy toiled away at left half and was one of 29 players of which no fewer than 17 made their debuts. Reeling off 25 games on the trot, Bill showed a disdain for injuries.

Macaulay valued this quality in a player and gradually started to assemble a side that not only rose from the lowest division the following season but did so in style.

By December 1963, he had landed Dave Turner from Newcastle who made the number 6 shirt his own. Bill donned number 10 and after Wally Gould and Jack Smith were signed, the team managed 19 wins for a comfortable eighth spot. In a more attacking role Bill scored six goals in 29 games.

Perhaps Bill tended to be overshadowed by the star quality of the side. But there was not the slightest doubt that his 24 appearances yielding 10 vital goals had an important bearing on the destination of the pennant.

He banged in the winner against Halifax on Boxing Day to delight a 19,000 Goldstone crowd.

Injury prevented him from figuring in all but two of the last 14 matches.

Old knocks were catching up. He came back after a hernia the previous season and then broke a small bone in his back and there was also a spate of knee problems.

By the summer of 1967, it was time for Bill to leave the Albion. Archie gave him a free transfer and Jimmy's career at the club was also up. Bill and his wife decided that a move to Southern League Chelmsford City would suit, but Jimmy had other ideas and went to Wimbledon.

The change of scene was to Bill's liking as he appeared in three successive Southern League championship teams beginning with Chelmsford and then at Cambridge United.

At Chelmsford, Bill achieved cult figure status.

At Cambridge, his Albion nickname of *Thunderboots* stuck as he scored 56 goals in 120 outings.

Ron Atkinson was Cambridge manager in 1971-1972 and he valued Bill Cassidy as a crash-bang-wallop centre forward and he was a key player for United when they entered the Football League.

During his time at Cambridge, Bill had a spell during the summer with Detroit Cougars. After United's initial season in the Fourth Division, he joined Kettering Town and then Ramsgate followed by a return to Scotland as player-manager of Ross County.

Then tragedy struck. At the still young age of 42, he was diagnosed with thrombosis and was registered as an invalid and struggled to keep up with basic living expenses.

Then in the 1980s, Bill was sentenced to a term of imprisonment after being convicted on burglary and handling charges.

Bill Cassidy's luck had run out and he died at his home in Oxford in 1995, aged just 54.

Jimmy Collins said: *"A man couldn't have had a better friend. He had his down spells, but he made you laugh. I loved that man."*

There can be few more amusing and tough players in the Albion's history than Bill Cassidy.

36

Jimmy Collins
(James Collins)
1937-2018
BHAFC 1962-1967
Inside Forward
Appearances: 221
Goals: 48

Jimmy Collins was one of the most talented and popular players to ever don an Albion shirt.

He also had a remarkable longevity and lasting fitness as a player and was still turning out competitively well into his 50s.

Jimmy was born in Sorn, a small village in East Ayrshire. He began his football career with nearby Lugar Boys' Club and Lugar Boswell Thistle.

The club was in the 1956 Scottish Junior Cup final where they lost to Petershill 4-1 in front of a bumper crowd of 64,702 at Hampden Park. Jimmy was capped twice at Scottish Junior level in the same year.

He was scouted by Tottenham Hotspur who paid £1,000 in June that year to secure the services of the youngster as a part-time professional, while Jimmy also completed his National Service in the Army and an apprenticeship as a bricklayer.

The speedy inside forward featured in two first team matches for Spurs in 1961 and made his senior debut against West Ham United on 23rd August 1961, aged 23.

Football coaches and analysts described Jimmy as a player with natural talent.

However, when he was with Tottenham, he lived in the shadow of legendary Spurs player and fellow Scotsman John White. So, Jimmy had to wait in the wings and made the First Division team only twice.

But his time with Tottenham eventually paid off. He was spotted by Brighton boss George Curtis who signed Jimmy for £9,000. He made his debut for the Albion in a 1-0 defeat against Carlisle United on 2nd October 1962.

After his debut Curtis said: *"It speaks well for the character of this player that, after sections of the press stated he was not prepared to come to the Goldstone Ground, he had never revealed such an intention to me.*

"And, on Monday, he signed forms and travelled overnight to Carlisle.

"We shall benefit from the great experience of this young and accomplished player."

But the Albion were relegated to the Fourth Division during his first season at the Goldstone, but Jimmy impressed with his unhurried and constructed skill in what was otherwise a poor side.

After Curtis left the club, new boss Archie Macauley set about consolidating the side, especially with Bobby Smith's unsettling departure from the Goldstone in the early stages of the Division Three campaign.

Macauley said Jimmy was the general of the team and a natural captain and the Scot rarely missed a game over the next three seasons.

Following back-to-back relegations, Jimmy captained the side during much of the Albion's Fourth Division title campaign in the 1964-1965 season and the principal playmaker also scored 17 goals.

Promotion was clinched in front of a crowd of 21,489 at the Goldstone in a 3-1 victory against Stockport County on 19th April. After Stockport went ahead, the Albion bounced back with an equaliser by Jack Smith. Then Jimmy Collins struck by hooking in a corner from John Goodchild, before Goodchild himself scored the third.

In a 3-1 win against Darlington, in the final game of the season before a bumper 31,423 crowd on 26th April 1965, there were gasps of awe as Jimmy opened the scoring.

Penalty king Jimmy Collins

The *Daily Mirror* reported: *"The opening goal (and Brighton's 100th of the season) came from a pass by Bobby Smith to Jimmy Collins. The inside right hammered the ball against the diving Hope and then cracked in the rebound."*

The following season (1965-1966) early results in the Third Division for the club were poor. When the side lost 2-1 at Walsall at the start of November, Brighton lay in 21st position and a relegation battle loomed.

Then the Albion thrashed Wisbech Town 10-1 in the 1st Round of the FA Cup, with Jimmy Collins grabbing one, Jack Smith and Bill Cassidy hitting two, and Charlie Livesey bagging a hat-trick.

Two games followed before Brighton then put Southend to the sword in an astonishing 9-1 Third Division victory at the Goldstone played on 27th November 1965, and once again Jimmy hit the newspaper headlines by scoring the first goal in the avalanche.

The *Daily Mirror* reported: *"Jimmy Collins opened the scoring in the sixth minute... and Southend never knew what hit them."*

Jimmy enthused everyone with his playmaking and his goals for a full five years at the Goldstone. His former Albion team-mates fondly recall Jimmy as one of the best players of his era.

Not only did he impress team-mates and fans as a player but he was also described as a friendly and lovable person.

Ex-player Norman Gall said: *"He was such a super guy. He came down from Tottenham and straight away was made captain.*

"He played really well. He was all over the place. He was a natural wing-half and he helped me out and told everybody how to play.

"He was always very straight with you. If you didn't do what you were supposed to, he would tell you. But he always played as well as he could. I think maybe he was disappointed to be moved out by Spurs, but he always gave his all for Brighton."

Sussex Sports commentator Peter Brackley said he had been a fan of Jimmy since he was a child.

"He is up there with my all-time favourites - the likes of Dave Turner, Wally Gould, Brian Powney, the Smiths and Norman Gall," he quipped.

Peter said when he played football at school he would always try to play like his idol.

He said: *"Playing at school, I would be either Jimmy, trying to trap a ball and pass like him or Denis Law with my sleeves hanging over my hands. Watching Jimmy Collins had inspired me to want to get a career in sports.*

"I always remember Jimmy coming out of training, signing my autograph book and then having a bite of my apple. Made my day."

Albion fan Alan Reynolds also has fond memories of Jimmy: *"As a kid I used to watch the Albion train at the Goldstone,"* he recalled.

"Sometimes the players would go to Hove Park after training and I remember on one occasion Jimmy Collins, Wally Gould and a few others were having a game of cricket.

"Somehow I was asked if I wanted to join in. One memory was of Jimmy pulling a shot that flew past my head with him shouting 'Catch it!' in his broad Scottish accent.

"Another was when they let me have a bat, and Jimmy nicknamed me 'Geoffrey' after Geoff Boycott, as I wore glasses and had a good forward defensive," he laughed.

But although employed as a sweeper during the 1966-1967 season with considerable success he became concerned about his future at the club.

Throughout his life Jimmy always had a smile for everyone

In the spring of 1967, he asked for a transfer and moved into the Southern League at the end of the season with non-league team Wimbledon, where he was immediately made captain.

He spent his spare time at Wimbledon training for the licensed trade while helping out in a friend's laundry business.

After spending four years at Pound Lane, he returned to Sussex and played for Southwick, Shoreham and Saltdean United.

He also played for the Corals in the Sussex Sunday League into his 50s while working in the building trade.

When he retired, he did not return to live in his native Scotland but stayed in Shoreham.

Norman Gall has fond memories of their time playing for Corals.

He said: *"When he came back down here we got together straight away to play Sunday football with another good lad, Paul Flood. We enjoyed it and had a good team.*

"We played snooker together as well and did quite well."

Norman continued his close friendship with Jimmy and visited him when his health declined.

He said: *"I still used to go and see him and he had been very poorly. I don't know if he understood everything but he was still able to smile.*

"He was one of the best players we have ever had – and a fantastic bloke."

Jimmy Collins died at his home in Shoreham-by-Sea in 2018, at the age of 80.

37

Mel Hopkins
(Melvyn Hopkins)
1934-2010
BHAFC 1964-1967
Left Back
Appearances: 58
Goals: 2

There can have been few Albion players more decorated and modest than Welsh international full back Mel Hopkins.

The son of a miner from Ystrad in the Rhondda coalfield, Mel was signed by Tottenham Hotspur at the age of 15, when spotted by Welsh scout Joe Fisher playing for his local boys' club.

The versatile and lanky teenager was taken on as a £3 a week apprentice after just one trial and made his debut in January 1952.

The former Tonypandy Grammar School pupil had already played for Spurs' B team in the London Midweek League by the end of that season.

During the following season the ever improving full back progressed up to the Spurs A team in the Eastern Counties League before then making his debut for the reserves against Bristol Rovers in the April of 1952.

Such was Mel's fine progress, he made his debut for Spurs' first team under the tutelage of manager Arthur Rowe in a league game against Derby County in October of 1952, the game finishing in a goalless draw.

Mel could play at left back, his preferred position, but could also play at centre half or in midfield if required.

Although he found his way to the left back position barred by Charlie Withers and Arthur Willis, he didn't have to wait long until those two stalwarts had given way and as a 17-year-old he was a regular in the side and had upped his earnings to £20 a week, while living in digs in Enfield.

Spending four seasons in the left back berth after replacing Withers, Mel showed good positional sense and a strong, fearless tackle making him one of the most highly regarded full backs in the country.

Being a youngster in the side did not faze him, bringing him experience at a time when the team were not doing so well and then later shining under the management of Jimmy Anderson and Bill Nicholson.

But then bad luck struck. In 1959, Mel suffered a serious injury while playing for Wales against Scotland following a collision with Ian St John, smashing his nose and upper jaw, an injury which would keep him out of football for two years and thus miss being part of the famous 1960-1961 Spurs double winning team.

In total, Mel played 219 games over 12 years for Spurs, before signing for Brighton & Hove Albion in October 1964.

In a glittering career, Mel's finest game was in the quarter-final of the 1958 World Cup in Gothenburg against Brazil.

He would play in each of the five matches in which Wales were engaged. In their first round group, he appeared against Hungary – a ghost of the great team which had thrashed England twice, in 1953 and 1954 – only drawing 1-1 in Sandviken.

Next, in Stockholm, he figured in another 1-1 draw, this time versus Mexico, followed by a goalless draw, again in Stockholm, against an under-strength Swedish team.

Mel Hopkins and the Welsh defence at large had already shown their resilience, but now, with Wales coming equal second in their group with the Hungarians, they had to meet them again in a play-off in Stockholm.

It proved to be a bruising game against a Hungarian team who kicked John Charles, the Wales centre forward, out of the World Cup. But Wales, a goal down at half-time, went on to win 2-1.

This pitted them in the quarter-final against a Brazilian team which, with the aid of the 17-year-old Pelé and the dynamic right winger Garrincha, had struck formidable form.

The Welsh held out against fierce pressure, with the towering Mel Hopkins facing Garrincha's dynamic pace and a magical swerve. Mel countered him superbly. Time and again, he anticipated Garrincha's bursts, something that would prove far beyond the capacities of Sweden's defence in the ensuing final. Brazil prevailed through a single, scrappy goal by Pelé.

But Mel had effectively marked legendary Garrincha out of the game, and as a result he was named man of the match.

Altogether, Mel would play 34 games for Wales between 1956 and 1962. Standing 5ft 11in, but weighing little over 11 stone, he was a mobile and intelligent full back.

Back before that incredible performance in Sweden, Mel's performances for Spurs had already made him regarded as one of the finest left backs in the country.

Racking up appearance after appearance for the Lilywhites (Mel made 240 for Spurs' first team in total) things were going well for the Welshman who was a key player under managers Arthur Rowe, Jimmy Anderson and Bill Nicholson.

Ever loyal to Spurs, he stayed at White Hart Lane until 1964, despite the disappointment of failing to play a single game when the team became the first of the 20th century to win the FA Cup and League double, in the 1960-1961 season.

In October 1964 when he joined Brighton & Hove Albion for £8,000, it was just 18 months since the 29-year-old Mel had won his 34th and final cap for Wales.

And he joined his former Spurs colleagues Bobby Smith and Jimmy Collins on the Albion's triumphant march to the Fourth Division championship that season.

Albion fan Philip Dennett recalls: *"Mel was getting on a bit when he came to the Albion, but he was sheer class in every game."*

While playing for the Albion, the versatile left back often played over on the other flank at right back.

Things took a downward turn the following term, though, and Mel requested a transfer in February 1966, but he remained at the Goldstone until July 1967, by which time he had notched up 58 appearances scoring two goals.

Spurs star player Eddie Clayton remembers Mel with great fondness as he used to be close to the Welshman.

He said Mel was a tough tackling wing half who was good on the ball and possessed good pace.

"He was probably the best left back in the country at the time up until his unfortunate accident when he lost his place," recalled Clayton who also went onto say that Mel loved to attack down the left flank.

On leaving the Albion, Mel enjoyed a brief spell at Ballymena United in Northern Ireland 1967, and this was followed by a move to Bradford Park Avenue in January 1969, where he played 30 games before retiring in 1970 and moving back to Sussex.

From the early 1970s, Mel lived in Shoreham-by-Sea and worked as a sports teacher at the Dorothy Stringer Secondary School in Brighton, coached works teams three nights a week and was appointed as secretary of the Sussex Coaches.

He later worked as a sports officer and coach for Horsham District Council.

It was while teaching in the 1990s that he arranged a trip for some of his students to visit the Goldstone Ground.

The Albion's Physiotherapist Malcolm Stuart remembers the visit well: *"When we were leaving the Goldstone Ground in the 1990s we had lots of requests for group visits.*

"One such group of school kids made their way into the gym followed by their teacher, who I immediately recognised. But he kept himself very much in the background.

"After a short but lively Q&A session I asked the kids if they ever questioned their teacher about his illustrious career for Spurs, Brighton and Wales.

Mel's daughter-in-law Julia Hopkins said that in later life he was the perfect grandfather and was adored by her children

"They all looked totally shocked and the teacher, a certain Mr Mel Hopkins looking somewhat surprised, admitted that he had never let on about his career prior to teaching.

"We then had a lovely chat about winning leagues and cups and even touched on the World Cup quarter-final with Wales.

"It was a very pleasant afternoon spent with a very reluctant hero of mine.

"He was such a quiet and unassuming bloke, yet when you look at what he achieved in the game most would have shouted it from the roof tops," added Malcolm.

In 2003, Mel was given a special merit award by the Football Association of Wales.

Melvyn Hopkins died on 19th October 2010, aged 75, in St Barnabas House Hospice in Worthing following a long illness.

38

Wally Gould
(Walter Gould)
1938-2018
BHAFC 1964-1967
Outside Right
Appearances: 193
Goals: 46

Wally Gould was an explosive and entertaining outside right and an Albion great who scored more goals than average for a winger.
A fixture in the Brighton side for four seasons Wally was a quick ball-playing winger who would often energise the crowd and was an integral member of the club's Fourth Division championship-winning campaign of 1964-1965 where he topped the scoring chart with 21 goals.

The title was clinched on the last day of the season back on 26th April 1965 against Darlington at the Goldstone where goals from Wally, Jimmy Collins and Jack Smith sealed a 3-1 win in front of 31,423 supporters.

Led by manager Archie Macaulay, the club won the title with a home record of 18 wins and five draws.

South Yorkshire-born, Wally represented Rother Valley Schools and became a junior with Rotherham United while working as an apprentice electrician, an occupation which caused him the loss of several fingers.

During his time at Millmoor he was loaned to non-league Rawmarsh Welfare, but in March 1958 he signed professional forms at nearby Sheffield United.

After just five Second Division appearances at Bramall Lane he moved to York City in February 1961, where his career really took off.

His 25 goals from 120 Fourth Division appearances caught the eye of the Albion scouts, and he headed south and signed for Archie Macaulay's resurgent side in a £4,000 deal in January 1964 and Wally quickly impressed.

Wally's consistently high level of performance in the blue and white endeared him to the Goldstone faithful. He rarely missed a match, creating many opportunities with his direct style and accurate crosses, while scoring many goals himself.

He went on to make 193 appearances for the Albion, scoring 46 goals.

Die-hard Albion fan Ray Noble said: *"Between 1965 and 1967 we had something of a golden period with two wingers who could both create and score goals.*

"With the younger Tiger Tawse on the left and the experienced Wally Gould on the right, there was always a belief that a goal could come from out of nowhere.

"It seemed to me that Wally was the sorcerer and Brian the sorcerer's apprentice," he added.

In February 1968, and much to the reluctance of the club, Wally was released by Brighton to pursue a highly successful career in South African football, featuring for Durban United, Hellenic and East London United.

In May 1968, Wally featured in an article in South African Soccer Monthly, titled *Boy from Brighton*, which celebrated how he was one of the country's leading goal-scorers at the time.

He was a forerunner for other Albion players such as Kit Napier and Brian Tawse who also emigrated to seek their fortunes in South Africa a few years later.

During his long and successful career as a footballer, Wally played 300 matches and scored 71 goals in the Football League.

In 2001 at the club's centenary Wally acknowledges the cheers of the Albion crowd at Withdean

He hung up his boots in the professional game after playing his last season at Chelmsford City in 1977, aged 39, and took to running a pub. But after just a few weeks as a licensee he was offered a coaching job with Stoke City alongside then manager of the side, George Eastham, at the start of the 1977-1978 season. He then became the reserve team coach for the side in 1980 before becoming number two at the club.

He was reserve team coach when Cyril Lea resigned in New Year 1980. Wally then stepped up to be number two to Alan Durban. He subsequently served Richie Barker when he became manager but left in March 1982.

There were rumoured to be differences between Wally and some of the senior players at this time, with one training ground incident resulting in Ray Evans, the captain, being suspended for two weeks. Days later Wally was replaced by Bill Asprey.

Former Albion chairman Dick Knight recalls: *"For me, Wally's legend is his major contribution to the Albion's reputation over the years of always trying to play fast, attacking football.*

"I'll never forget his dazzling, jinking wing play sending defenders in a spin. Very few players would score goals at the rate Wally did.

"His contribution to the enjoyment of the crowd showed he was a true entertainer on the football pitch."

Mr Knight likened him to Liverpool's Mohamed Salah and former Manchester United great George Best because of the way he played his football.

He added that Wally attended many events at Brighton Racecourse held during Dick Knight's time as chairman and was a great friend of Brighton & Hove Albion.

Off the pitch Wally was a family man who had a love for golf, horses, cars and dogs… and not necessarily in that order!

His son Ian recounts one story that is typical of the man that his dad was: *"One day while he was at Brighton my dad was invited to a farm somewhere in Sussex where my uncle lived, for a rabbit shoot.*

"Then armed with a shotgun he was unfortunately apprehended by the local police.

*"The front page of the **Evening Argus** reported his arrest with the headline: Albion Striker in Shotgun Incident."*

"It was made worse in that he hadn't told mum and the first she knew about it was when she read the report in the Argus!"

In another incident Wally was definitely not guilty.

"Another funny incident was he was taking our pet dog Pyrenean Mountain dog out for a walk when he dropped off at the Goldstone Ground to collect something, leaving the dog in his Black Vauxhall Cresta," recalls Ian.

"He returned to the car an hour later to find all the seats and dashboard ripped to pieces and the dog had eaten the tax disc!"

"Dad always seemed to have little mishaps… don't mention the Halloween witch's mask which frightened all and sundry," he laughed.

Wally died in March 2018, following a short period of illness after battling with dementia for many years.

39

Charlie Livesey
(Charles Edward Livesey)
1938-2005
BHAFC 1965-1969
Inside Forward
Appearances: 146
Goals: 37

**In the mid to late 1960s the
North Stand at the Goldstone
Ground would regularly rock
with the empowering chant
of:** *"Sha la la la Livesey"*
**which deliberately mimicked
the Small Faces 1966 Top
Ten hit** *"Sha la la la lee"*.
And if that failed to ignite
the match, it was closely followed by the whole ground singing:
"Charleee, Charleee, I'd go a million miles for one of your goals… oh Charleee"
to the music hall tune of Al Jolson's *My Mammy*.

Eastender Charlie Livesey was already a star with Southampton
and Chelsea where over five years he scored a combined 32 goals in
67 competitive matches long before he joined the Albion.

He had also enjoyed stints at Gillingham and Watford (where he
scored 26 goals in 64 games) before arriving at the Goldstone as a
27-year-old in September 1965 for a £7,000 fee from Northampton
Town.

At times wayward off the pitch, Charlie started off as a youth
with his local side West Ham and played for the Custom House
United in the Essex league. He also had a trial with First Division
Wolves.

But it was Southampton for whom he signed as an 18-year-old in 1956.

Scoring freely for the Saints reserves and keeping hours that shocked his flat-mates, Tony Godfrey and Denis Pring, Charlie had had to wait two seasons for a start.

That came about, in August 1958, when the prolific Southampton centre forward Derek Reeves broke a toe. Initially slow to grab his chance, Charlie then scored six times in two games, also breaking a toe in the process.

When the respective toes mended, Saints' manager Ted Bates opted to play Charlie at Number 9 with Reeves at inside right.

But it did not work. In 14 games as a pair, they never both scored in the same match and aggregated only seven goals.

Reeves expressed his unhappiness, but the Board couldn't decide what to do with Charlie. In February, they tried in vain to sell him; in March, they increased his wages; but in May, they were ready to let him go – with one director, Rex Stranger, resigning in protest.

Chelsea's manager, ex-Saint Ted Drake, now wanted Charlie, after all. Charlie wasn't keen to leave – unless he could *"go home"* to West Ham – but the Southampton directors helped Bates to get a better deal from Chelsea.

It proved to be an *"amazing deal"* – in Bates's own words – for Southampton, who effectively acquired three new players out of it.

By the time Charlie reached the Goldstone Ground he proved to be one of the cleverest forwards to play for the Albion since the end of World War Two.

A powerful runner with a great eye and keen anticipation, Charlie was not a prolific goal scorer but this Brylcreem blonde pin-up boy was certainly a popular player with the fans.

He started out under manager Archie Macaulay as a centre forward but subsequently operated as inside forward and became a regular for the next four seasons, during which time he was acknowledged as the club's most talented player.

It took Charlie only three matches to get off the mark for the Albion, netting the second goal in a 2-2 draw with Millwall at the Goldstone.

Of his 14 goals that season, 11 came in an astonishing 12-match run that began with an FA Cup tie against Wisbech Town in November 1965. Charlie helped himself to a hat-trick in a 10-1 thrashing of the non-Leaguers.

Albion fan Simon Todd said: *"Even if he didn't score, there was always the expectation that he was going to score when he got the ball, hence the excitement he created."*

His ability was such that England manager Alf Ramsey had him watched in the build-up to the World Cup finals in 1966 despite Albion being mid-table in the Third Division at the time.

And it was Charlie who often hit the newspaper headlines, starting a late avalanche of goals in Albion's record equalling 9-1 victory against Southend on 27th November 1965.

The **Sunday Mirror** reported: *"The late rush was started by Livesey in the 85th minute, with Smith smashing in his third three minutes later and Livesey powering in a great goal in the last minute."*

In Brighton's League Cup run in the 1966-1967 season Charlie was on target. The 1-0 second round win against Norwich City at Carrow Road in September 1966 was reported by the **Daily Mirror** under a headline: *Livesey Slams Brighton Home.*

The report read: *"A goal three minutes from time by centre forward Charlie Livesey put Brighton through to the third round of the league Cup.*

"Livesey seized on a ball kicked wildly upfield and from 20 yards sent in a scorching shot which goalkeeper Kevin Keelan had no chance of saving."

And the Albion went one better in the next round on 11th October beating Coventry City 3-1 away at Highfield Road.

Peter Ingall at the **Daily Mirror** reported: *"Brighton were streets ahead of a struggling Coventry side who scored first in the ninth minute.*

"But Brighton equalised seven minutes later when Bill Cassidy sent a shot against the post and the always dangerous inside right Charlie Livesey hammered in the rebound."

But one of Charlie's most gloried moment came in a third round replay of the FA Cup on 1st February 1967 with Brighton beating Aldershot 3-1 in front of a bumper 29,208 crowd and thus setting up a fourth round meeting with high flying Chelsea.

Under a banner headline: *Sunk by sub called Charlie*, George Harley at the **Daily Mirror** again reported: *"Charlie Livesey, much the freshest* *player on the field, made certain of a fourth round tie against his old club Chelsea last night.*

"He had come on as a substitute for inside left Eric Whittington midway through the second half of this tough, rough replay.

"And with the Aldershot defence retreating wearily, the lively Livesey burst through the middle to head home a centre by Brian Tawse, for the crushing third goal six minutes from the end."

Charlie's flair never deserted him and in one game in October 1967 he showed what he was all about.

In a 3-1 drubbing of Grimsby at the Goldstone a brace of Livesey goals had the crowd in delirium, as the **Daily Mirror** reported: *"One of the finest goals seen on the Goldstone Ground restored Brighton's lead after 50 minutes.*

"Livesey picked up a loose pass near the half-way line and dribbled through the entire Grimsby defence to the penalty area. He gave a short pass to Kit Napier, took the immediate return, and drove the ball home.

"Six minutes from the end, Livesey volleyed another grand goal from a Napier centre."

Albion fan Brian Long recalled: *"Charlie would glide past opponents with seeming ease. He was also the first 'sung' hero… nobody else had their own North Stand song at the time."*

Long-time friend Peter Keene added: *"Charlie was a big man with a big heart and was everybody's favourite. He was a bit of a lad, very outgoing and very popular with the crowd."*

Albion supporter Ray Noble said: *"One of my most abiding memories of Charlie, outside his obvious ability as a footballer was seeing him taking the last puffs of a cigarette before running out at the start of a match."*

Fellow fan Simon Levenson: *"I remember a story about Charlie throwing a boy his car keys during a five -a-side training session and asking him to: 'get my fags out the car'…. He had a quick smoke and resumed training!"*

Kit Napier's first wife Pat Hunter was friends with many of the Albion players' girlfriends and wives during the late 1960s, where they often swapped stories about their footballing partners.

"Charlie Livesey was a great character, cockney boy and a real Jack the lad," she said. *"If he'd been out drinking and got home late, he would often undress downstairs and walk into the bedroom backwards.*

Charlie leads the Albion team out in a game against QPR, closely followed by left winger Brian Tawse

"If his wife woke and he was caught he would apologise for waking her and tell her he was on the way to the loo."

After being released by the Albion in April 1969, aged 31, Charlie had one season at Crawley Town before finally hanging up his boots.

Over 13 years he had played in all four divisions of the Football League in a career spanning 329 League games and 106 goals.

Following retirement from playing Charlie returned to his beloved East End of London where he became a humble painter and decorator.

He died at St Bartholomew's Hospital in London in February 2005, aged 67, after a short illness.

40

Nobby Lawton
(Norbert Lawton)
1940-2006
BHAFC 1967-1971
Left Half
Appearances: 127
Goals: 16

**Like fellow Busby Babe,
fellow Albion legend and
close friend Alex Dawson,
Nobby Lawton excelled as a
professional footballer
wherever he played.**

Indeed, he was already a
legend at both Manchester
United and Preston North End
when he signed for Brighton & Hove Albion in 1967, aged 27.

Born in Newton Heath in North East Manchester, Nobby
attended a school where one of the teachers was also a scout for the
Old Trafford club.

After representing Lancashire Schoolboys it was a short step to
joining his local league club as an amateur in 1956 at the age of 16,
training on two evenings a week while working for a coal merchant.

Nobby was part of Manchester United's successful FA Youth
Cup winning team in 1957. Lawton and Dawson were both on the
scoresheet when United beat West Ham 3-2 in the first leg of the
1957 FA Youth Cup and Dawson scored twice in the 5-0 second leg
win.

Then following the Munich air disaster in 1958, the 18-year-old
Nobby gave up his job with a local coal merchant to sign
professional forms with Manchester United.

However, while playing for the club's reserve team, Lawton succumbed to a heavy bout of the flu, leading to double pneumonia and the temporary loss of the use of his legs.

He was out of action for several months but eventually made his debut for the first team on 9th April 1960, playing at inside left in a 3–2 win over Luton Town at Kenilworth Road.

Matt Busby kept faith with the fledgling talent and by the middle of the following season, he was a first team regular.

Over the next couple of seasons, Nobby forged a partnership with Bobby Charlton on the left side of the United forward line, scoring a hat-trick against Nottingham Forest on Boxing Day 1961, and by the 1962-1963 season he was increasingly deployed as a wing half.

Nobby was ever-present in United's run to the semi-finals of the FA Cup, where they were well beaten by Tottenham Hotspur, but somehow his confidence was never quite on a par with his abundant ability, and soon, in the face of inevitably brisk competition for midfield places, he slipped out of Busby's plans. This resulted in his sale to Second Division side Preston North End in March 1963 for a fee of £11,500, after a total of 44 games and 6 goals for Manchester United.

He was appointed captain by Preston at the age of 23 and inspired them to a third-place finish, just missing out on promotion to the First Division, and to the 1964 FA Cup Final where they lost to First Division West Ham United in a close game by 3-2.

Nobby remained Preston captain even though he was hampered by serial knee problems and he later admitted: *"I came back after two knee operations at Preston, but I was a shadow of the player I was in 1964. I was butchered really."*

After 164 league and cup appearances and 23 goals for North End, in September 1967, he dropped a further grade, joining Third Division Brighton & Hove Albion for a £10,000 fee.

He was signed by Archie Macaulay, but just over a year later found himself helping to select the team as part of a committee for two matches after Macaulay stepped down.

It wasn't long though before a familiar face took the helm in 1968 in the shape of his former Old Trafford playing colleague Freddie Goodwin.

Nobby was no-nonsense and cultured in his approach to playing and became Albion's midfield general for his entire time at the Goldstone Ground.

The classy left half inherited the captaincy of Brighton's Third Division side and on the pitch led by example and his experience was a big factor in the side's improvement under the new boss.

He also played a major part in the exciting, but ultimately unsuccessful 1969-1970 promotion campaign, when the Albion finished fifth, just five points from a promotion place.

Although most of his work was grafting in midfield and providing chances for the strikers, he will also be forever remembered for an astonishing 40-yard goal against Shrewsbury Town at the Goldstone in February 1969. The unlucky visiting goalkeeper was future Brighton player John Phillips.

Nobby played a total of 127 games for the Albion before he lost his place in the side, and Goodwin's successor, Pat Saward, transferred him on a *"free"* to Fourth Division Lincoln City in February 1971, together with striker Alan Gilliver.

Former Albion midfielder John Templeman, who played alongside Nobby for four seasons, has fond memories of his old team-mate.

"Nobby loved cricket, as did Alex Dawson, and they brought their cricket club from Manchester down to play three friendly matches in West Sussex," he recalls.

"One of them was at Ford Prison and the prisoners absolutely loved them both," he added.

Simon Francis also remembers that Nobby had a funny side to his personality.

"I remember him finding out that the BBC radio team were broadcasting the second half of a match," he said.

"Nobby spent the whole of half-time telephoning friends and relations to tell them to listen in!"

While at the Goldstone, Nobby served on the executive committee of the PFA (Professional Footballers' Association).

Nobby made just 20 more league appearances, when in 1972 at 32, he retired after a surgeon warned him another injury could cripple him for life.

The following March, Nobby Lawton was the beneficiary of probably one of the best-ever testimonial matches to take place at Sincil Bank, with a Lincoln City XI taking on an All-Star XI.

The PFA chairman at the time was the well-known Wolves and Northern Ireland centre forward Derek Dougan, and the Doog took part in the match along with other top players including Johnny Giles and Peter Lorimer from Leeds, Bobby Moncur of Newcastle United, his former Preston team-mate Alex Dawson, Nobby Stiles from Manchester United and City boss David Herd.

Bobby Charlton was also present at the game but did not play. A crowd of over 10,000 saw a win for the All-Stars by 9-7.

Nobby took several jobs outside football before returning to Newton Heath in 1977 to work for an export packaging firm.

He died from cancer in April 2006, shortly after his 66th birthday.

Upon his death England World Cup hero Nobby Stiles paid an immediate tribute to his former team-mate. The pair had played together for five years.

"We both came from the city and knew each other very well when we were growing up," he said.

"He was a great lad, a lovely guy. On the pitch he was a tough player but off it he was a smashing lad.

"He was an attacking wing half and a very good one at that.

"We were both called Norbert, which was especially good, but the difference was that he was a bit more graceful than me!"

41

Alex Dawson
(Alexander Downie
Dawson)
1940-2020
BHAFC 1968-1971
Centre Forward
Appearances: 65
Goals: 29

**He was big, grisly and
bruising, and ran out into
every game casting fear into
the eyes of which ever
defender was given the task
of marking him.**
Alex Dawson scored goals
like no other centre forward
who had worn the blue and white of Brighton & Hove Albion.

The Black Prince, as he was affectionately known, left opposition
defenders and goalkeepers quaking in their boots at the physical
battering they were about to take at the hands of this take-no-
prisoners centre forward.

He was a bustling presence who scored wherever he went,
racking up 212 goals from 393 career appearances.

Alex could head a ball with more power than he could kick it and
he would run through a brick wall for his team. If somebody tossed
a cross into the box, he would find a way to be on to the end of it
no matter how many innocent opponents he had to rampage
through to get there.

He was the perfect centre forward in a goal-laden three years at
the Albion and had enduring popularity with the Goldstone Ground
crowd.

Alex was born in Aberdeen and went to the same school as Manchester United legend Denis Law, but his parents moved to Hull and such was his footballing talent that Alex joined United straight from Hull Schoolboys, where he spent four years before joining nearby Preston North End in 1961.

Julian Denny recalled how Alex once scored three hat-tricks in a row for a United reserve team that was regularly watched by crowds of over 10,000.

He scored on his United first team debut against Burnley in April 1957 aged just 17, and in each of the final two matches that season (a 3-2 win at Cardiff and a 1-1 draw at home to West Brom) to help win the title and secure United's passage into Europe's premier club competition.

They were the first of 54 goals in 93 United appearances.

But as with many United players and staff everything changed with the Munich air disaster of 6ᵗʰ February 1958.

Following the crash, which claimed 23 lives, among them eight Manchester United players and three club officials, Alex was one of the young players who was asked to step up and fill the void.

Thirteen days after the accident, Alex took his place beside survivors Bill Foulkes and Harry Gregg and scored one of United's goals as they beat Sheffield Wednesday 3-0 in the fifth round of the Cup.

He scored again as United drew 2-2 with West Brom in the sixth round.

He scored yet again in the quarter-finals of the competition against West Brom and then notched a hat-trick in a 5-3 semi-final replay win over Fulham at Highbury.

He was just 18 years and 33 days old on 26ᵗʰ March 1958 when his perfect treble (header, right foot and left foot shots) for a makeshift post-Munich Manchester United helped to secure a 5-3 win over Fulham in a replay in front of 38,000 fans at Highbury.

Alex Dawson still holds the record as Manchester United's youngest ever hat-trick scorer.

Years later Alex recalled: *"In our first game with Fulham, Bobby Charlton scored twice in a 2-2 draw, and I was put on the right wing. I was a centre forward really and, when we played the replay at Highbury four days later, I was back in my normal position.*

"Jimmy Murphy said before the game: 'I fancy you this afternoon, big man. I fancy you to put about three in.' I just said: 'You know me Jim, I'll do my best,' but I couldn't believe it when it happened.

"The first was a diving header, I think the second was a left-footer and the third was with my right foot.

"I'm a proud man to still hold this record. Even when it goes, nobody can ever take the achievement away from me."

Also in the United side that day was future Albion manager Freddie Goodwin and future Preston and Brighton team-mate Nobby Lawton.

Against all the odds and thanks largely to Dawson's goals, United had made it to the FA Cup final just three months after the Munich disaster. Sadly, the fairy tale ended at Wembley in a 2-0 defeat to Bolton Wanderers.

In an interview in the ***Daily Record*** in 2008, on the 50th anniversary of the crash, he recalled: *"I used to go on those trips and had a passport and visa all ready but the boss just told me I wasn't going this time. I had already been on two or three trips just to break me in. I know now how lucky I was to be left in Manchester. The omens were on my side."*

He went on to describe the disbelief and the feelings they had at losing eight of the team, including Duncan Edwards, several days later: *"We were all so close and Duncan was also a good friend to me before the accident. Duncan was such a good player, there is no doubt about that. He was a wonderful fellow as well as a real gentleman.*

"I will never, ever forget him because he died on my birthday, 21st February, and before that he was the one who really helped me settle in."

Alex remained a regular scorer at Old Trafford over the next three seasons, scoring 54 goals in 93 appearances. Despite that impressive record, there has always been this feeling that he could have achieved much more at United.

How different things might have been had he not been thrown in at the deep end as a teenager, trying to cope with the loss of so many colleagues at the same time as being charged with replacing his good friend Duncan Edwards in the starting line-up.

Those challenges may have impacted on young Alex Dawson in ways nobody will ever know. They did however help form his quirky, positive personality as a man who was grateful for the opportunities that came his way.

Preston was his next port of call and after being sold to the Deepdale club for £18,000 in October 1961, he scored 114 goals in 197 matches for the Lilywhites, whose supporters dubbed him The Black Prince.

Alex also scored in the 1964 FA Cup Final for Preston, picking up his second runners up medal as second tier North End fell to a 3-2 against a West Ham United side led by Bobby Moore.

Some 21 goals in 50 matches for Bury followed and it was from Gigg Lane that Alex Dawson arrived at Brighton in December 1968 with the club deep in relegation trouble, one place off the bottom of the third tier.

Archie Macaulay had resigned as manager with his place taken by Freddie Goodwin. It did not take Goodwin long to identify the Albion's problems – scoring goals and a lack of physicality. He needed even less time to formulate a solution, paying £9,000 to Bury to make his one-time Old Trafford team-mate Dawson his first signing as Brighton boss.

And it didn't take the new man long to make an impression at the Goldstone Ground scoring on his home debut as Reading were beaten 2-0 on Saturday 20th December 1968.

The goals flowed from that point on. Over the next three years, the sight of Alex Dawson in a Brighton shirt scaring the life out of a visiting goalkeeper with his powerful finishing with either feet or head became a staple part of an afternoon at the Goldstone.

And he always played with a smile on his face.

A typical Alex Dawson performance came against Portsmouth in a First Round League Cup tie at the Goldstone on 13th August 1969.

His attacking style was ably reported in the **Evening Argus**:

"After a succession of Albion corners, a cross was whipped into the crowded Portsmouth box from the left. With the ball seeming to hang under the lights, big Alex Dawson – who looked like a scarred nightclub bouncer - leapt above his marker and powered a header destined for the back of the net.

"But it cruelly rebounded off the crossbar and was eventually scrambled clear.

"A few minutes later another Dawson header, this time assisted by a dink into the box by Lawton, was saved by Portsmouth keeper John Milkins."

Then with just 10 minutes of the second half played Alex struck again.

"Full back Willie Bell found Dawson on the edge of the box and his shot had too much power for Milkins, who got a hand to it but could only watch as it soared into the top of the net."

Despite only being present for half of the 1968-1969 season, Alex still managed to finish the campaign as top scorer with 17 goals from 23 appearances. Included in that total was a four-goal haul as the Albion won 5-2 away at Hartlepool on Saturday 22nd February 1969.

Having sat 23rd in Division Three South when he arrived, Brighton ended the campaign in 12th spot. That upward trajectory continued in the 1969-1970 season when Dawson and Kit Napier formed a partnership which for much of the year looked like it would fire the Albion to the title.

As late as Good Friday, Goodwin's Seagulls topped the table until a spectacular collapse saw them win one and lose four of their final five games, blowing any chance of promotion to fall away and finish fifth.

Freddie Goodwin departed for Birmingham City at the end of the campaign and his replacement Pat Saward didn't fancy the look of Alex Dawson, despite his obvious goal scoring talents.

Alex featured only three times under the new manager in the 1970-1971 season, joining Brentford on loan where he scored six goals in 10 outings.

The Bees were going through financial hardship at the time and despite wanting to keep Dawson, they were unable to match Brighton's asking price.

As a result, Alex was stuck in the reserves at the Goldstone for most of the campaign. It was an unedifying way to treat a player who had never given less than 100% in his time with the Albion.

But Dawson being Dawson, he of course took it all in his stride. He was released in the summer of 1971, spending the next two seasons with Corby Town.

Relaxed Alex at the wheel of his car

Needless to say, Alex top scored for the Southern League club in both those campaigns before retiring to become their trainer.

You can imagine what he passed onto the amateur players of Northamptonshire in that role. How to head as if your skull is made from cement. How to finish with both feet into the bottom corner. How to become universally popular yet frighten the life out of opposition goalkeepers and defenders at the same.

And around such a legend as Alex Dawson stories were created.

But one such tale that he drank a double whisky before every match was scotched as *"utter nonsense"* by former team-mates.

"Alex liked a drink, but he was also a consummate professional," said one former Albion player.

But other stories were true.

"*Alex Dawson said he would never shave on match day as he said he wanted to look as menacing as possible to his opponents,*" said Albion supporter Rob Denny.

Another story was that Alex only had to smile to terrify an opponent.

Albion fan Simon Francis recalls: "*I remember when we played Swansea. The Swans had a young debut keeper. Dawson ran past as the lad claimed the ball. Returned to the pitch and I presume said boo to the keeper who promptly dropped the ball and watched in horror as Alex rolled it into the goal.*"

Graham Simmons said: "*He was the best diving header of a ball to ever play for the Albion and I swear he could head a ball harder than he could kick it!*"

Terry Pierce agrees, adding: "*He took many goalies in the net with the ball… he was a real Nat Lofthouse type.*"

Ricky William Wainwright added: "*Alex Dawson would stoop very low to head the ball in rather than kick it.*

"*But not every goal was a header. One great goal he did score was against Walsall in the FA Cup was in front of the North Stand… the winger crossed the ball and it was going between Alex and the goal keeper, a young Phil Parkes. Alex stepped forward letting the ball go behind him and flicked his right leg up behind him and kicking the ball in past the helpless goalkeeper.*"

But away from football Alex Dawson was a gentle and affable guy.

Former Albion midfielder John Templeman, who played alongside Alex for three seasons, has fond memories of his old team-mate.

"*Alex was a gentle giant off the pitch,*" he said. "*He was a boyhood hero of mine as I loved Manchester United from before the Munich Air crash.*

"*Alex and Geoff Sidebottom started a small window cleaning business in the Shoreham area. They would generally have a liquid lunch at the Shoreham Labour Club and then head for home.*

"*Well on this particular day Alex was driving his Jaguar with the ladders on a roof rack northbound up Kingston Lane towards the Old Shoreham Road. Out of nowhere he unfortunately drove into the back of a parked car. Luckily, he had slowed down, and it wasn't too serious.*

"They were quickly invited into a woman's home as she saw the accident and was concerned about their health.

"They accepted her invitation and when inside asked her if she had a whisky or brandy as they needed one to calm down.

"A few minutes later a police car arrived having been called by the owners of the car who lived next door.

"When they wanted Alex to give a breathalyser test the woman told the police officers that she had given them an alcoholic drink!

"That comment saved Alex's driving license and put an end to the window cleaning business," he added.

When Alex retired from football in 1973, he worked as a fork-lift truck driver at the British Steel plant in Corby, Northamptonshire.

Alex Dawson died after a short illness on 17th July 2020, aged 80.

42

Kit Napier
(Christopher Robin
Anthony Napier)
1943-2019
BHAFC 1966-1972
Forward
Appearances: 291
Goals: 99

Kit Napier was arguably the most complete forward to ever play for the Albion.

He was a hero of the Goldstone and the club's leading post war goal scorer until Glen Murray beat his record in October 2018 – just a few months before Kit's death.

Kit was born in Dunblane and raised in West Linton, just south of Edinburgh.

He was a nephew of Celtic player Tommy McInally and played youth football with Linton Hotspur before joining Blackpool's ground staff straight from school and turned professional on his 17th birthday in 1960.

Kit only played twice in the league before joining their arch-rivals, Preston North End, for the 1963-1964 season. After a single appearance in the Second Division, and still only 20 years old, he moved on to his third club, Workington, newly promoted to the Third Division.

He scored twice as Workington eliminated First Division Blackburn Rovers from the 1964-1965 League Cup by 5-1 and scored the equaliser as his club earned a deserved replay against eventual winners Chelsea in the quarter-final.

Such results, added to 25 goals from 58 League matches, attracted the attention of bigger clubs.

In November 1965, First Division Newcastle United paid £18,000 for Kit's services, but he struggled to adapt to the higher level, and the signing of Welsh international centre forward Wyn Davies marked the end of the road at St James Park for Kit.

A Newcastle United report says: *"Kit was seen as a forward who had great potential. Unfortunately, he struggled to come to terms with the First Division and despite having all the tricks he could not put the ball into the net.*

"But being given only eight games to prove himself, one wonders whether he was given a real chance or not before Wyn Davies arrived."

Kit's first wife Pat Hunter, who he first met while playing at Workington recalled: *"Kit only played 10 games at Newcastle, but one against Moscow Dynamo he whacked a scorcher from virtually the halfway line and it missed by inches. He said afterwards that if it had gone in, he would have been made… but it was not to be."*

In 1966, Brighton & Hove Albion's manager Archie Macauley, paid £8,500 to take Kit south to the Goldstone Ground, where he would enjoy the best spell of his career.

The Albion were struggling in the bottom half of the Third Division when Kit arrived, and he made an instant impact scoring twice on his debut in a 5-2 win over Peterborough.

It was the perfect start to what was to be the most successful period of his career.

Over Easter in 1971, Kit scored in all three of Albion's matches – a 1-0 home win over Aston Villa on Good Friday, a 2-0 home win over Reading the following day, and a 3-2 away win at Bradford City on Easter Monday.

The matchday programme for the following home game declared: *"This gift of marksmanship blends very nicely with his ball control and general skill in possession. Not to mention the times when he lets fly at goal from outside the penalty area.*

"We've seen some thrilling thunderbolts from him, including several during 1967-68 season when he broke Albion's post-war individual scoring record with 30 goals, 24 of them in the league."

He was top goal-scorer in five of his six seasons with the club and, by the time he left, he had netted 99 goals in just short of 300 appearances, including 19 in the 1971-1972 promotion-winning side. Against Shrewsbury at the Goldstone, on 30th October 1971, he netted his 100th career league goal. At that time, his Albion tally was 75.

Kit is rightly considered an Albion legend. He was a ball-playing attacker, skilful with both feet, and packing a fierce shot, he had a tremendous talent for goalscoring.

He played in all the forward positions, as a centre forward, as a supporting striker and as a winger during his six years at the Goldstone.

His class, quick-witted play and ability to surprise with a deft touch endeared him to the crowds.

Indeed, he is the only Albion player in peacetime to have scored 10 or more goals in six consecutive seasons.

The 1967-1968 season saw the mercurial Kit at his best, as he equalled Albert Mundy's post war goal-scoring record netting 28 goals in league and cup games.

His performance was all the more remarkable when you consider that Mundy was part of a team that scored 112 league goals, while the team that Kit played for only managed 57 league goals and spent much of the season mid-table.

But aside from the run of the mill goals, Kit had an amazing talent for scoring direct from corners with either foot from both the left and right corner flags by the South Stand.

The first of these memorable corners was in a Third Division home fixture against Barrow on 22nd March 1969 in front of a 9,997 crowd, when the Albion went on to win 4-1.

Brighton supporter Steve Mead remembers it well.

"It was probably my favourite Goldstone game from the 1960s," he said. *"Probably because of Kit's remarkable goal."*

Fellow supporter Colin Belsey added: *"That was very special to me as it was my first ever game at the Goldstone and there began a lifetime of ups and downs."*

**Kit aka *The Silver Fox* enjoys a beer at his
older son Robin's 21st birthday**

Nine months later, on 27th December 1969, Kit was at it again,
this time scoring direct from the other corner in front of 13,383 fans
in a 2-0 home win against Bury.

Albion fan Ricky William Wainwright remembers: *"I was there for
them both. After that at every corner we in the North West corner sang: Who
kicks the corners, Kit kicks the corners."*

Brighton & Hove Albion's official historian Tim Carder notes:
*"A feature of the season was the chaos that Kit Napier was able to create in
opposition defences with his beautifully flighted in-swinging corners from either
flag."*

Pat Hunter said he was really proud of his corners. *"I know at one
time he held the record for goals scored from corners, not sure if it still stands, but
Kit was proud of it,"* she added.

But it was in the normal run of play where Kit also excelled with his ability to outwit opponents.

Even if games were tough, you could bet your last sixpence that Kit would score. At times, he might look a little lazy but then he'd throw in a body swerve or a burst of pace and be away from whoever had been given the unenviable job of marking him.

Then came one of his most remarkable goals in a regulation Third Division home game against Chesterfield on 27th November 1971 in front of 10,179 fans.

The game was tightly poised and suddenly a whistle sounded.

Thinking there had been a foul or other infringement the Chesterfield goalkeeper Alan Stevenson put the ball down in the penalty area for a free kick. But Kit was waiting behind him and swiftly ran round the keeper to poke the ball into the net!

The whistle had come from the crowd and the referee blew his own whistle to acknowledge Kit's cheeky goal.

Albion fan Steve Harrington recalls: *"I rarely was at the South end and this was the end we were attacking. There was a whistle sounded in the East Terrace and all bar Kit thought it was the ref. Hence everyone left the penalty area and the goalkeeper thought it was a free kick… then Kit pounced. The Chesterfield team went nuts when the ref gave the goal."*

Fellow supporter Stephen Roberts added: *"It was very funny, but the Chesterfield players were livid."*

The Albion went on to win the game 2-1.

But Kit's *Boxing Day* (it was actually 27th December) goal that season against Bournemouth in front of a bumper 30,600 crowd was far from controversial and instead was described by most who saw it as *"one of the best goals ever seen at the Goldstone Ground."*

But not every Kit Napier moment turned out as it should.

Kit's friend, fellow Scot and playing colleague Brian Tawse has many memories of their time together at the Goldstone Ground.

But none can be so bitter-sweet as the FA Cup 4th Round tie against the mighty Chelsea in front of a bumper 35,000 crowd on 18th February 1967 when the Albion held for a 1-1 draw thanks to a goal by Dave Turner. But it could have been so much more.

Brian takes up the story: *"We had been pressing Chelsea and had them on the ropes.*

"A long ball from our defence was contested between Kit and Chelsea's centre back.

"Kit won the header and glanced the ball to me. The volley was a perfect height and I struck it sweetly. Bonetti never saw it and I was sure we had the winner.

"But the ref gave an infringement against Kit saying he had jumped on the defender's back.

"It was some time before the players and the supporters realised that the goal was disallowed because of the immediate roar in the stadium.

"I wonder what VAR would make of it today," he added.

Another missed moment came at one home game against Preston North End on 27th February 1971. The Albion were awarded a penalty in front of the South Stand.

But when Kit – who was a regular penalty taker – paced back to take the spot kick, brash Geordie forward Alan Duffy promptly stepped forward, pushed his team-mate out of the way and took the penalty himself. But the ball hit the bar and the penalty was missed!

The game ended as a disappointing draw, so not only was an important point lost, but in hindsight it might have prevented Kit scoring 100 career goals for the Albion, rather than the 99 he finished with.

Pat Hunter said Kit was furious with what Alan Duffy had done.

Brian Powney, the Albion keeper later said: *"Alan was hit and miss, a bit madcap.*

"He had a lot of talent and, had he applied himself, he would have had a longer career. He was a good player but not such a good pro."

As for the penalty fiasco, Powney said: *"The manager went mad at him afterwards."*

Manager Pat Saward promptly dropped Duffy to the bench for the next two matches.

And it wasn't all plain sailing for Kit either. The following season, in a home game against Wrexham, Kit had been having a bit of an off day and the crowd were getting on his back.

Much later in life Kit at the wedding of his younger son Chris

Eventually Saward subbed him off and, as he trudged towards the tunnel, rather than the polite applause that tends to accompany substitutions there were lots of ironic cheers to greet his withdrawal.

Kit responded by waving a two-fingered salute to all corners of the ground, something which may well have led to a fine and suspension in today's game.

But Kit's 16 goals helped Albion win promotion to the Second Division in 1972, in second place behind Aston Villa.

With Albion promoted, new manager Pat Saward knew he needed to strengthen the side and he clearly didn't think Kit was up to playing at the higher level and put him on the transfer list.

Although he made a handful of starts in the 1972-73 Second Division campaign, by the end of August he'd been sold to Blackburn Rovers (who were in the Third Division at the time) for

£15,000 as Albion sought to recoup some of the £29,000 record fee they spent bringing former England international Barry Bridges to the club from Millwall.

Kit had two seasons at Ewood Park and brought down the curtain on his English league career with a further 10 goals in 54 appearances and a career of 380 senior games and 119 goals.

In 1974 he emigrated with wife Pat and young son Robin to South Africa to play for Durban United.

After retiring from playing, Kit enjoyed a career in the motor trade in the Natal capital alongside his former Albion team-mate and friend Brian Tawse. Both men also turned out for a local Sunday league side in Durban. Kit enjoyed the South African lifestyle, playing a lot of golf off a 5 handicap and was a frequent competitor in local Pro-Ams. His greying locks earned him the nickname *The Silver Fox* in his new homeland.

He re-married and in 1982 he and his new wife Diana had a second child who they named Christopher, after Kit's first name.

Whereas Kit's older son Robin (named after his middle name) thrived with theatre and music, Chris inherited his dad's love of football.

Chris says his one regret is that he was too young to ever watch his father play.

"He always supported Brighton & Hove Albion and would watch every match he could via satellite," he added.

"He also never stopped playing football in his dreams as the bruises on mum's shins did testify," he laughed.

Sadly, Kit, who as a younger man was a regular smoker, suffered from the lung condition emphysema, which blighted his final years.

Christopher Robin Anthony Napier, died in his adopted South Africa on 31st March 2019, aged 75.

43

Brian *Brom* Bromley
(Brian Bromley)
1946-2012
BHAFC 1971-1974
Midfielder
Appearances: 55
Goals: 3

**Brian Bromley only served
Brighton & Hove Albion for
two and a half seasons, yet he
remains one of the most
respected, skilled and
influential midfielders to ever
wear the blue and white of
the club.**

He was also one of the key
players in the Albion's famous 1972 promotion-winning team.

Born in Burnley, *Bromley* or *Brom*, as he was affectionally known
by all his friends, started his career at local rivals Bolton Wanderers.
He made his debut in March 1963 as a raw 16-year-old apprentice
against Sheffield United. In July 1963 he signed professional forms
and won England youth honours the following year. In total he
made 184 appearances in all competitions for the club, scoring 26
goals over five years.

In November 1968, he joined Portsmouth for a fee of £25,000
and stayed at Fratton Park for a further three years. However, a
serious knee injury hampered his career with Pompey before he
joined the Albion on loan in November 1971.

He was enlisted by manager Pat Saward to give impetus to
Brighton's push for promotion,

He made his debut as sub for Dave Turner away to Chesterfield. He started the next game and kept his place.

He had a profound influence on the side. Cool, strong and determined, he proved an inspiration and although he went back to Portsmouth in January 1972, he soon returned to the Goldstone on a permanent transfer in exchange for a £14,000 fee.

Having played most of his career in the second tier, he brought a touch of guile and class to the midfield – and a couple of important goals – as the team gained promotion from the old Third Division.

A powerhouse in the middle of the park with his non-stop running, Brom formed an impressive partnership with John Templeman, allowing his team-mate to push forward while he anchored the midfield.

John Vinicombe wrote in the ***Evening Argus***: *"His transfer was a giveaway and to this day Portsmouth fans still bemoan his departure."*

Bromley's first goal was the decider in a 1-0 win away to Mansfield Town, but it was the opener in a 2-0 home win over Tranmere Rovers that lived long in the memory. He took the ball from his own half on a lung bursting run before smashing it past Tommy Lawrence, the former Liverpool keeper.

After the game manager Pat Saward said: *"I think all followers will agree that Bromley's goal was one they will remember for a long, long time.*

"It came early in the game, at just the right time for us, and I have to search way back in my memory to recall such an exciting goal, with Bromley starting his run in his own half, after a neat bit of tackling, and finishing with a brilliant shot from the left which left even that experienced campaigner Tommy Lawrence flatfooted."

He said that signing Bromley was *"the best move I've made"* adding: *"He's an exceptional player, one who instils and builds confidence in those around him. He can do anything I ask for because he has both ability and character."*

Brom took over the captaincy when John Napier was dropped before some key matches in March 1972.

As the excitement grew towards the promotion goal, one of his best performances was a night game when Blackburn Rovers were beaten 3-0. Bromley scored the third goal, and it was again lauded by John Vinicombe in the ***Evening Argus***: *"Eighty-nine minutes: After*

Irvine was fouled just outside the box, Napier executed a brilliant free kick and Bromley read it expertly. Jones was slow off his line as Bromley raced in to head home, 3-0."

A **Goal** magazine article revealed how special it was to Bromley. When he had been transferred from Portsmouth earlier in mid-season there was talk that injury might end his career.

"I was heartbroken at the time," Bromley said. *"I really felt my career might be finished. But now I've led a side back into the Second Division and everything is just great."*

In an August matchday programme he wrote: *"Although the majority of my footballing career has been spent in the second division, my debut came in the First Division with Bolton Wanderers when I was only 16 years old.*

"And one of my greatest ambitions now is to play in the First Division again – with Brighton & Hove Albion."

"When I joined Brighton last season, first as a loan player and then permanently, I was impressed with the standard of Albion's play and the attacking football that was adopted.

"I believe now that the Albion have the ability to do well in the Second Division. Everyone here thinks like a big club and we are ambitious.

"An early look through the teams doesn't appear to throw up any exceptional outfits. Blackpool impressed me very much last season. They're a good side and it will be interesting to see how Nottingham Forest and Huddersfield go.

"But in my opinion, Albion have nothing to fear. We could be a surprise side but are unlikely to win by four and five goals away like we did in the Third Division."

But it was to be a disastrous season as the team shed loads of goals and appeared to be cannon fodder away from home where they lost 17 games including 6-2 against Blackpool, two 5-1 losses to Carlisle and Fulham and 4-0 reverses against Bristol Rovers, Sunderland and Preston. It ended with an automatic return to the Third Division.

However, the new season was only a couple of months old when Brom was reunited with his former Pompey team-mate George Ley.

Several years later Ley recalled: *"One of my best mates, Brian Bromley, had gone to Brighton and they had just won promotion.*

"He used to play just in front of me in midfield when I was at full back, that was one of the reasons why I left – to go and play with Brom again in that position."

But Brom, hampered by injury, had lost the captaincy to Ian Goodwin and played less than half of Albion's games in the Second Division. He was drafted back into the team when they returned to the Third Division at the start of the 1973-1974 season.

Saward was struggling to get the side to gel, though, and after only three games, a 2-0 defeat at home to Bournemouth was Bromley's last in Albion colours and he moved to Reading in September 1973, only two months before Brian Clough was made Albion manager and began his wholesale clear-out of the Saward players.

Brian Bromley had played 55 games for the Albion in total, plus three as a sub, but he made his mark when it mattered.

His midfield partner John Templeman remembers Brom with fondness both as a player and as a friend.

"Brom was such a good midfielder. His skills and passing ability were so important to us getting promotion in 1972," he said.

"Due to serious knee problems we were so fortunate to have Brom on the pitch as many times as we did. The problems didn't allow him to train between games as his knees were so badly damaged. He had to have treatment and rest between games. It was a miracle that he played so many games for us that promotion season.

"He was also great to spend an evening with him at a local pub. It's no secret that he enjoyed a pint of beer and a day out at Fontwell Park races.

"He made many friends in Brighton in the pubs and restaurants. I can remember arriving back in Brighton after a victory away from home. It was very late and Brom suggested we go for an Indian meal.

"As we were walking to the Indian restaurant, I noticed that all of the other restaurants were closed and I suggested he was unaware of how late it was.

"But as we approached this one restaurant with no lights on, all of the lights suddenly came on, the door opened and two Indian guys welcomed us inside. Within a few minutes, drinks were served followed by a very nice curry.

"When we left, we asked for the bill but they told us: it's on the house!

"Apparently Brom had been a regular and provided the guys at the restaurant with complimentary tickets for our home games. In return Brom would eat free of charge.

"I had some wonderful times with Brom and will always remember his ability on the pitch and his humour off it."

Brom spent the 1974-1975 season with Reading but only made 14 appearances for Charlie Hurley's side and was sent out on loan to Darlington.

The following season he moved on to Wigan Athletic, who at that time were in the Northern Premier League, and in a season with the Latics played 23 times.

In 1976-1977, he linked up with his former Pompey team-mate David Munks at Southern League Waterlooville.

After Brom finished playing, he did what many players of that generation did and moved into the licensed trade.

At one time he was the landlord of the Black Dog in Arundel Street, Portsmouth, and the large White Hart pub in Portchester.

But his last years were beset with a battle against cancer.

On Wednesday 7th March 2012 he was suddenly taken to the Queen Alexandra Hospital in Portsmouth and transferred to Southampton General Hospital the next day.

Brian Bromley passed away on Friday 9th March 2012. He was 11 days short of his 66th birthday.

44

Steve *Pipes* Piper
(Steven Piper)
1953-2017
BHAFC 1972-1978
Defender/Midfielder
Appearances: 190
Goals: 9

There can be few Albion players more loved and respected by fans and colleagues alike than Steve Piper – always known fondly as *Pipes*.

Speaking about Steve during his brief tenure as Albion manager, the legendary Brian Clough said: *"They were difficult times when I first arrived, and I needed all the help from the players.*

"Unfortunately, not too many of them wanted to play for Brighton when I got there, but there was one or two we could rely on, and none more so than Steve Piper, who was one of the most honest and genuine lads, if not the most genuine, we had on the books."

Brighton-born Steve came through the youth ranks at the Goldstone Ground alongside fellow local boy Tony Towner.

He was a Sussex lad through and through, later playing non-league football for five different clubs across the county, after a serious knee injury brought his professional playing career to a premature end when he was aged just 26.

Steve attended Longhill School in Rottingdean and developed his skills as a youngster in Albion's youth team.

He also played for both the Sussex and Brighton Boys teams and even had an England trial at the age of 14.

He signed full-time professional terms for the Albion in September 1972, under the management of Pat Saward. A couple of months later, aged just 19, he made his debut for the first team in a 1-0 home defeat against Burnley. It was one of his only 10 games during the 1972-1973 season.

It was a real baptism of fire though as the Albion battled against relegation for the entire season before dropping down to the Third Division the following May.

But over the following three seasons, Steve became a regular in the side showing real defensive consistency as either a right back or central defender under the management of Saward, Clough and Peter Taylor, before new manager Alan Mullery chose to give Steve a chance as a ball winning and deep lying midfielder.

Mullery recalls how after his initial training session at the Albion in July 1976, there was a full-scale practice match and he saw something in Steve and how he should play.

"In the second period of the practice game I changed Ian Mellor from being a wide midfield player to playing up front with Peter Ward at centre forward," he recalled some years later.

"And I brought Stevie Piper, who was a big centre half in the reserves, to sit in front of the back four... and it worked."

It is somewhat ironic that when Peter Ward scored his debut goal for the Albion against Hereford United some four months earlier, it was Pipes playing in a utility role in midfield, who was the first to congratulate him.

Steve's hard tackling efforts in his newfound position were a great success and he is famed for not missing a single game in the 1976-1977 promotion season.

He is fondly remembered for scoring the goal which secured promotion against Sheffield Wednesday... one of only nine goals he scored during his time with the Albion.

But having played in the opening 15 games in the 1977-1978 season in the Second Division, Steve lost out to new signing Paul Clark and was put on the transfer list at his own request.

Steve helps celebrate Peter Ward's debut goal against Hereford United in March 1976

Portsmouth paid £20,000 for Steve's signature in February 1978 to play in his now familiar midfield role.

But it was after being switched to Pompey's defence he began to shine. He operated alongside Steve Foster at the back, helping Fozzie's education as he went on to play for England.

But his career at Fratton Park was effectively ended after just 29 League games when he sustained a bad knee injury nine months later in the first half of a home clash with Hartlepool.

It was initially thought he would never play again but following an operation he returned to Pompey's reserves before the knee broke down for a second time.

Football historian and Portsmouth stalwart Barry Harris remembers Steve as an affable character who delivered impressive performances when moving into his side's back-line.

Harris said: *"Steve was a good utility player and a nice fella as well.*

"He came as a midfield player but Frank made him a defender – and he looked good there.

"He played his best football there alongside Steve Foster and aided Steve as he went on to be sold for big money and play for England."

Steve subsequently returned to his native Sussex and played non-league football for Worthing, Littlehampton, Whitehawk, Steyning Town and Southwick.

He also represented the Sussex county side while later working in the mortgage and insurance industry and had brief spells as joint manager at Worthing and assistant manager at Littlehampton.

Albion legend Peter Ward said Steve was one of his favourite players.

"I loved the guy. He was part of our promotion team in 1979 and along with Andy Rollings and Brian Horton was the backbone of the side… a really good player," he recalled.

"And he seemed to be friends with everyone… he was such a lovely fella."

One good friend Brendan Quirke recalled: *"I played for a pub side The Queens Head in Division 8 of the Sussex Sunday League*

"In late 1971 we were struggling and one of the lads brought Steve Piper along. He was an apprentice at Brighton at the time but had no hesitation in helping us out. And so began a lifelong friendship. He was such a lovely man."

John Coomber added: *"Steve was a really great person. He trained a Sunday team I played for, and I was really chuffed that a real Brighton player was training us, and he became a good friend.*

"Steve called me 'Little John' as there were three of us and me being the smallest the name was obvious. My work colleagues were really jealous that I knew an Albion player personally.

"My late father used to come and watch me play and Steve would often give his car keys to him and say: 'park my car please Vic', which my dad loved doing.

"On one occasion we went to watch an Albion match at Aldershot, and my mum came to her only ever match. During the warm-up Steve spotted me and my father at the front of the stand and he came over to meet my mum and shake hands… it was such a lovely thing to do.

A young Steve Piper (back row far left) turned out for the The Queens Head in Division 8 of the Sussex Sunday League

"Steve was a lovely and genuine man who gave me some great memories," he added.

Famed local newspaper and radio journalist Ian Hart said: *"They say you should never meet your football heroes as they often disappoint.*

"I went totally the other way, Pipes was in the first Albion side I ever watched in April 1973, and far from disappointing when we later met, we became friends."

Despite the fact he could not continue playing football after retiring, Steve still loved to watch football as much as possible in his later life.

He had been battling illness and was with his wife and children when he died aged 62, on Tuesday, 26th December 2017.

Following his death Old Brightonian and former chairman of the campaign for Falmer, Paul Samrah said: *"Steve Piper was a class act on and off the pitch. One of my childhood heroes, who always gave 100%.*

"Steve never complained if things weren't going his way. The Albion family will never forget him… a hero and a local one as well."

45

Michael Robinson
(Michael John Robinson)
1958-2020
BHAFC 1980-1983
Striker
Appearances: 133
Goals: 43

Michael Robinson was one of the finest strikers ever to play for Brighton & Hove Albion and remains a legend of the Goldstone and in his adopted Spain, where he was treated as a hero for more than 30 years.
Michael was born in Leicester to local publican Arthur Robinson, and he followed in his father's footsteps in playing for Brighton.

Arthur played for the club during World War Two when in the army, and also played for Leyton Orient.

When he was four, Michael and his family moved to Blackpool where his parents took over the running of a hotel in the popular seaside resort. The young Michael first played football on Blackpool beach with his brother.

After leaving Thames Primary School, at Palatine High School Michael first got involved in organised football, and, before long, he caught the eye of the local selectors and represented Blackpool Schools at under 15 level, even though he was only 13.

Amongst his team-mates at that level was George Berry, who ironically was Michael's opponent at centre half in his first Albion match, against Wolverhampton Wanderers.

The young Robinson also played for Sunday side Waterloo Wanderers in Blackpool and when still only 13 he was invited for trials at Chelsea, by assistant manager Ron Suart, who had played for and managed Blackpool.

Although he was asked to sign schoolboy forms, Michael's dad thought it was too far from home.

Coventry, Blackpool, Preston and Blackburn were also keen, and the North West clubs had the edge because he wouldn't have to leave home.

Eventually he chose Preston North End, just 15 miles from his Blackpool home, and on his 16th birthday signed as an apprentice.

At the time, Mark Lawrenson was also there, training with the youngsters, and Gary Williams was already on the books.

After two years as an apprentice, Michael signed professional forms and began to push for a first team place with the Lilywhites.

With former World Cup winner Nobby Stiles in charge, in 1978-1979, Michael scored 13 goals in 36 matches, was chosen Preston fans' Player of the Year.

His goals and all-round form attracted the attention of several bigger clubs.

He had already built his reputation on the field as both a strong and skilful attacking player.

That prompted Malcom Allison's Manchester City to spend an astonishing £756,000 on Michael in the 1979 close season, making him the second most expensive English player of all time.

Allison was also making unsuccessful overtures to Brighton to sign Peter Ward to complete his dream striking duo.

The Robinson fee meanwhile was an eye-watering amount for an unproven 20-year-old striker who had played fewer than 50 games for Preston in the Second Division and it is often credited as being one of the deals that sparked such rapid inflation in the transfer market.

Understandably, Michael struggled to live up to expectations although he did still finish as top scorer in his one season at Maine Road.

The move didn't work out and after scoring only eight times in 30 appearances for City.

Michael later admitted: *"I'd never kicked a ball in the First Division and the fee was terrifying.*

"If I had cost around £200,000 – a price that at that time was realistic for me – I would have been hailed as a young striker with bags of promise."

He was never truly happy at City and so Alan Mullery swooped in to sign him for half of what City had paid a year previously.

It proved to be an astonishingly good bit of business for the Albion.

"I received the go ahead to make some major signings in the summer of 1980," recalled Mullery in his autobiography.

"I could see Michael had lost confidence at City and I made a point of praising him every chance I got," he added.

"When I signed him, it was because I thought Ward was struggling in the First Division and that Robinson could help take the pressure off him. Robinson was big, strong, and powerful and I asked him to lead the line like an old-fashioned centre forward and he did the job very well."

Ironically, Allison's dream striking partnership came together at Brighton when Peter Ward lined up alongside Michael Robinson in the opening league game of the season, at home to Wolves.

Although Ward could not add to the five goals that he had scored against Wolves during the previous season, a comfortable 2-0 win for the Seagulls was an encouraging start.

Slowly as the season progressed Michael began to outscore the legendary Ward and before the Christmas presents were wrapped Ward was transferred to Brian Clough's Nottingham Forest.

Meanwhile, leading the attack in a buccaneering style the burly new striker excited supporters with his power and determination, and of course, his goals.

Michael Robinson top scored in his first season at Brighton with 19 league goals and a total of 22 goals in all competitions in 1980-1981.

That was an outstanding return in a side that looked doomed to relegation until a run of victories in the final month of the season resulted in a last gasp escape from the drop.

**Michael celebrates scoring the winner against
Sheffield Wednesday in the 1983 FA Cup semi-final**

Michael was overwhelmingly voted as Player of the Year at the end of the campaign and made his Republic of Ireland debut, going onto win 24 caps for the nation he qualified through via his grandmother.

Michael scored 11 times in the 1981-1982 season despite missing a large chunk of the campaign through injury.

His goal scoring feats meant that he was constantly linked with other clubs, but he remained at the Goldstone, scoring another 10 goals in the 1982-1983 season which ended under the Twin Towers of Wembley.

Three of those goals came in the run to the FA Cup Final, including Brighton's second in the semi-final win over Sheffield Wednesday.

When asked many years later to describe his proudest moment in football, he maintained: *"Scoring the winning goal in the FA Cup semi-final that meant that a bunch of mates at Brighton were going to Wembley in 1983."*

It was Michael's trademark skills of speed and physicality – he was remarkably strong for someone a little over six foot tall – which teed up Gordon Smith for the infamous *"And Smith must score"* chance in the final minute of extra time against Manchester United.

His final Brighton career numbers read 43 goals in 133 appearances… 37 of those goals in the First Division. Michael Robinson will always be fondly remembered for his scoring exploits on the south coast during one of the greatest periods in the club's history.

Without him and his goals, the Albion's first top-flight adventure would never have lasted the four seasons it did. His buccaneering style lit up the Goldstone and what's more, everyone who ever talked about him never did so without referring to what a great man he was.

Peter Ward played only a few games alongside Michael but one of his abiding memories is quite amusing and shows the gentle humour of the dressing room.

"He was a very nice guy and I liked the fella a lot," he said. *"It seemed funny at the time, but he had man boobs and when we came in from training, he'd put on a bra!"*

"When he first arrived it was always Mick that or Micky this, but with footballers' humour you can imagine the nicknames he got called back then."

Michael was too good to slip into Division Two with the Albion following relegation in 1983. The books needed to be balanced too and so he was sold to Liverpool for £250,000.

Although Michael only spent 18 months at Anfield, he still managed to win the League title, the European Cup and the League Cup.

Despite showing his innate ability, Michael was often on the substitutes' bench, and so moved on to QPR at the end of 1984. There, he was an unlucky loser at Wembley again, in the 1986 Football League Cup Final 0–3 defeat by Oxford United.

However, during the run up to the decisive match, he earned himself a place in QPR fans' hearts when he scored a 40-yard goal against arch-rivals Chelsea in the quarter-final replay at Stamford Bridge.

In January 1987, Michael moved to Spain to play for CA Osasuna, with ex-Liverpool team-mate Sammy Lee joining in August.

He retired in summer 1989, at the age of 31, with a knee injury, after making 58 La Liga appearances for the club and scoring 12 goals, two of which came in the 1987-1988 campaign as the Navarrese overachieved for a final fifth place.

A measure of the man was that as soon as Michael knew he was unlikely to play again, he ripped up his contract with the Spanish club so that they would not have to pay his wages.

He stayed in Spain after retiring and completely embraced the Spanish way of life, learned the language sufficiently to be an analyst for a Spanish TV station's coverage of the 1990 World Cup, and then took Spanish citizenship.

His on-screen work grew, and the stardom Michael achieved on Spanish TV attracted some of the heavyweight English newspapers to head out to Spain to find out how he had managed it.

He had his own show which was watched almost religiously by football fanatics who loved his integrity and his broken Spanish.

In an interview with Spanish-based journalist Sid Lowe in 2004, Michael told how the FA Cup semi-final goal against Sheffield Wednesday in 1983 was the proudest moment in his football career, and that Steve Foster was his best friend.

In June 2017, his TV programme marked the 25th anniversary of Barcelona's first European Cup win at Wembley, with some very studious analysis. Michael produced and presented La Liga's first ever highlights show *El Dia Después* which aired on Mondays and was hugely popular.

Spanish viewers took him into their hearts; acceptance was rubber-stamped, literally, when the makers of the country's version of *Spitting Image* made him one of its principal latex puppets.

Michael later became the doyen of Spanish TV sport

In December 2018, Michael announced publicly that he had been diagnosed with a malignant melanoma – an often deadly skin cancer.

Tributes flowed from across the sporting world when he died on 28th April 2020, aged 61. His death was on the front page of every Spanish newspaper and led the TV news.

The 19-time tennis Grand Slam winner and Spanish hero Rafael Nadal said: *"We woke up with the sad news of the death of one of our own. You were the one who always made us happy about sport. We are grateful to you."*

Barcelona FC paid tribute in a tweet that described him as *"A person who loved football and who knew how to explain it with knowledge and ingenuity"*.

Albion chairman Tony Bloom led the tributes from his former club, where his talents had really shone.

"For Albion fans of a certain vintage, we remember Michael at the Goldstone playing with enthusiasm, tenacity and endeavour, yet always with a big smile on his face" he said.

And his former Liverpool team-mate and Brighton star Mark Lawrenson, said: *"I used to call him 'the wall'. He was very good at holding the ball up and causing defenders all sorts of problems – they couldn't have a moment's peace against him. Then he turned himself into the Des Lynam of Spanish football."*

Albion supporter Guy Brooks added: *"I remember getting Michael Robinson's autograph on a Shoot magazine picture which included him, Bobby Shinton with Malcolm Allison in between.*

"He put a Red Cross on Allison's face and called him something very unpleasant with a chuckle in his voice."

Few Albion players were loved quite as much as Michael Robinson.

46

Tony Grealish
(Anthony Patrick Grealish)
1956-2013
BHAFC 1981-1984
Midfielder
Appearances: 121
Goals: 8

If any player could ever be considered the heart and soul of a Brighton & Hove Albion team it would surely be 1983 FA Cup Final captain Tony Grealish.

Tony was truly a players' player, someone who did the hard work in the engine room of the team to enable players with more flair to shine, so it is incongruous that he was nicknamed *Sleeper* by his team-mates

Born in Paddington, London, Tony qualified to play for the Republic of Ireland through his father, Packie, a publican who was born in Athenry, Galway, and his mother Nora's parents, both from Limerick.

Tony represented West London Schools, but was playing Sunday football for Beaumont FC on Hackney Marshes when he was discovered by Orient manager George Petchey.

After an apprenticeship he signed as a professional at Orient in July 1974 and went on to make 171 League appearances for the O's, one of the last being a memorable 3-3 draw against Brighton in 1979.

The previous year he had been part of the Orient side that made it through to the FA Cup semi-final against Arsenal, played at Stamford Bridge, but they were beaten 3-0.

In 1979, David Pleat signed him for Luton Town for £150,000 for whom he played 78 games in two seasons.

A managerial upheaval at the Goldstone Ground in the summer of 1981 saw the arrival of Mike Bailey in place of Alan Mullery, and one of his first moves was to pay more than £100,000 and bring in the combative 24-year-old Tony Grealish as part of a swap for Brian Horton, the ageing, inspirational captain who had led Brighton from the old Third Division to the First Division.

Tony was already an accomplished midfield performer – and a seasoned Irish international with 23 caps - when he joined the Albion.

But he had to endure a lot of criticism from the terraces before winning over the Goldstone fans with consistent sterling displays.

It was always going to be hard for the player who had replaced the hugely popular Brian Horton, but Tony had a fine pedigree for the job and was admired by all who played alongside him.

And it was in the Albion's famous 1983 FA Cup run that Tony Grealish really shone.

It was Tony who rolled the ball to Jimmy Case to smash home that memorable opening goal in the semi-final against Sheffield Wednesday.

He relished his team-mate's strike, saying: *"It wasn't just the power, it was the way the ball swerved away from the keeper that did it."*

Reaching the cup final was a special moment for Tony and he found himself thrust centre stage as team captain due to captain Steve Foster's suspension from the first match.

Fans remember how Tony wore the trademark Foster headband as he led Brighton out. *"It was a small protest over Steve's exclusion from the final,"* he said after the game.

Before the big match, Foster positively purred about his stand-in. *"Sleeper is the man I'd want on the other side of me in a war,"* he said.

Tony leads out the Albion team at Wembley wearing
a mock Steve Foster headband

*"He's so honest, he accepts responsibility even when it's not his fault. Tony is
a natural leader. He thrives on responsibility."*

In fact, Tony was involved in both Brighton's goals in the 2-2
draw at Wembley.

And with the clock ticking down, and Manchester United 2-1 up,
it was Tony who drilled the ball hard into the penalty box where
Gary Stevens controlled it and fired the ball past Gary Bailey to net
the equaliser.

241

Tony lived in Peacehaven during his time with the Albion and clearly enjoyed the social life with his team-mates.

"The atmosphere at Brighton is particularly good," he told Tony Norman in a club programme feature. *"There's always plenty going on. I enjoy our Wednesday golf games. There's often as many as 10 of the players there. That's always a laugh."*

Albion supporter Dave Wilcock remembers how Tony enjoyed the odd drink and was the life and soul of events when away from the Goldstone.

"I was on a stag do at The Sussex Coaster in Peacehaven at a time when Rory was the DJ and you had the barmaids dancing on the bars," he recalls.

"This night we were all drinking and we noticed a little guy in the middle of the dance floor absolutely smashed. I thought I recognised him as he looked vaguely familiar.

"Anyway, he had made a move on a lady and this other guy had taken exception to it.

"Suddenly I worked out it was none other than Tony Grealish. I moved in to separate them as the other guy threw a punch and caught me on the shoulder.

"I took hold of Tony's arms and marched him over to the seating areas. "I'll have him mate he kept saying."

"Then a bouncer came over and wanted him out. I persuaded him that I would look after him and through a haze of alcohol he thanked me for pulling him away as Jimmy Melia would have fined him for fighting and drinking.

"After a while I left him and about 30 minutes later the manager came over and said: "I think your mate needs to go home".

"So, I walked Tony outside, put him in a taxi and gave the cab driver a tenner. He seemingly knew where Tony lived as he was a "regular".

"Never got my tenner back... bless his heart!"

Following relegation to the second tier, the Albion squad was broken up bit by bit Gary Stevens and Michael Robinson going first.

Tony Grealish lasted a little longer and played two thirds of the 1983-1984 season before being sold to West Brom in March 1984 for £95,000.

In total, he had played 116 games, plus five as a sub, for Brighton, and his last game for the Seagulls saw him score in a 1-1 home draw with Manchester City, who he would subsequently join in 1986-1987.

He played 65 games for West Brom, and 11 times for City, who also had former Brighton player Neil McNab in their line-up.

In 1987, Tony moved to Rotherham United and played 110 games for the Millers before moving to Walsall.

Albion fan Simon Todd said: *"Grealish was the heart and soul of the Brighton team. He was totally unselfish, and the team was always much better with him than without him."*

By the time the curtain came down on his playing career at non-league Bromsgrove Rovers in 1995, he had played a total of 589 league games, plus 45 for the Republic of Ireland; 17 of them as captain.

Although spending his entire playing career – and indeed his life – in England, Tony never forgot his Irish roots and turned down an England Youth cap to play for the Republic of Ireland.

He was given his international debut against Norway in 1976 by the legendary Johnny Giles, who knew a thing or two about midfield play.

In fact, it was Giles, in his second spell as WBA manager, who took Tony to The Hawthorns in 1984.

Years later Giles said: *"I obviously knew him at that stage from the Ireland set-up and knew what to expect.*

"He wasn't the classiest of players but he was one of the most hard working and you knew exactly what you were going to get.

"He was a great lad; a social animal who liked a drink after a game but gave you absolutely everything during it."

When he died from cancer on 23rd April 2013 at his home in Ilfracombe in Devon, aged just 56, the Football Association of Ireland paid a warm tribute.

FAI president Paddy McCaul said: *"He will be remembered as a great servant of Irish football who was part of the international set-up under John Giles and Eoin Hand that came so close to qualifying for major tournaments and helped change Ireland's fortunes at that level of the game."*

FAI chief executive John Delaney added: *"Tony Grealish was one of my footballing heroes when I was a child and I always remembered him as a great competitor who always gave his all for Ireland."*

"He was a great character," said Hand. *"I don't think I ever selected a team during my time in charge that didn't have him in it.*

"I'd say he was a great club player but the commitment he gave for Ireland; he just couldn't have given that on a twice weekly basis playing club football. He gave absolutely everything.

"He contributed so much, had an infectious enthusiasm for it all. If ever there was someone who showed how proud he could be to represent his country, then Tony was it. He was very much part of it all; a great ambassador; very generous."

Hand added: *"He was a great example to others in the way he dealt with people; other players, supporters, kids… a really wonderful guy. I was very lucky to have him around when I was manager."*

For so many reasons Tony Grealish will forever remain an Albion legend.

47

Justin Fashanu
(Justinus Soni Fashanu)
1961-1998
BHAFC 1985-1987
Forward
Appearances: 20
Goals: 2

Justin Fashanu is remembered more for his personal life outside football and his tragic death than for many of the amazing things he achieved on the pitch.

Yet he remains a legend of the game.

Justin was the son of a Nigerian barrister living in the UK and a Guyanese nurse named Pearl. When his parents split up, he and his younger brother John were sent to a Barnardo's care home.

When he was six, he and John were fostered by Alf and Betty Jackson and were brought up in Shropham, Norfolk. Justin excelled at boxing as a youth and was rumoured at one time to be pursuing a professional boxing career instead of his footballing career.

Justin played for a variety of football clubs between 1978 and 1997.

He was known by colleagues at his early clubs to be gay, and came out publicly later in his career, becoming the first professional footballer to be openly gay.

As a footballer, Justin began his career as an apprentice with Norwich City, turning professional towards the end of December 1978.

He made his league debut on 13th January 1979, against West Bromwich Albion, and settled into the Norwich side scoring regularly and occasionally spectacularly. In 1980, he won the BBC Goal of the Season award, for a stunning goal against Liverpool.

He managed a total of 103 senior appearances for Norwich, scoring 40 goals. While at the club he was also capped six times for England at under-21 level, although the anticipated call-up to the senior side ultimately never happened.

He scored 19 league goals in the 1980-1981 season, but it wasn't enough to prevent the Canaries from being relegated.

Justin's name had been linked with bigger clubs for some time, and his inevitable departure from Carrow Road came in August 1981 when he became Britain's first £1 million black footballer, when he signed for Nottingham Forest.

But his career stalled as his professional relationship with manager Brian Clough deteriorated. Clough was disturbed by the rumours of Justin's visits to gay nightclubs and bars.

His goals and confidence dried up as he failed to fit in with the playing and lifestyle demands of Clough. After being sent off in his first game in a mini tournament against Real Zaragoza he scored just three goals in 32 league games for Forest in 1981-1982.

Albion legend Peter Ward, who played with Justin at Forest, said his time there was troubled, particularly after he came out as gay.

He recalls: *"I remember the rumours about his lifestyle were circulating widely and one day we were all sitting in the changing room and one of the players – it was either Kenny Burns or John Roberston suddenly said: "There's a rumour going round that you're gay? Then it went round the room and lots of the other lads said: "I've heard it too."*

"Fash just shrugged and said: "Well, what do you think?"

"It was shortly after that he came out and boy was it tough for him. He seemed to put up a tougher exterior on the pitch and got quite aggressive... and he was a big lad to start with.

"One match at Forest against Man City we had a corner and John Robertson was lining up to take it and I was at the near post and Fash was behind me.

"Just before the ball came over, I heard a loud crack. I turned round to see Tommy Caton (a City defender) lying on the floor with his nose broken… there was blood everywhere. Fash had just elbowed him.

Peter continued: *"However, once off the pitch I liked Fash, he was a nice lad. But he had a nightmare at Forest. Some of the young apprentices in training used to deliberately mess up their ball control and when challenged by the coach would reply: "We're controlling it the Fashanu way!"*

In December 1982, Justin was sold to local rivals Notts County for £150,000. He scored 20 times in 64 games for the Magpies, although he was unable to prevent them suffering back-to-back relegations, before he moved to Brighton & Hove Albion in June 1985 for a fee of £115,000.

When he signed for the Albion, many fans held their collective breath to see if the wonder boy from five years earlier could recapture the form from his Norwich City days.

But because of some notorious clashes with Albion players before he joined the club, Justin never became popular with all the supporters and a subsequent lack of form – just two goals in 20 games – did little to help his cause.

When making his name at Norwich City, Fash had broken the nose of Brighton defender Andy Rollings as the Canaries won 4-2 at the Goldstone in October 1979. Rollings went onto swing a punch at Justin, earning a red card in the process in what sadly proved to be his penultimate appearance in the stripes.

Then there was the game in August 1984, when Brighton beat Notts County 2-1 and Justin was involved in incidents which resulted in the Albion's central defenders Eric Young and Jeff Clarke both being hospitalised.

Given all that, his arrival was greeted with more than an air of suspicion. Even manager Chris Cattlin had his concerns before committing to sign Fashanu, to the point where the Brighton boss invited the striker to move in with him for four nights to try and establish whether Justin's reputation for trouble was justified.

Cattlin said at the time: *"Justin had a reputation of being a bit of a problem player with his other clubs but that is all in the past. In my dealings with him I've found him to be a smashing person and the sort of player our supporters will take to."*

Cattlin was right – supporters did eventually take to him, although unfortunately we never really got the chance to see him in action.

There were also doubts about Justin's fitness when he first came to the Goldstone and an exploratory operation on his left knee side-lined him for a month.

On his return, though, it became evident that it was the right knee which was the real problem and after four months at a rehabilitation centre, he was forced to retire in July 1986 at the age of 25. Following a legal battle over insurance, Justin's contract was eventually paid up in January 1987.

It appeared to be a sad end to a career that at one time promised so much.

But Justin was not finished and fought his way back to fitness in the USA and began playing again, first with Los Angeles Heat and then to Canada with the Edmonton Brickmen and with the Hamilton Steelers.

He returned to England in 1989 and tried to resurrect his top-level playing career, joining Manchester City on 23rd October 1989, and played twice in the First Division, but on 20th November, barely a month after joining the club, he moved to West Ham United, later having a trial with Ipswich Town.

He joined Leyton Orient in March 1990 and subsequently non-league Southall as player-coach, before spending the summer of 1991 back in North America with Toronto Blizzard. After leaving Toronto, he returned to England again to sign for semi-pro team Leatherhead.

Then in October 1990, Justin suddenly agreed to an exclusive interview with *The Sun* newspaper to come out as gay. They ran the headline as: *£1m Football Star: I AM GAY* on 22nd October. In the front page story he claimed to have had an affair with a married Conservative MP, whom he first met in a London gay bar.

"We ended up in bed together at his London flat", he claimed in the story.

Nine months later, Justin was then interviewed for the July 1991 cover story of *Gay Times*, where the situation was summarised that *The Sun* had dragged out the tale with titillating stories of sexual encounters with unnamed MPs, football players and pop stars, which, he claimed, were largely untrue.

The revelations earned him a considerable sum of money, but he later admitted that he wasn't fully prepared for the backlash that followed and his career in football suffered *"heavy damage"*.

Although fully fit, no club had offered him a full-time contract after the story first appeared.

He was also forced to deal with abusive comments and chants from crowds at clubs that he did manage to get contracts with.

In October 1991, he began a trial with Newcastle United and made one first-team appearance as a sub against Peterborough United.

One month later he signed for Torquay United in the Third Division. And once again he was the centre of media attention while at Plainmoor: in particular, his relationship with Coronation Street actress Julie Goodyear featured in tabloid newspapers. But he managed to impress on the pitch, playing 21 league games that season and scoring 10 goals, though he was unable to save Torquay from suffering relegation from the Third Division.

Then on 13th April 1992, things went from bad to worse as Justin received a £265 fine and a 28-day driving ban after being found guilty of speeding and failing to produce his driving licence.

In February 1993, with Torquay battling against a second successive relegation, from the new Division Three to the Football Conference, Justin left the club, having scored 15 goals in 41 games for the Gulls.

He went on to play for Airdrieonians but was unable to save them from suffering relegation from the Scottish Premier Division.

He left Airdrie in 1993, playing in Sweden with Trelleborg, before returning to Scotland, joining Hearts in July 1993, but then had his contract terminated in February 1994 for *"unprofessional conduct"* and returned to the USA to coach youth football in Georgia.

He later moved to Ellicott City to coach the Maryland Mania, a new professional team in the second division USL A-League, and officially announced retirement from the professional game.

It was while he was in Maryland, in March 1998, a 17-year-old boy claimed to police that he had been sexually assaulted by Justin after a night of drinking. Homosexual acts were illegal in the state of Maryland at the time, and the youth stated the act was not consensual but being performed as he awoke. The assault was alleged to have taken place in Justin's apartment in Ellicott City, Maryland.

He was questioned about this by the police on 3rd April, but he was not held in custody. The police later arrived at his flat with a warrant to arrest him on charges of second-degree sexual assault, first-degree assault, and second-degree assault, but he had already fled to England.

On the morning of 3rd May, he was found hanged in a deserted lock-up garage he had broken into, in Fairchild Place, Shoreditch, London.

In his suicide note, he denied the charges, stating that the sex was consensual, and that he had fled to England because he felt he could not get a fair trial due to his homosexuality, and he added: *"I realised that I had already been presumed guilty. I do not want to give any more embarrassment to my friends and family."*

An inquest held in London on 9th September 1998 heard evidence from a Scotland Yard detective that the US police made no request for Justin to be found or arrested, and the coroner stated that he was not a wanted man at the time he hanged himself. The inquest recorded a verdict of suicide.

Justin's remains were cremated, and a small ceremony was held at City of London Cemetery and Crematorium.

Long-time Albion supporter and Yorkshire born Chris Worrall has fond memories of Justin Fashanu.

"I remember talking to him and getting his autograph several times outside northern grounds," he recalls.

"One time at Barnsley I was outside the players entrance and he got off the coach and headed straight towards me and my dad and called us by name (we'd seen him not long before elsewhere). This was a measure of the class of the man.

"He never turned down a chat, a photo or an autograph and he was quite simply the nicest footballer I'd ever met and a real gentleman.

"He actually got into trouble that day as Ron Pavey stuck his head out the door and shouted Justin! He needed to go and get changed to warm up, but he

stayed talking to supporters for as long as it took, then he just said: "I'd better go!" and gave everyone a big smile and a thank you."

In March 2009, a football team, **The Justin Fashanu All-stars**, was named at a special event in Brighton, supported by the FA. The team, named in his honour, was created by the Justin Campaign against homophobia in football, which promotes the inclusion of openly gay players in football.

In 2020, Justin Fashanu was inducted into the National Football Museum Hall of Fame.

48

Dale Jasper
(Dale William Jasper)
1964-2020
BHAFC 1986-1988
Defender/Midfielder
Appearances: 60
Goals: 8

Dale Jasper was one of the most naturally stylish footballers to ever play for the Albion and was likened to David Luiz for his defensive midfield passing abilities.

Although he could play anywhere in defence, he was known for being a creative, box-to-box midfielder and scored eight goals in 60 appearances during three seasons at the Goldstone Ground.

Croydon born Dale was a Chelsea fan since he was little and joined the club as a 11-year-old in 1975.

Having been considered one of their best prospects as a youth-teamer by star player Alan Hudson, the tall and elegant ball player signed professional terms at Stamford Bridge in January 1982, and he captained the Chelsea Reserves in The Football Combination.

He was handed his debut by manager John Neal during the Second Division championship-winning season of 1983-1984 in an away match at Cardiff City.

His first game, when he played centre back, could hardly have been more dramatic. Chelsea were losing 3-0 with less than 10 minutes to go before showing incredible fortitude to draw 3-3.

"I can't believe what took place out there, I'm just shell-shocked at the moment. It's hard to believe it was the same match in the second half," Dale said afterwards.

He also started the game at Grimsby when the divisional title was secured at the end of the season and was one of the big hopes for the future.

The trend for Jasper appearing in the most dramatic games of the era continued that season at Sheffield Wednesday. Neal's team again came back from being 3-0 down to draw a League Cup quarter-final tie 4-4 although the semi-final at Sunderland went less well. Dale replaced injured Joe McLaughlin early in the game on a frozen pitch but he conceded two penalties, although one was not converted.

He retained his place for a few games after that but barely featured under new manager John Hollins the following season.

After that Dale found it difficult to break into the first team, partly because the two established centre backs were captain Colin Pates and Joe McLaughlin, who were ever-present.

During the period 1982-1986, Dale made just 10 senior League appearances for Chelsea.

He interested Stoke City having been recommended by Alan Hudson, the ex-Chelsea star. However, Dale's father did not want his son leaving London, so no move to Stoke ensued.

One of his team-mates during his Chelsea days, club legend Pat Nevin, said: *"Dale was about as much fun as you could find wrapped up in one person. He had a brilliant personality in the dressing room at Stamford Bridge and was always up for a surreal laugh with all of us, particularly when he was with his great friends Colin Pates and John Bumstead.*

"I looked forward to seeing and hearing the madness that would ensue every single day when they would walk into the changing rooms. I admit openly those were the three whose company I always sought out first.

"On the field he was graceful in the way Glenn Hoddle was. He could ping beautiful long passes not unlike Glenn or maybe even like David Luiz did in the modern game for Chelsea.

"It was harder then with the poorer pitches, but he always tried to play good football, even if those around him were sometimes more likely to just lump it long. Dale was too good for that.

253

Dale signs for the Albion in 1986 as manager Alan Mullery looks on

"He was capable of playing at centre back in much the same way as many of us think of David Luiz.

"My adoration of David stems from the love of Dale and that similar outlook on the game. They also shared a love of a harmless silliness with a big dash of passion in every part of life.

"He seemed to giggle at every given opportunity, and it was infectious.

"He always interested others and delighted in asking me what I was doing on the team coach. I was reading the plays of the Russian literary giant Anton Chekhov one day and Dale, much to my surprise, said he knew Chekhov's work well. He then said he was surprised that I was a Star Trek fan!

"I recall out of the blue, one day he said to me, "I think I'll get married." An extremely good-looking lad, I wondered who the lucky girl was.

"I dunno yet," came the answer.

"So why do you want to get married, Dale?"

"I think I just want to knock out a sprog," came the dead-pan reply.

At age 23, Dale moved on a free transfer to Brighton & Hove Albion in 1986 under Alan Mullery's second spell in charge.

Within three days of signing, he was walking up the steps of a British Caledonian jet and heading off for the trip of a lifetime to Hong Kong.

254

"That was quite a start to my days at the Goldstone," he later recalled.

"I had been determined to get away from Chelsea because I wanted regular first team football. Quite a few clubs showed an interest in me, including Reading and Charlton, but when Brighton came in for me, that was it. I knew right away this was the club I wanted to play for.

"I signed on the Monday and three days later I flew out to Hong Kong with the team, so it wasn't a bad week, was it? We played an exhibition match over there. I was a bit disappointed when a goal I scored was disallowed, but I was smiling by the end of the game, because we won 3-1.

"We were away for about a week and it was a very good way for me to meet the rest of the players and get to know them."

Looking a little fragile in the hurly burly midfield of the English Third Division, Dale was never able to establish himself on a regular basis in the team, despite oozing with class and often playing defence splitting passes, as well as scoring a few crucial goals.

Albion supporter Chris Stratton and others remember that one of Dale's eight goals for the club was one of the most remarkable and illegal goals ever seen at the Goldstone Ground.

In a Division Three evening fixture against Chesterfield on Wednesday 17th February 1988, in front of a crowd of 8,182, Dale emulated the famous Diego Maradona.

"We were losing 1-0 and not playing well," recalls Chris.

"Then in front of the North Stand a ball was crossed in and Dale rose and literally punched it into the net for the equaliser. Probably only three people who missed the handball that night were the ref and the linesmen!"

The game ended 2-2 with Garry Nelson scoring the other goal.

Brighton were promoted at the end of the season in second place behind Sunderland and just two points better off than third placed Walsall.

Dale listed his football ambition in a club programme as *"winning the Sussex Senior Cup"*. In May 1988, the joke backfired on the wiry midfielder when, having been out of first team reckoning for several weeks, he was in the reserve side which lifted the cup for the very first time... just a few weeks before he was released by manager Barry Lloyd.

While at the Albion Dale had his own home near East Croydon railway station just 40 minutes up the line from Brighton and popped in to see his mum and dad every day, who in turn travelled all over the country to watch him play.

Dale subsequently moved to Crewe Alexandra in 1988 and was part of the side that won promotion to the old Third Division in 1989. He made more than 100 first-team midfield appearances as *"a stylish passer and creator"* under manager Dario Gradi, helping the team win promotion in his first season.

Following three years at Gresty Road, Dale returned to Sussex by securing a move to Crawley Town in 1992 and spent a season there during the club's Southern League days before ending his career at Kingstonian.

Dale Jasper died suddenly on 30th January 2020 at the age of 56 after suffering a heart attack.

Former Albion goalkeeper, John Keeley, who signed for the club at about the same time as Dale said: *"I'm gutted. Dale was really well-liked by everyone. He had some real talent and was a top, top lad."*

49

Bernie Gallacher
(Bernard Gallacher)
1967-2011
BHAFC 1991-1993
Left Back
Appearances: 50
Goals: 1

Bernie Gallacher was a cool, reliable and highly respected full back whose football career and indeed his life ended far too soon.

Bernie was born in Johnstone, near Paisley and he played as a pacey winger for his school teams, St Peter's Primary and St Aelred's High and played for Renfrewshire Schools.

His brother John played for Scotland Schoolboys, but Bernie missed out because he broke a leg just before a big game.

But scouts from Leicester City and Aston Villa had been tracking him and in 1983, aged just 16, he chose to join Villa, who had won the European Cup the year before.

At Villa Park Bernie rose through to youth and reserve teams to sign a professional contract in March 1985 and become a first-team regular making 57 appearances.

"Football was his life and he often played two or three games a day when we were growing up in Johnstone," his other brother Charlie said.

"I'll never forget his debut for Villa because it was against Manchester United at Old Trafford and I remember thinking it didn't get any better than that."

It was the final game of the 1986-1987 season and in front of 35,000 at Old Trafford, Villa were heading back down to Division Two.

Having successfully made it through the apprentice ranks, Bernie's introduction to the first team came under Graham Taylor.

"Bernie was a young boy at a club going downhill fast and therefore it was very difficult for him and the other lads," said Taylor.

"He was reliable, wanted to do well and was never going to cause any trouble. He was a manager's dream.

"He wanted to do his best and he wasn't going to cause me any problems on or off the pitch.

"When we went out on the pitch, he gave a standard of performance that he very rarely dropped below.

"There are a number of players who don't get recognised in football and Bernie was one of those," he added.

Formerly a winger, Bernie was converted to an attacking left back and in Villa's promotion campaign of 1987-1988 he missed only one league game, amassing 50 appearances in league and cup.

He formed a useful defensive partnership with right back Kevin Gage which was pivotal in the club's return to the top-flight.

Bernie missed only one game as Villa stormed to promotion back to the First Division in the 1987-1988 season - Taylor's first season in charge.

Bernie made a total of 72 appearances for Villa between 1985 and 1990, but former Villa team-mate, Pat Heard, recalled: *"Bernie became a cult hero during the 1987-1988 promotion season and never gave less than 100 per cent every game."*

But he struggled to adapt to First Division football and following a knee injury Bernie only played 13 more top-flight games for Villa, seven of which came in the 1989-1990 season when the Midlands club were runners up behind Liverpool, seven points ahead of third-placed Tottenham Hotspur.

His final appearance in a Villa shirt came against Chelsea at Stamford Bridge in November 1990.

His only goal in Villa colours was in a 6-0 rout of Birmingham City in the Simod Cup.

He had a month on loan at Blackburn Rovers from November 1990 and played a couple of games for Doncaster Rovers before heading south to join Barry Lloyd's second tier Brighton & Hove Albion in the autumn of 1991.

He quickly impressed with his cool displays and took over the left back slot from Ian Chapman. He made his debut in a 1-0 defeat away to Blackburn on 2nd November.

He also captained the side in the absence of Dean Wilkins and Gary Chivers and kept his place through to the end of what proved to be a disastrous season with Albion relegated in 23rd spot.

While defending was his priority, Bernie got on the scoresheet in a 2-1 Boxing Day defeat at Leicester City.

Albion fan Barry Johnson recalled: *"The ball was played to him on the left touchline. He cut inside one, went past a defender and unleashed a shot from the edge of the area… it was a superb goal."*

Bernie lost his place to Ian Chapman the following season and made only occasional appearances before being released by the club in May 1993.

As a dependable overlapping full back Bernie had played 50 games for Brighton before joining Northampton Town as a non-contract player in 1994. But he only played five games for the Cobblers towards the end of the 1993-1994 season when his career was cut short by a terrible cruciate ligament injury.

During the next campaign he turned out for Conference side Bromsgrove Rovers on a non-contract basis and played some football in Hong Kong.

Albion fan Tim Hodges remembers one bitter-sweet moment during Bernie's time at the Goldstone Ground.

"I used to work with Robert Codner pre signing for us, so I got in the players' lounge quite a bit and got to know Bernie Gallagher quite well," he said.

"I remember Bernie turning up on a match day in the 1992-1993 season without the manager Barry Lloyd having spoken to him all week in training. Mrs Gallagher accompanied him and Bernie's intention, not having featured for a while in the team, was to do his pre match duty of turning up.

"Then having promised he was going to lavish his Mrs with a shopping expedition and nice late lunch in the Lanes, the reality of being a professional footballer hit home.

"Sadly, for Bernie, Lloyd had named him as one of two subs. Bernie was livid but not as livid as his wife!

"Later, as a non-playing sub, Bernie was still trying to console his wife in the players' lounge afterwards."

Following retirement from playing at the age of just 27, Bernie stayed in the English Midlands and later worked in the probation service.

Following a short illness Bernie Gallacher died in Good Hope Hospital, Sutton Coldfield, near Birmingham on 28th August 2011, aged 44, leaving behind his partner Sheila, daughter Amy and two sons James and Charles.

At his funeral at St Mary and St John Catholic Church in Birmingham, Father Gerard Lennon told of his early talent as a footballer.

He also spoke of Bernie's work in the probation service, his passion for golf, fireworks, finding bargains, cooking and his volunteer work, including one occasion when he found him re-painting the zebra crossing outside the church on Gravelly Hill North because he felt: *"It needed to be done"*.

50

Paul *Macca* McCarthy
(Paul Jason McCarthy)
1971-2017
BHAFC 1988-1996
Defender
Appearances: 217
Goals: 8

**There can't be many players
who are considered a legend
at three different clubs, but
Paul McCarthy – known as
Macca to his many friends –
is certainly one of them.**
     Born in Cork in the Republic
of Ireland, the defender began
his career as a trainee with
Brighton & Hove Albion, making more than 200 appearances in a
seven-year stretch.
     He stood out as a consistent and classy operator at a time when
off-the-pitch turbulence often gained more column inches than the
performances on it.
     Paul played hurling and Gaelic football – representing Cork
Schools – but he also played soccer for the local Rockmount club
alongside Manchester United legend Roy Keane, where he gained
Irish international caps at various age levels.
     It was while he was a member of the Irish under 16 squad that he
attracted the attention of Albion scout Ted Streeter and was
brought to the Goldstone as a trainee in July 1988 – the fee to
Rockmount was a couple of match balls!

Bernie, second from right at the local Rockmount club in Ireland, alongside a diminutive Roy Keane

Having gone on to win further caps at under 17 and youth levels, Paul signed as a full professional with the Albion in April 1989.

He made his first team debut in March 1990, coming on as a substitute forward late in the game to create the winning goal for Dean Wilkins in a 2-1 win against Bradford City.

Over the next few seasons injuries and contractual disputes led to him being in and out of the side. In December 1991, he had a trial with Scottish Premier Division club Ardrieonians.

But the return to the Goldstone of club legend Steve Foster in 1992 helped bring out the best in the young Irishman and he developed into a sound central defender.

Macca was a physical presence not to be messed with – rugged, strong, but not short on quality.

Nominated more than once as Barclays Young Eagle of the Month for the region, Paul won his first cap for the Republic's under 21 team in a game against England in November 1990, and subsequently skippered the side from November 1992. He eventually won 10 under 21 caps.

In November 1993 he was named Republic of Ireland under 21 player of the year and was third in the 1993-1994 Albion player of the season award.

Continuing to mature in the absence of Steve Foster, Paul took over the club captaincy from his partner and performed bravely as Brighton battled vainly against relegation during 1995-1996, before he was injured for the last two months of the campaign.

Former Albion player Dominic Shepherd has fond memories of Paul.

"I played with Macca in the 1990s and he was a real gent," he said. *"Also, a really funny guy who liked a good drink."*

Raymond Hardwick added: *"Paul was one of the nicest human beings I had the pleasure to have met and become friends with."*

Albion physio Malcolm Stuart remembers Paul's sparkling humour even when times were tough.

"I had Paul in the treatment room for a knee injury at a time when I was being hassled by a salesman trying to sell a magnetic therapy unit to me," he recalled.

"We were just winding up for the day when the said salesman put his head through the open window of the gym to plead his case to me again.

"Paul and one of the other lads said go on let him in and let's see what his got. As he walked in the treatment room Paul was about to ice his knee but the salesman pleaded with him to try out his magnets on his knee to show us the benefits.

"Paul with his lovely Irish drawl agreed, so the gentleman set about placing magnets all around the leg whilst keeping up a constant dialogue with anyone who would listen about the miracles we could achieve if we purchased the system.

"Twenty minutes in I thought it time to call a halt so the magnets were taken off and the salesman took Paul through a number of movements and with a massive grin asked Paul if he felt any pain at all in the knee.

"None at all said Paul to the delighted salesman and then totally deflated him with the next comment: but it's the other knee that is the problem.

"Exit one deflated salesman never to be seen again.".

Strong in the air and deceptively quick, Paul turned down several offers of a new contract before signing for Wycombe Wanderers in the summer of 1996, looking for security which was sadly lacking at the Albion during the Bellotti/Archer/Stanley years.

The fee settled by a tribunal, was £100,000 and the 25-year-old quickly established himself in the Second Division side.

He made over 250 appearances for Wycombe in seven seasons at the club, helping the club to a FA Cup semi-final against Liverpool in April 2001.

He scored Wycombe's first goal in their quarter-final giant killing win over Premier League side Leicester City, paving the way for Roy Essandoh to score the winner.

Paul was one of a number of new faces at Adams Park in the turbulent era that followed Martin O'Neill's exit from the manager's post. Many of those new arrivals failed to reach the high standards set by those players who had achieved success in the years that had gone by... but Paul McCarthy was different.

In his first season at Wycombe he was the one constant in a much-changed backline as he settled into the club with 45 appearances and one goal.

An injury sustained in February 1998 cut short his second season, but he returned to feature 36 times in the following campaign, starring in both wins over Manchester City.

Paul was an established and hugely respected member of the side by the time the 2000-2001 campaign came around and he had begun to develop a canny knack of scoring vital goals.

He netted an extra-time winner over Barnet in the first round of the League Cup and sealed a home victory over Notts County that October.

But his next five goals ensured his name would be written into Wycombe Wanderers folklore for eternity, playing his part in the incredible run to the semi-final of the FA Cup.

The first was a stylish overhead kick to see off Millwall in a second round replay. Wycombe had never scored an FA Cup third round goal in their history, but he put an end to that with an equaliser against Grimsby at Adams Park, and then opened the scoring in the replay success.

He then scored a last-gasp equaliser at full-stretch in the fifth round replay at Wimbledon, forcing a penalty shootout in which he converted his spot-kick in an 8-7 triumph.

Next up were Leicester City in the quarter-final when he nodded home the first before Essandoh's fairytale last-minute winner.

Wycombe eventually went out bravely 2-1 in the semi-final at Villa Park against a Liverpool side containing Robbie Fowler, Michael Owen and Emile Heskey, before attentions turned the following year to winning promotion.

Macca played 32 times as the side fell away from the play-offs towards the end of the year and found himself a victim of measures to cut costs and reduce the average age of the squad the following season.

He helped keep a clean sheet in what was to be his final game for the Chairboys against Huddersfield Town before moving on to Oxford United on loan in March 2003, signing for the club on a permanent basis at the end of the season.

After 35 appearances for Oxford, he was released on a free transfer in summer 2004 and joined non-League club Hornchurch.

He then became available after Hornchurch ran into financial trouble and signed for Conference National club Gravesend & Northfleet (now Ebbsfleet United) in November 2004.

He became club captain and by the end of the 2007-2008 season, had made over 110 appearances for Ebbsfleet and collected a winners' medal when they won the FA Trophy in May 2008. He signed a new one-year contract in June 2008 and a year later he was appointed as player-assistant manager at the club. Paul left Ebbsfleet in July 2013 following a change of owner. He subsequently signed with Crowborough in August 2013.

The never say die Macca was still playing, aged 41, for Ebbsfleet United in 2012. He was also a regular in the East Stand at the Amex right up to his sudden death in February 2017.

He was a hugely popular player both on and off the pitch for each of the clubs he played for and is regarded as a legend not only at the Albion, but also a Wycombe and Ebbsfleet.

McCarthy died suddenly on 19th February 2017, aged 45, of a heart attack.

Ian Chapman played with McCarthy for eight years at Brighton said: *"He was a very close friend of mine. We used to room together on away games, we would travel to training together, and we socialised outside of the game.*

"He was a lovely man, a real good friend and his death was an utter tragedy.
"Paul McCarthy was one of the greats."

Following his death, Ebbsfleet United FC issued a statement which summed him up as a player and a man: *"Quite apart from going down in Fleet history as the man who lifted the Trophy at Wembley in 2008, Paul was a well-loved and popular figure throughout his long association with the club."*

Paul was not the most recent Goldstone legend to pass on to the Field of Dreams. But as his playing career for the Albion ended less than a year before the Goldstone Ground was demolished, his story seems a perfect bookend to a tale which began 94 years earlier with the redoubtable Arthur Hulme.

Rest all their souls in loving memories.

Bibliography and Resources

Billy Wright's Book of Soccer – Various (1960)
ISBN None
Jonathan Livingstone Seagull – Richard Bach (1972)
ISBN 978-0-00-649034-0
Up, Up and Away – John Vinicombe (1979)
ISBN None
Shoeless Joe – WP Kinsella (1982)
ISBN 0-395-95773-7
Football's Strangest Matches – Andrew Ward (1989)
ISBN 1-86105-292-8
Fever Pitch – Nick Hornby (1992)
ISBN 0-575-05919-9
Seagulls: The Story of Brighton & Hove Albion FC – Tim Carder & Roger Harris (1993)
ISBN 0952-1337-0-9
Albion A-Z – Tim Carder & Roger Harris (1997)
ISBN 095-21337-1-7
Park Life – Nick Varley (1999)
ISBN 978-0-14-027828-X

The Ultimate Drop – George Rowland (2001)
ISBN 07524-2217-0
Albion: The First 100 Years – Paul Camillin & Stewart Weir (2001)
ISBN 970-0953-2045-02
His Way – Patrick Murphy (2004)
ISBN 978-1-86105-849-2
Brighton's War – Helen Roust & Teresa Dennis (2005)
ISBN 9-781857-703023
The Best of Charles Buchan's Football Monthly (2006)
ISBN 1-905-624-04-2
Football Handbook: The Glory Years – Various (2006)
ISBN 0-462-00681-6
Alan Mullery: The Autobiography – Alan Mullery & Tony Norman (2006)
ISBN 0-7553-1481-6
Brighton & Hove Albion: Miscellany – Paul Camillin (2006)
ISBN 1-84196-188-4
Brighton & Hove Albion: On This Day – Dan Tester (2007)
ISBN 781-905-411658
Footballing Fifties – Norman Giller (2007)
ISBN 978-1-906217-25-9
Match of My Life – Paul Camillin (2009)
ISBN 978-1-84818-000-0
English Football League & FA Premier League Tables – Michael Robinson (2009)
ISBN 978-1-86223-184-9
He Shot, He Scored – Peter Ward & Matthew Horner (2009)
ISBN 978-0-9562769-0-2
The Illustrated History of English Football – Tim Hill (2009)
ISBN 978-1-907176-04-3
In and Out of the Lion's Den – Julie Ryan (2013)
ISBN 9781-481081-993
Mad Man – Dick Knight (2013)
ISBN 978-1-907-637582
Football History Told Through Newspaper Headlines (2016)
ISBN 978-1-906688-66-0
Bloody Southerners – Spencer Vignes (2018)
ISBN 978-1-785-90436-3
Death in Grimsby – Nic Outterside (2019)
ISBN 9781-095979754

The Daily Mirror/The Sunday Mirror (1904-20012)
The Evening Argus – John Vinicombe (1962-2001)
The Albion Mag – Dan Tester (2016-2018)

www.brightonandhovealbion.com/club/history/club-history
www.theargus.co.uk/news
www.thebeautifulhistory.wordpress.com/clubs/brighton-hove-albion
www.seagullpedia.com
www.inparallellines.wordpress.com
www.mybrightonandhove.org.uk/topics/topicsport/football/brighton-and-hove-albion-fc
www.thegoldstonewrap.com
www.footballandthefirstworldwar.org/brighton-footballers-served-in-the-first-world-war
www.wearebrighton.com/albionfeatures/lest-we-forget-brighton-nine-great-war-dead
www.shorehambysea.com/more-shoreham-characters/
www.brightonjournal.co.uk
www.sussexpast.co.uk/
www.theseagulllovereview.blogspot.com
www.thetweetingseagull.com/

Thanks and Acknowledgements

Alan Reynolds
Alan Willard
Barry Harris
Bill Spencer
Brendan Quirke
Brian Tawse
Charles Wright
Chris Dunster
Chris Napier
Chris Stratton
Chris Worrall
Colin Wood
Dave Wilcock
Dean Wilkins
Dick Knight
Dominic Shepherd
Gary Stevens
George Ley
Gill Outterside
Henry Wood
Ian Gould
Ian Hart
Ian Hine
John Ansbro
John Coomber
John Templeman
Julia Hopkins
Julie Ryan
Katie Westcott
Kee-Wah Cheungipswicz
Malcolm Boyes
Malcolm Stuart
Mark Raven
Maureen Abbott
Mick Fox
Nick Turrell
Pat Hunter

Paul Gunn
Peter Beatle
Peter Langley
Peter Ward
Phil Dennett
Ray Eggleton
Robin Napier
Ricky Wainwright
Russ Poore
Simon Francis
Simon Levenson
Simon Todd
Steve Cowdry
Steve Harrington
Steve Mead
Steve Ringwood
Tim Carder
Tim Hodges
Vaughan Woolley

Picture Credits

Brighton & Hove Albion Managers

John Jackson	1901-1910
Frank Scott-Walford	1905-1908
Jack Robson	1908-1914
Charlie Webb	1919-1947
Tommy Cook	1947
Don Welsh	1947-1951
Billy Lane	1951-1961
George Curtis	1961-1963
Archie Macaulay	1963-1968
Freddie Goodwin	1968-1970
Pat Saward	1970-1973
Brian Clough	1973-1974
Peter T. Taylor	1974-1976
Alan Mullery	1976-1981
Mike Bailey	1981-1982
Jimmy Melia	1982-1983
Chris Cattlin	1983-1986
Alan Mullery	1986-1987
Barry Lloyd	1987-1993
Liam Brady	1993-1995
Jimmy Case	1995-1996
Steve Gritt	1996-1998
Brian Horton	1998-1999
Jeff Wood	1999
Micky Adams	1999-2001
Peter J. Taylor	2001-2002
Martin Hinshelwood	2002
Steve Coppell	2002-2003
Mark McGhee	2003-2006
Dean Wilkins	2006-2008
Micky Adams	2008-2009
Russell Slade	2009
Gus Poyet	2009-2013
Óscar García	2013-2014
Sami Hyypiä	2014
Chris Hughton	2014-2019
Graham Potter	2019-

English League Club Nicknames

Accrington Stanley	Stanley
Aldershot Town	The Shots
Arsenal	The Gunners
Aston Villa	The Villa
Barnsley	The Tykes
Barrow	The Bluebirds
Bolton Wanderers	The Trotters
Bournemouth	The Cherries
Birmingham City	The Blues
Blackburn Rovers	Rovers
Blackpool	Seasiders
Bradford City	The Bantams
Bradford Park Avenue	Avenue
Brentford	The Bees
Brighton & Hove Albion	The Seagulls
Bristol City	The Robins
Bristol Rovers	The Gas
Burnley FC	The Clarets
Cambridge United	The U's
Cardiff City	Bluebirds
Carlisle United	The Blues
Charlton Athletic	The Addicks
Chelsea	The Pensioners
Cheltenham Town	The Robins
Chester City	The Seals
Chesterfield	The Spireites
Colchester United	The U's
Coventry City	The Sky Blues
Crawley Town	The Reds
Crewe Alexandra	The Alex
Crystal Palace	The Eagles
Derby County	The Rams
Doncaster Rovers	The Rovers
Everton	The Toffees
Exeter City	The Grecians
Fulham	Cottagers
Gillingham	The Gills
Grimsby Town	The Mariners

Halifax Town	The Shaymen
Hereford United	The Bulls
Huddersfield Town	The Terriers
Hull City	The Tigers
Ipswich Town	Tractor Boys
Leeds United	The Peacocks
Leicester City	The Foxes
Lincoln City	The Imps
Liverpool	The Reds
Luton Town	The Hatters
Manchester City	The Sky Blues
Manchester United	The Red Devils
Mansfield Town	The Stags
Middlesbrough	The Boro
Millwall	The Lions
Newcastle United	The Magpies
Newport County	The Ironsides
Northampton Town	The Cobblers
Norwich City	The Canaries
Notts County	The Magpies
Nottingham Forest	Forest
Oldham Athletic	The Latics
Orient	The O's
Oxford United	The U's
Peterborough United	The Posh
Plymouth Argyle	The Pilgrims
Portsmouth	Pompey
Port Vale	The Vale
Preston North End	The Lilywhites
Queens Park Rangers	QPR
Reading	The Royals
Rochdale	The Dale
Rotherham United	The Millers
Scunthorpe United	The Iron
Sheffield United	The Blades
Sheffield Wednesday	The Owls
Shrewsbury Town	The Shrews
Southampton	The Saints
Southend United	The Shrimpers
Southport	Sandgrounders

Stoke City	The Potters
Swansea City	The Swans
Swindon Town	The Robins
Sunderland	The Rokerites
Torquay United	The Gulls
Tottenham Hotspurs	Spurs / Lilywhites
Tranmere Rovers	Rovers
Walsall	The Saddlers
Watford	The Hornets
West Bromwich Albion	The Baggies
West Ham United	The Hammers
Wigan Athletic	The Latics
Wimbledon	The Dons
Wolverhampton Wanderers	Wolves
Workington	The Reds
Wrexham	The Reds
Wycombe Wanderers	The Chairboys

Afterword

For most birds flying is just a means of finding food, but for a Seagull, flying is life itself.
Richard Bach

The terrace was uncovered and it was a very cold and wintry day. It was windy and rainy, and the second half was played in semi-darkness because it was before the days of floodlights.
Dick Knight

The North stand was noisy, they'd bollock everybody. Unforgiving. They expected a goal with every attack.
Paddy McIlvenny

It used to be a tenner for the day and non-stop singing, supporting players as ordinary as the fans standing watching them.
Park Life

Football is a sport and if a team through the cause of an injury suffers it is very unfortunate, and it is only right and proper to take these setbacks sportingly. Again – no substitutes.
Billy Lane

When I left the Goldstone that afternoon, I went down to the seafront for a stroll to clear my head before driving home. As I walked on the pebble beach and gazed out to sea all my footballing memories flashed through my mind.
Alan Mullery

While the details here are unique to me, I hope they will strike a chord with anyone who has found themselves drifting off, in the middle of a working day to a left-foot volley into the top right-hand corner, 10 or 15 or 25 years ago.
Nick Hornby

The game ends and the players begin to drift off toward their exit, but the dreams and the memories will never end.
WP Kinsella

279

About the Author

Wet Socks and Dry Bones is written and edited by Nic Outterside, and published by his independent publishing house ***Time is an Ocean Publications***.

Nic has been a fervent supporter of Brighton & Hove Albion since watching his first game at the Goldstone Ground in September 1967.

His previous book about the Albion: ***Death In Grimsby*** became an Amazon best-seller in 2019.

Nic is also an award-winning journalist and creative author, who over 34 years has worked across all forms of media, including radio, magazines, newspapers, books and online.

Among more than a dozen awards to his name are *North of England Daily Journalist of the Year, Scottish Daily Journalist of the Year, Scottish Weekly Journalist of the Year* and a special award for investigative journalism.

In 1994, 53 MPs signed an Early Day Motion in the UK House of Commons praising Nic's research and writing.

In 2016 Nic was awarded an honorary doctorate in written journalism.

Wet Socks and Dry Bones is his 26th published book.

Author and Editor:

The Hill - Songs and Poems of Darkness and Light
Another Hill - Songs and Poems of Love and Theft
Asian Voices
Asian Voices - the Director's Cut
Blood in the Cracks
Don't Look Down
Luminance - Words for a World Gone Wrong
Death in Grimsby
Bones
Hot Metal – Poems from the Print Room
Poets Don't Lie
Contacts
The Man's a Tart
Western Skies
Reality Cornflakes
A Moon Magnetized This Screeching Bird
The Arbitrary Fractals of an Oracle
Dissect My Fragile Brain
Sonnets
Spiced Dreams and Scented Schemes
Minotaur and Other Poems
An Alpine State of Mind
Blue Note Poems
Love Like a Rose
Under the Weight of Blue

Printed in Great Britain
by Amazon